M. Erasmus
mob.# 07985197283

PERS
CENT
FACILI

PROCESS, THEORY AND PRACTICE

THIRD EDITION

PERSON-CENTRED FACILITATION

PROCESS, THEORY AND PRACTICE

HANKA GROBLER • RINIE SCHENCK

OXFORD
UNIVERSITY PRESS
SOUTHERN AFRICA

OXFORD
UNIVERSITY PRESS

SOUTHERN AFRICA

Oxford University Press Southern Africa (Pty) Ltd

Vasco Boulevard, Goodwood, Cape Town, Republic of South Africa
P O Box 12119, N1 City, 7463, Cape Town, Republic of South Africa

Oxford University Press Southern Africa (Pty) Ltd is a subsidiary of
Oxford University Press, Great Clarendon Street, Oxford OX2 6DP.

The Press, a department of the University of Oxford, furthers the University's objective of excellence in research, scholarship, and education by publishing worldwide in

Oxford New York

Auckland Cape Town Dar es Salaam Hong Kong Karachi
Kuala Lumpur Madrid Melbourne Mexico City Nairobi
New Delhi Shanghai Taipei Toronto

With offices in

Argentina Austria Brazil Chile Czech Republic France Greece
Guatemala Hungary Italy Japan Poland Portugal Singapore South Korea
Switzerland Turkey Ukraine Vietnam

Published in South Africa
by Oxford University Press Southern Africa (Pty) Ltd, Cape Town

Person-centred facilitation: Process, theory and practice

Third edition

ISBN 978 0 19 598636 5

Third edition published 2009
Eighth impression 2012

Publishing manager: Alida Terblanche
Assistant commissioning editor: Marisa Montemarano
Managing editor: Lisa Andrews
Editor: Louise Banks
Designer: Jade Minords
Illustrator: Richard Commin
Cover design: Judith Cross
Indexer: Clifford Perusset
Cover photo: The Bigger Picture

Set in Adobe Caslon Pro 10.5 pt on 13 pt by Mckore Graphics
Printed and bound by ABC Press, Cape Town
118846

Acknowledgements
The authors and publisher gratefully acknowledge permission to reproduce copyright material in this book. Every effort has been made to trace copyright holders, but if any copyright infringements have been made, the publisher would be grateful for information that would enable any omissions or errors to be corrected in subsequent impressions.

Contents

Foreword to the third edition

Person-centred Facilitation was written to meet the needs of lecturers, students, social workers, psychologists, counsellors and other engaged citizens around the world who are increasingly challenged with the diverse personal, social, economic and political processes inherent in the realities that people must manage in their daily lives.

South Africa and the world are facing unprecedented challenges that threaten the livelihoods and wellbeing of society. The persistence of poverty, unemployment, and the high incidence of HIV and Aids, as well as other associated socio-economic problems, are contributing factors. These challenges do not only require appropriate policies and interventions, but also the training of adequate and skilled professionals for the helping professions.

In developing this book, the authors have succeeded in bringing the person-centred approach to life. The book is easy to read. It is interactive and is illustrated with valuable practical examples. The text provides hands-on theoretical and practical knowledge. It encourages an understanding of the theory, practice and value base that underlie a person-centred approach in working with individuals, groups and communities.

Choosing to write a book based on the philosophy of the person-centred approach can be seen as a product of time, growth and changes in the global context. As cultures in South Africa and the world grow less homogeneous, they consequently also give less support to the individual. Individuals can no longer simply rest comfortably upon the ways and traditions of our society, but find many of the basic issues and conflicts of life centring in themselves. Each person must resolve within him- or herself issues for which society previously took more responsibility. It would, however, be a mistake to explain the choice of the person-centred approach solely as a product of cultural and political changes. This approach covers the beliefs, values, assumptions, norms and standards that serve as the philosophical and moral foundations for many of the helping professions.

A person-centred approach enables us to overcome the limitations or influences of different cultures to a great degree. In addition to this, the approach can be applied to many other fields such as education, organisational development, group process and developmental work in communities. It can be used to facilitate the process when dealing with problems such as inter-racial tensions.

This book will make a meaningful contribution towards the empowerment of individuals, groups and communities, and will assist the development of knowledge and skills in a variety of helping professions.

Ida van Dyk
Department of Social Work, University of South Africa

Acknowledgements

We would like to thank our colleagues who were available to discuss and think about their and our ideas about this approach. It underlined the proposition that the self (in this case, our professional selves) is formed in interaction with others. Our colleagues are not the only significant others in this regard, as our students, with their unique perspective and contributions, were valuable collaborators in our continuing journey of exploration of the person-centred approach. We would like to continue this journey in interaction with others, including you, the reader, and therefore we are thanking you in advance for your ideas and perspectives.

As the approach was initiated and originally documented by Carl Rogers, we owe him a great debt for providing us with the basic tenets of a theory that we have found helpful in understanding and working with people in a humane and respectful way.

We would like to extend a very special word of thanks to Dr Dries du Toit, who was part of the original development of the book. He was a contributing author of the two previous editions of this book.

We would also like to thank all the people involved in the actual preparation of this book, as well as and especially our families, who supported us in our quest and patiently put up with our meandering minds and, sometimes, physical absence from home.

Our thanks also go to the supervisors and students of Unisa for their comments on the first and second editions. Implementation of these comments and suggestions makes the third edition even more student-friendly.

Hanka Grobler
Rinie Schenck

Introduction

This book describes the process of facilitation according to the person-centred approach. We will begin by exploring what this process entails and then give a brief introduction to the approach.

What is meant by the facilitation process?

The facilitation process can be described as what happens between a facilitator and his or her client (an individual, a group or a community) from the beginning to the end of the relationship. As the process involves both the facilitator and the client, it follows that the process also includes what is happening inside the facilitator and the client. The facilitator uses what is inside him or her (theory, values and professional skills) to enable the client to explore what is inside him or her.

The facilitation process could be described as a road on which the facilitator walks with a client, accompanying that client on his or her journey of self-discovery. The process makes it possible for the client to explore issues such as: 'Who am I?', or: 'What are the thoughts, perceptions, feelings, needs, behaviour and values that make me who I am?', or: 'What prevents me from being who I want to be or living to my full potential?'

The facilitator cannot walk this road for the client. Only the client can know what it feels like under his or her feet and how it feels to walk in his or her shoes. Only the client can know where he or she is going or wants to go. Only the client can know where he or she does not want to go or which roads are too steep for his or her legs.

This journey of self-discovery is not predictable. It may have many twists and turns, and no two journeys are the same. The travellers might encounter high mountains and wonder whether they will be able to climb to the top. They might encounter blind curves where they cannot see the road ahead. The journey may be scary and demanding for the client as well as the facilitator.

In spite of its unpredictability, this journey can be divided into four broad phases:

- The beginning phase, where the facilitator tries to make sure that everything is in place for a safe journey, including establishing a relationship that is conducive to mutual trust during the rest of the journey

- The second phase, during which the travellers (facilitator and client) explore what hampers the client's self-discovery
- The third phase, in which the travellers work together to sort through the issues that were uncovered in the previous phase
- The fourth and final phase, where the travellers near the end of their journey together and are ready to go their separate ways.

The facilitator carries various provisions for the journey. These provisions include the theory, values and skills that equip them to accompany a client on the journey and assist the client with the process of self-discovery. This book describes how the facilitator can use the person-centred theory as well as the values and skills that flow from it to facilitate a client's journey of self-discovery.

It is important to note right from the beginning that the person-centred approach deals with people who encounter problems and not with the problems that people encounter. A reader who is inclined to focus on a client's problem, behaviour or cognition will probably find the person-centred approach frustrating. The problem is part of the facilitation process, but not the sole focus of it. Metaphorically speaking, if you called in an electrician to fix a broken geyser, you would not care about the electrician as a person, only that he or she can fix the problem. The electrician would also not care about you as a person, only whether you would be able to pay for his or her services.

Activity

Think back to an occasion when you had to call in a person to repair an appliance (for example, a TV, fridge or stove) in your house.

1 Can you remember the person's face?
2 Do you know whether the person was married or not?
3 Do you know whether he or she was a happy person?
4 Do you know whether he or she was an outgoing person?

The two of you would probably not engage in a relationship other than one that allows the electrician to concentrate on and fix the problem.

During the process of facilitation, it is usually a problem experienced by the client that brings the client and the facilitator together. However, the problem is not separate from the person who brings it to the facilitator's attention. The facilitator and the client cannot look at the problem in the same way as the two people in the illustration on the next page are looking at the broken geyser. They cannot look at the problem as if it is not connected to either of them.

The problem is part of the client as a person. It is not an entity in itself. The problem indicates that the person is battling with something within him- or herself, not an outside entity (although a client may initially perceive it as such). If the client thought he or she was able to deal with the problem on his or her own, the client would have done so.

How do we fix this problem?

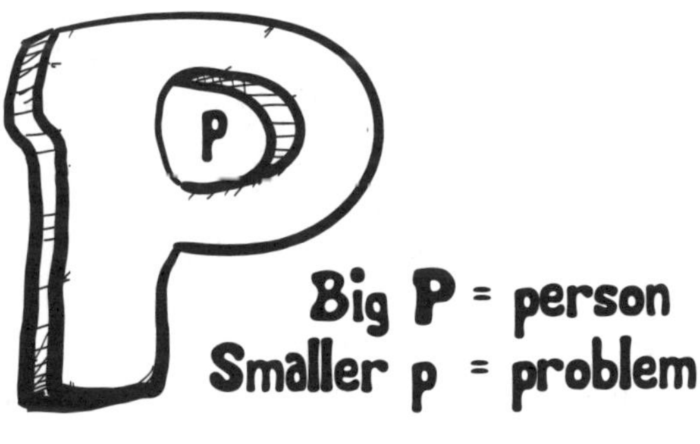

The problem is part of the inner world of the person.

The client may think that he or she wants the facilitator to solve the problem, as the client experiences him- or herself as incapable of solving it. This could be an indication that the client has lost faith in him- or herself and in his or her ability to sort matters out. The client might also be unsure about what would be in his or her best interests, and need reassurance from an outside source. This idea that an outsider may know better than the client implies that the client does not trust what his or her inner voices are saying.

If the facilitator then solved the problem for the client, it would confirm to the client that he or she was incapable of solving the problem. It would also deprive the client of an opportunity to explore what had prevented him or her from solving the problem.

The person-centred approach aims to enable people to discover for themselves what they are struggling with and then find their own unique way forward.

What is the person-centred approach?

The best way to answer this question is with the words of Carl Rogers, who developed the approach. According to Rogers, the facilitator in the person-centred approach tries to understand how the client sees him- or herself.

> *Psychotherapy deals primarily with the organisation and functioning of the self. There are many elements of experience that the self cannot face, cannot clearly perceive, because to face them or admit them would be inconsistent with and threatening to the current organisation of self… In the therapeutic experience, to see one's own attitudes, confusions, ambivalences, feelings and perceptions accurately expressed by another … paves the way for acceptance into the self of all the experiences that are now more clearly perceived. Reorganisation of the self and more integrated functioning of the self are thus furthered.*
>
> [Rogers 1987: 40–41]

The person-centred approach deals with the self or identity of a person, group or community. It looks at those experiences that the client cannot allow into his or her conscious mind, because the experiences threaten the client's perception of who he or she is (the client's self). To be able to deal with these threatening experiences in the context of facilitation, the client needs to be accepted by the facilitator and enabled to see him- or herself and all of his or her experiences more clearly.

A few salient themes emerge from this description:

- The self – what it is and how it is experienced by the client
- Experiences that the self can face
- Experiences that the self cannot face and why
- What the therapeutic relationship must provide to enable the client to reorganise his or her self
- What could happen if the client's self were reorganised
- What knowledge, values and skills the facilitator needs to be able to create the therapeutic relationship required for this reorganisation of the self to take place.

These themes are covered by the nineteen propositions originally formulated by Carl Rogers. The propositions are listed here for easy reference.

Rogers' nineteen theoretical propositions

Proposition 1: Human experiences at a conscious and unconscious level

There are three important elements to this proposition:

- The experiential world of every person is central, unique and personal.

- This personal world is constantly changing.
- The experiences that constitute this world can be conscious or unconscious.

Proposition 2: Human perceptions

Like experiences, perception (or observation) of the world or reality is an individual matter. People behave according to their experiences and perceptions.

Proposition 3: Wholeness

The person, group or community responds to the world as an organised whole.

Proposition 4: Self-determination

The person, group or community has one basic tendency and striving; to actualise, maintain and enhance the self.

Proposition 5: Needs and behaviour

Behaviour essentially consists of purposeful endeavours by the person, group or community to satisfy the needs that person, group or community experiences in the world.

Proposition 6: Emotions

Emotions accompany and facilitate intentional behaviour (Proposition 5). The intensity of the emotion correlates with the importance that the person, group or community attaches to the behaviour in terms of self-preservation and self-enhancement (Proposition 4).

Proposition 7: Frames of reference

The best way to understand behaviour is to view it from the person, group or community's frame of reference.

Proposition 8: The self

A portion of the total perceptual field gradually becomes differentiated as the self.

Proposition 9: The self and significant others

As a result of interaction with the environment, and particularly as a result of evolutional interaction with others, the structure of the self is formed, together with values attached to these concepts.

Proposition 10: Values: Own and adopted from other people

Values attached to experiences form part of the self and may be shaped by the person, group or community's own experiences. They may also be taken over from others and assimilated into the self as if they had been experienced personally.

Proposition 11 [a and b]: Dealing with experiences at a conscious level

As experiences occur in the life of the individual, they are either symbolised, perceived and organised into some relationship to the self, or ignored because there is no perceived relationship to the self-structure.

Proposition 11 [c and d]: Dealing with experiences at an unconscious level

As experiences occur in the life of an individual, they are either denied or distorted because the experiences are inconsistent with the structure of the self. One of the characteristics of therapy (and perhaps one of the most important changes that can result from therapy) is the bringing into the awareness of experiences of which the client has not previously been conscious.

Proposition 12: Self and behaviour

Most of the ways of behaving that are adopted by the organism are those that are consistent with the concept of self (Rogers 1987: 507).

Proposition 13: Behaviour and unconscious experiences

Behaviour may, in some instances, be brought about by organic experiences and needs that have not been symbolised. Such behaviour may be inconsistent with the structure of the self. In such instances, the behaviour is not owned by the individual.

Proposition 14: Psychological tension

Tension is created by unsymbolised experiences or distorted symbolisation of experiences that cannot be incorporated into the self.

Proposition 15: Reconstruction of the self

A person becomes well adjusted when all or a maximum of experiences can be symbolised congruent with the person's self-perception.

Proposition 16: Defence of self

Experiences that conflict with the person, group or community's self-perception are considered threatening to the self. The greater the number of such experiences, the more intent the self-structure becomes on self-preservation.

Proposition 17: Conditions for change

Under certain conditions, primarily involving complete absence of any threat to the self-structure, experiences that are inconsistent with the self may be perceived and examined. The structure of the self may then be revised to assimilate and include these experiences.

Proposition 18: Acceptance of self

When a person is able to symbolise most of his or her experiences, and to integrate them into a total self-concept, that individual will display greater understanding of others and be able to accept them as separate, unique individuals.

Proposition 19: Developing your own valuing process

As a person comes to perceive and symbolise more of his or her sensory experiences, integrating these experiences into his or her self-concept, the person's value system, which was previously based mainly on distorted symbolisation of other people's values, will make way for a process of determining that person's own values.

Why does this book emphasise Rogers' nineteen propositions?

Books on the person-centred approach tend to focus on the attitudes of the facilitator: the so-called core conditions of empathy, congruence and unconditional positive regard. Although these core conditions will be discussed in more detail later in the book, they need further discussion here because they are so often the starting point of any discussion on this approach.

The core conditions lead us to think about how we regard people. In other words, when we observe a person, what do we perceive and think? What does the word 'person' mean or encompass? This becomes even more relevant when the person we are observing is experiencing some kind of difficulty or problem. Is our vision filled with the issue at hand and our need to alleviate the pain the person is experiencing? If so, then we are observing and thinking not primarily about the person, but about the difficulty (pain or problem) he or she is experiencing. We must ask ourselves who the person is behind or in this difficult situation. How do we think about people and what do we take into consideration when thinking about them? Do we see and think primarily about their feelings of pain and the situation in which they experience the pain? Do we see and think about their behaviour, and what do we make of this behaviour?

The core conditions also set us thinking about the attitude of the facilitator. What does 'positive regard' imply? Is this just a passive acceptance of any person as 'good', even though we do not really think the person (or what he or she does) is good? How then do we stay congruent? Or, as some people argue, is positive regard an acceptance of the person, but not the behaviour that we find 'not good'? This implies that we do not accept the whole person, as we exempt the behaviour from our acceptance.

But what does acceptance mean? The Oxford dictionary defines it as 'approval, belief, toleration' (Sykes 1982: 6). If we go along with this view, then judgment is implied, even if it is a positive judgement. That is, if we agree with (or approve of) what the other person does, our own values come into play. We decide what is good or positive and what is not. On the other hand, acceptance could also mean taking the person and whatever he or she does as given, without judging it in any way. Whether or not the person's actions are positive or negative then depends on that person.

When we turned to Rogers' writings and interviews for some guidance in this regard, we saw that he looks at much more than people's feelings or behaviour. He often refers to the self, the values and needs of the people he works with. This wider view (and why Rogers uses it) became clear from the theoretical ideas he formulated by way of nineteen propositions. For instance, Proposition 3 states that when taking a person-centred approach, we have to look at and understand the whole person. But what would or could some of the dimensions of a 'whole person' be? The other propositions give concrete examples of what these experiences might entail. They thus serve as a reminder or guide to what else can be explored and understood while we are involved with another human being. (For example, Proposition 2 refers to perceptions, Proposition 5 refers to needs and behaviour, Proposition 6 refers to the emotions, Proposition 8 refers to the self, Proposition 9 refers to interaction with others, and Proposition 10 refers to the values and the valuing process.)

These propositions about being human and what possibly motivates people, on various levels of consciousness, provide tentative guidelines for facilitators in their efforts to understand, think about and make sense of what we can observe of others, like what they think, say, do and feel when we encounter them. Even if you do not agree with these ideas, considering them could enable you to think more broadly about other people. For example, you could have an experience like: 'I never thought of people like this before', or: 'I never thought of it quite like this before', or: 'I do not think of people like this, but rather like ...', adding your own perspective to the matter under discussion. It is for these reasons that we decided to use Rogers' propositions as a starting point in this book.

However, remember that the propositions are by no means all that there is to human beings. There are other dimensions we can think of, like their physical and spiritual experiences. We must therefore bear in mind that people are not the propositions, but the propositions can help us explore and consider a spectrum of possible dimensions in which people can be understood.

It is also important to keep in mind that the ideas (about the theory, values and skills) discussed in this book are ways of thinking, believing and acting that the facilitator can develop. They are not prescriptions for our clients. In other words, we cannot expect the people we work with to know this theory or to believe in the values we as professional facilitators need to uphold. We cannot expect our clients to act in accordance with the skills we describe in later sections of this book. These ideas cannot be imposed on our clients, as the approach holds that they have the right and the ability to grow and develop in their own unique ways. No one can even force you, the reader, to agree with what is written here. These ideas are for you to explore. You must decide for yourself whether you think they will be useful to you in your future interaction with people.

How can these propositions be used practically?

What does this kind of approach mean to the people we encounter if they are not aware of our attitudes? In this regard, we were guided by Proposition 1. A person's experiential world is private and known only to him or her, unless shared with others in some way or another. The facilitator thus has to share his or her experiences (perceptions, thoughts and attitude) with the people encountered. How can this be done?

The communication skills discussed later in this book are seen as a way (and by no means the only or correct way) for the facilitator to demonstrate his or her understanding of the whole person, and his or her respect for that person.

However, the facilitator may encounter people in a variety of settings, and the understanding and respect that need to be demonstrated will differ in each setting. We have therefore divided the possible setting for the facilitation process into three categories:

- Encountering and relating with one other person, an individual

- Encountering others in groups
- Community settings.

The way in which the facilitator thinks about people, his or her attitude towards people and the demonstration of these experiences is basically the same in all three situations. However, there are some variations in each situation, which is why each situation is discussed separately.

The whole process of facilitation (all four phases) are discussed in terms of the relevant theoretical propositions, values and skills for each phase. They are discussed firstly with regard to individuals, then with regard to groups and finally with regard to communities. As groups and communities consist of individual people, Section A, which deals with individuals, is the most comprehensive. All the ideas about the theory, values and skills discussed in Section A are also applicable to the other constellations. We will explore the specific challenges in working with groups in Section B. Section C addresses the implications for working with communities.

In order to share our own ideas and understanding of the theory (propositions), values and skills (actions of the facilitator) with you, the reader, we have used several examples from our own and our colleagues' practice. We have also included various activities. These provide an opportunity for your involvement. They are intended to enable you to see whether these ideas are helpful to you as a person and to stimulate you (both as a reader and as a facilitator) to contemplate and question the issues discussed. We would appreciate any comment and illustrations of these examples and activities. Please send your feedback to the address provided on p. 252 of the book.

Structure of the book

The book is divided into four sections.

Section A: Working with individuals

The four phases of the facilitation process with individuals are discussed in six chapters. The first three chapters deal with the first phase, as creating a safe environment is such an important part of the process of facilitation. Chapter 4 describes the second phase, while Chapter 5 and Chapter 6 deal with the third and fourth phases respectively.

Section B: Group facilitation

Here too, the first phase is described in the first three chapters. Chapter 10 looks at the second phase of the facilitation process when working with groups, while Chapter 11 and Chapter 12 address the third and fourth phases respectively.

Section C: Person-centred facilitation in communities

Once again, the first phase is described in the first three chapters. Chapter 16 looks at the second phase of the facilitation when working with communities, while Chapter 17 considers the third and fourth phases.

Section D: Some special considerations

In the final three chapters of the book, we discuss some special situations that might stretch the ingenuity of the facilitator to its utmost: cross-cultural communication, working with people in conflict and the self of the facilitator.

We hope that you will enjoy reading and using this book, and will find it helpful in your encounters with others.

SECTION

A

Working with individuals

In this section, we will describe the four phases of the process of facilitation with individuals. We will consider how these phases unfold in relation to the theory (Carl Rogers' nineteen propositions), the professional values and the communication skills advocated by the person-centred approach. The theory is used to help the facilitator to understand his or her clients as people and as human beings. The professional values assist the facilitator in developing a professional attitude towards his or her clients. The skills provide the facilitator with some guidelines on how to demonstrate his or her understanding and acceptance of them to clients. We will also explore the aims of doing so. We will start with the beginning of the first phase of the process in Chapter 1 and will end with the final phase in Chapter 6.

CHAPTER

1 Creating a safe space for facilitation (Phase 1)

1.1 Introduction

The people-centred approach takes the view that who people are or how they perceive themselves to be is primarily contained in the person's self-structure. The self-structure is the person's idea of 'I' or 'me'. We can also express this idea as: 'This is who I am', or: 'This is how I see myself'. As we explore the theory in more depth, it will become clear that this concept of personhood or self is central to the person-centred approach.

It needs to be clear from the outset that the facilitator working from this perspective does not try to change people, their identities or their selves. Instead, he or she tries to create conditions in which people can explore themselves and decide if they need to change, and if they do, what needs to change. Any changes made come from the client, while the facilitator simply facilitates the process.

In our consideration of where to start in creating these conditions, we will begin with the theory developed by Rogers. In Chapter 2, we will discuss some of the values associated with this theory. We will look at some of the skills that can be used to implement the theory in Chapter 3.

1.2 The theory of Carl Rogers

In this chapter, we will examine thirteen of Rogers' nineteen propositions and find out how they can help us to understand people and create a safe space for facilitation.

1.2.1 Proposition 17: Conditions for facilitation

> *Under certain conditions, involving primarily complete absence of any threat to the self-structure, experiences that are inconsistent with it may be perceived, and examined, and the structure of self revised to assimilate and include such experiences.*
>
> [Rogers 1987: 517]

You may well ask: 'What do these conditions entail?' The basic principle outlined in this quotation is that the facilitator should not, in any way or under any circumstances, threaten the self-structure of clients. In other words, he or she should not threaten people's ideas of themselves or who they perceive themselves to be. The facilitator needs to create a safe environment where clients are free to express themselves fully and thus explore themselves in depth.

This implies total understanding and acceptance of people, with all their experiences. The facilitator needs to demonstrate this acceptance to all clients through his or her physical attitude, mental attitude and behaviour.

If the facilitator wants to create a safe space for the process of facilitation, it follows that he or she has to avoid certain behaviours and practise other behaviours. We will discuss the behaviours and basic communication skills that are conducive for creating a safe space later in this chapter.

However, it is also important to explore what the facilitator should avoid or try not to do when interacting with clients.

Activity 1.1

1 List some of the behaviours you think would scare clients.
2 List some of the behaviours you think would insult clients.
3 List some of the behaviours you think would anger clients.

Activity 1.2

Consider the following possible behaviours by a facilitator. Decide if each behaviour would help to create a safe climate for facilitation.

1 A facilitator judges clients (including their behaviour).
2 A facilitator rejects clients (including their behaviour).
3 A facilitator argues with clients.
4 A facilitator fights with clients.
5 A facilitator confronts clients.
6 A facilitator pities clients.
7 A facilitator asks clients a lot of questions.
8 A facilitator gives clients advice.

It is not easy to create a safe space for the process of facilitation.

Example 1.1

A nature lover walking in the veld comes across a pupa. The pupa has already changed into a butterfly that is thrashing around desperately to escape from the cocoon. Out

>>

of kindness, the man picks up the pupa and very gently makes a small hole in it to help free the butterfly. But once it is freed, the butterfly is unable to fly. It wriggles around on the ground without any coordination. The struggle inside the cocoon was essential for the butterfly to strengthen its wings sufficiently for flight.

It is important to remember that these conditions (this safe space) must prevail throughout the process of facilitation. The facilitator cannot start by creating safe conditions, and then, when the client begins trusting him or her, place the client under pressure (by asking a lot of questions, for example, or by being confrontational).

Proposition 17 reminds the facilitator of the responsibility to accept and understand all clients as whole people at all times. In other words, the facilitator should recognise the self-structure of the client, or how the client is structured. The facilitator must see his or her clients as people in their own right, not just in terms of their problems. The problem does not define the person or the approach, but each person defines him- or herself. This approach maintains that the facilitator needs to create a safe space or relationship in which clients can explore all their experiences and get to know themselves more fully. They must feel safe enough to explore even those experiences that scare or confuse them and the facilitator.

We will explore the following dimensions of this proposition in more detail as we go along:

- What the self-structure is and what it consists of in terms of the propositions or theoretical principles that Rogers formulated (Chapter 1)
- The attitudes (values) and behaviours (skills) the facilitator can use to achieve complete absence of threat (Chapter 2 and Chapter 3)
- What can constitute a threat to the self (Chapter 4)
- How to enable clients to examine or explore these threatening experiences (Chapter 4)
- How the self-structure can be revised (Chapter 5).

1.2.2 Proposition 8: The self

> *A portion of the total perceptual field gradually becomes differentiated as the self.*
>
> [Rogers 1987: 497]

On page 498, Rogers gives a more detailed description of the self as 'an organised, fluid, but consistent conceptual pattern of perceptions of characteristics and relationships of the "I" or the "me"'.

A section of the individual's total perceptual field is gradually differentiated to become the self.

Example 1.2

A teacher teaching an adult literacy class asked her students to write down the figures 1 to 10. One man inverted the figure 7, reproducing a mirror image. When the teacher pointed this out, the following dialogue ensued:

Teacher: That is not the figure 7.
Student: When I'm standing up, who am I?
Teacher: You are Mr Phatudi.
Student: And when I'm sitting down, who am I?
Teacher: You are Mr Phatudi.
Student: And if I bend sideways to the left or the right, who am I?
Teacher: You are Mr Phatudi.
Student: So if I remain Mr Phatudi whether I am sitting, standing or bending sideways, then that figure on the page remains the figure 7 whichever way I write it.

The self means the person's conception (perception and experience) of who he or she is, as a person, a unique human being. The perception we have of ourselves links to all our experiences. In other words, our perception links to our thinking, behaviour, needs, emotions and values. So, to understand the person, we have to understand the self, or the perception of who that person believes him- or herself to be, in the here and now. This is because that belief links to all other experiences, including behaviour. This approach holds that if we know who we are, we will also know how to behave and what we believe in, and we will find our own way forward.

The concept 'total' implies that the self emerges from all our experiences, or put differently, all our experiences are part of who we are. As our experiences are always changing (as we will see in Proposition 1), the self is also changing. That is why it is described as a 'fluid' picture, not a static one.

It is also vital to note that this picture of ourselves is our own perception of our identity. (You will learn more about perceptions in Proposition 2.) We determine our perceptions and who we are as we move through life. The important issue of determining the self will be discussed further under Proposition 4.

We must remember that, although the self is changing, it is not an easy process. If we are to avoid a total sense of confusion, of not knowing who we are, or whether we are coming or going, then we need a sense of stability and continuity about ourselves.

Activity 1.3

You perceive yourself to be a heterosexual person. One night at a party, you feel attracted to someone of the same sex. Would your whole self change? If you think: 'Yes', say how. If you think: 'No', say why not.

Example 1.3

Imagine you were in an accident and woke up with amnesia (loss of memory). You would not remember who you are, what you like or dislike, what you do or believe in, what relationships you have and which people are important to you. If someone were to tell you about yourself, you would have to look inside yourself to see whether what they were saying was anything like you think you are, should be or want to be. You would have to find out for yourself, as it would be impossible to believe blindly what another person says about who you are.

In the same way, we need to understand that their sense of identity is important to our clients, and we cannot tell them who to be, or what to do or believe in. It has to come from them. It is possible that clients might not believe in their own potential to do so. If this is the case, it is even more crucial for us to keep on believing in them. As we use our skills to understand who our clients are at present, we enable them to find their own sense of self in a changing world of experiences.

If you reflect on yourself over the years, with all the changes that have happened, is there a central core that you can identify as peculiarly you? Or are the people that you were at the ages of 18, 25, and 30 completely different people? Individuals always retain some part of themselves in the midst of day-to-day change (Proposition 1).

What are all these experiences referred to above? Proposition 1, Proposition 2, Proposition 5, Proposition 6 and Proposition 10 explain them in more detail. We will start by examining Proposition 1.

1.2.3 Proposition 1: Human experiences at a conscious and unconscious level

> *Every individual exists in a continually changing world of experience of which he is the centre.*
>
> [Rogers 1987: 483]

There are three principal elements to this proposition:

- The experiential world of every person is central, unique and personal.
- This personal world is continually changing.
- The experiences that constitute this world can be conscious and/or unconscious.

Rogers uses the word 'experience' as an umbrella concept for all possible experiences. He does distinguish between particular experiences, but this distinction is not to be confused with separation. In other words, although particular reference is made to experiences like perceptions, needs, behaviour, emotions and values, this does not imply that one experience can be separated from another experience, or from the person experiencing them.

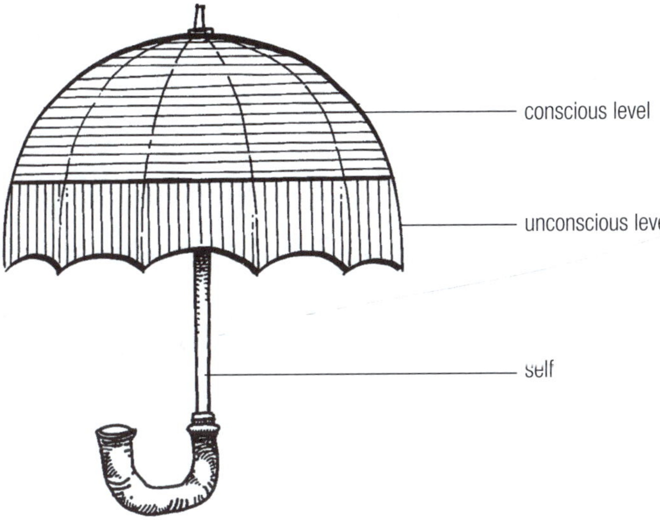

Symbolic representation of the self and experiences

One of these experiences is perception, that is, how people perceive themselves and their world, and how this perception constitutes their reality.

The experiential world includes both conscious and unconscious experiences. This is knowable only to the individual, which means that an outsider can only form an idea of an experience if the individual shares it with that person. Think of going to the doctor because you have a stomachache. The doctor cannot know what you are experiencing simply by looking at you. Doctors have apparatus, such as X-ray machines and ultrasound, which they can use to probe people's physical attributes. Sometimes surgery is performed for this purpose.

We cannot fathom people's inner worlds mechanically.

Unfortunately, we cannot fathom people's inner worlds mechanically. By the same token, the experiential world cannot be 'cut open' while the client is under anaesthetic. Only the individual can give an outsider a glimpse of what is going on inside his or her private world.

Example 1.4

A mother and daughter consulted a facilitator because they could not get along. Each felt that the other person did not hear or understand what she was saying. Proposition 1 will help the facilitator to understand that each of the two people is living only in terms of her own experiential world. This will enable the facilitator not to become impatient or judgemental. It is the facilitator's task to attempt to understand and become part of the experiential worlds of both mother and daughter.

The mother is central to her own world. Her perception of herself, of her task as mother and of her daughter changes continually. The way in which the daughter is experiencing herself and her mother is also changing continually. Such changes are not synchronised, and changes in the one may give rise to anxiety in the other. The facilitator should ask him- or herself how each individual is experiencing her own world, including the changes and even the unconscious experiences.

These experiences can be explained in more detail as our perceptions (Proposition 2), our needs and behaviour (Proposition 5), our emotions or feelings (Proposition 6), our interactions with others (Proposition 9) and our values (Proposition 10).

We might wonder why some experiences are conscious, while other experiences are unconscious. The self plays a major role in this, as explained in Proposition 11. We will start by considering the conscious experiences, since the facilitation process starts with these experiences. The unconscious experiences will be discussed in more detail at a later stage.

1.2.4 Proposition 11 [a and b]: Dealing with experiences on a conscious level

This approach assumes that our experiences manifest at two levels, namely the conscious level and the unconscious level. In both instances, the difference lies in the self and whether a particular experience fits with the self or not.

Although Rogers (1987: 503) deals with both these kinds of experiences in one proposition, we think that the difference between these experiences becomes more apparent if this proposition is discussed in two parts. In this chapter, we explore the process of symbolisation (consciously giving meaning to an experience) and how we deal with experiences that do not threaten the self, but rather fit with the self. In other words, these experiences are in line with how the self is being perceived. They do not contradict that perception.

> *As experiences occur in the life of the individual, they are either [a] symbolised, perceived and organised into some relationship to the self [b] ignored because there is no perceived relationship to the self-structure ...*
>
> [Rogers 1987: 503]

There are two key aspects to this proposition: the process of symbolisation and the relationship to the self.

> *The human being deals with much of his experience by means of the symbols attached to it. These symbols enable him to manipulate elements of his experience in relation to one another, to project himself into new situations, to make many predictions about his phenomenal world.*
>
> [Rogers 1987: 144 and 145]

During our lifetimes, we have different experiences and begin to attach particular symbols to them. These can be any kind of sensory experience, like a mother who shows a picture of a tree to her child. The child sees a tree and attaches the symbol or word 'tree' to it. Linking feeling to symbols is a bit more difficult. If a child falls down and hurts his knee, the mother will probably say a pain word, like 'hurts' or 'sore'. In this way, we learn to differentiate between what we like and what we don't like. We combine an experience with a symbol for like/not like.

We thus make sense of our experiences by attaching symbols to them. In the case of our conscious experiences, we have to place them in some kind of relationship to the self, or we can ignore them because they are not relevant to us at present.

The first way that individuals deal with experiences is to integrate the symbolised experience with the self. As a rule, these experiences are congruent with and affirm the self-structure. Thus individuals tend to admit to their consciousness (symbolise) those experiences that affirm the self.

It is important that you have a clear understanding of these two quite difficult concepts: 'symbolised experiences' and 'unsymbolised experiences'.

Symbolised experiences

Symbolised experiences are those experiences that have a physical presence. To use a metaphor, we can say they are 'above the water'. People can express their opinions on the subject. They can express their concerns and share what worries them with the facilitator. They can express what makes them happy, what makes them sad, what they are concerned about and what they are proud of.

Unsymbolised experiences

Unsymbolised experiences are the experiences that people are not aware of. They are still under the surface, just as fish are under the water. These experiences are not expressed (these issues are unspoken, but are implied). However, these unexpressed values, experiences and perceptions might influence the behaviour of people. For example, people may express the need to have a job or an income (symbolised), but what they are actually referring to is their dignity (unsymbolised).

We will focus on how we can facilitate the symbolisation process in Chapter 4.

Unsymbolised experiences

This illustration shows us the symbolisation process, when the unsymbolised experience becomes symbolised. We can compare the symbolisation or becoming-aware process with the process in which a fisherman takes a fish out of the water. This process will be described in Chapter 4 and Chapter 5.

Activity 1.4

Check which visual stimulation (books or films) you understand and remember best. Is it the material that corresponds with your own ideas and needs, or the material that differs from your ideas and needs?

The second way of handling experiences means that certain experiences do not even register. Consider what happens when you go through a supermarket with a shopping list. Of all the available commodities, you usually notice only those that you need to buy.

If people were to ask you afterwards which other commodities were available and on which shelves they can be found, you would probably not be able to tell them.

Selective shopping

The experiences referred to above can be any one or more of the experiences described in the following propositions:

- Perceptions: Proposition 2
- Needs and behaviour: Proposition 5
- Emotions: Proposition 6
- Values: Proposition 10
- Interactions with others: Proposition 9.

1.2.5 Proposition 2: Human perceptions

> *The organism reacts to the field as it is experienced and perceived. This perceptual field is, for the individual, reality.*
>
> [Rogers 1987: 484]

Like experience, perception (or observation and creation of meaning) of the world (or reality) is an individual matter. People respond in terms of both experience and perception.

Different lenses result in different views.

Look at the three figures below. What do you perceive in each of them?

[Hanson 1961: 13]

[Compton and Galaway 1984: 110]

[From Parnes 1981: 37]

- The first picture could be a small buck with long horns, or a bird with a long beak, or ...
- The second picture could be a vase, or two profiles facing each other, or ...
- The third picture could be an aeroplane in the process of landing, or is it taking off?

None of the above perceptions is either true or false, unless we believe that our own perception is the only admissible one.

Example 1.5

A mother and her fifteen-year-old son are watching the film *2001: A Space Odyssey* together. She asks him whether he recognises the background music and he answers that it is a waltz. She remarks that it is interesting that such an old tune should be so appropriate in a modern film. 'Modern?' her son responds, questioning her comment. 'That film was made way back in 1968!'

The experience or notion of what is 'modern' is relative to the individual's perception. It is futile to try to judge whether the mother or the son is right. Each of their perceptions is real and relevant, and they are both entitled to their own perceptions. The facilitator may find him- or herself in situations where one member of a family is complaining about another family member. This is when it is especially important to remember that all parties have the right to their own experiences and that we cannot judge or condemn anyone. All people perceive their world (including themselves and their interaction with others) in a uniquely individual way.

Example 1.6

A facilitator has to deal with a mother and her adolescent daughter who argue over issues concerned with rules and liberties. It is essential to bear in mind that both

>>

mother and daughter are individuals with their own perceptions or experiences of rules and freedom. The facilitator has to find out how each of them sees the issue, without taking sides with one or the other. This is difficult because the facilitator also has his or her own perception of rules to contend with. The facilitator may, for instance, believe that the parent is always right and that children are obliged to obey their parents until such time as they leave home. Or the facilitator may feel sorry for the daughter and believe that she should be supported, or that adolescents are entitled to more freedom. Can you guess how these ideas might influence the facilitator's actions, regardless of the contribution made by the clients? It is important to hear, however, how the mother and daughter, respectively, perceive and experience their experiential world, because it is their reality that is at issue.

Here you must also keep in mind that, if you speak to one person, and that person talks about another person, it is only the frame of reference, or perceptions, of the person speaking to you that you are hearing. These perceptions do not tell us anything about the person spoken about, because that person will have his or her own perceptions, known only to him- or herself. A facilitator cannot get to know one person by talking to another about that person. Let's consider the example of the mother and daughter mentioned above. If the mother came to see you alone, without her daughter, and talked about her daughter, it would be vital to remember that you were dealing with her perceptions, and not the daughter's perceptions. If, for instance, the mother said something like: 'My daughter is very naughty these days. She does not listen to me anymore and wants to do everything her own way,' you could not assume that the daughter was naughty, or know anything else about the daughter. The mother was sharing her own perceptions, which are unique to her. These perceptions reveal something about her mother-self and the changes taking place in this self.

1.2.6 Proposition 5: Needs and behaviour

> *Behaviour is basically the goal-directed attempt of the organism to satisfy its needs as experienced in the field as perceived.*
>
> [Rogers 1987: 491]

Behaviour is made up of deliberate efforts by individuals to satisfy the needs that they personally experience. These needs may not be obvious to an outsider, but the individual's behaviour mostly makes sense to him or her in its context.

In terms of this proposition, behaviour is associated with needs. Individual needs motivate behaviour. If we bear this in mind, it becomes clear that all behaviour (however odd it may appear to an outsider) has some motive, reason or goal.

Nest in shoe – motive?

So whenever the facilitator encounters clients whose behaviour seems strange, the facilitator can ask him- or herself: 'What need is this person trying to meet in this way?'

> ***Example 1.7***
>
> A teenage girl from an average-income home engages in shoplifting. At face value, this is perplexing. When we look more deeply into the matter, it turns out that she is giving the stolen items to her friends. In such a situation, the underlying need (whether symbolised or not – see Proposition 11) may be to gain the approval of her peer group. Possibly, she does not believe that they really like her (self-perception, Proposition 8, Proposition 9 and Proposition 12) and therefore tries to 'buy' their friendship and acceptance. Once her underlying need is understood, the apparently peculiar behaviour becomes more understandable.

1.2.7 Proposition 6: Emotions

> *Emotion accompanies and in general facilitates such goal-directed behaviour, the kind of emotion being related to the seeking versus the consummatory aspects of the behaviour, and the intensity of the emotion being related to the perceived significance of the behaviour for the maintenance and enhancement of the organism.*
>
> [Rogers 1987: 492]

Emotion accompanies and facilitates the purposeful behaviour mentioned above. The intensity of the emotion or feeling correlates with the importance that the person attaches to the behaviour in terms of self-preservation and self-enhancement (Proposition 4).

The intensity of emotions varies from one person to another and from one perceived situation to the next. For instance, if you are alone at home and you hear a strange noise, you will probably experience some measure of anxiety. The resultant behaviour may vary from keeping quiet and listening, to getting up and investigating. If you were to see someone climbing in through the window, the perceived threat to the self would probably be even greater and your behaviour would be correspondingly more strongly directed at self-preservation.

Thus, the girl who shoplifted in our example may experience anxiety at the thought of being caught shoplifting, but may feel even greater (more intense) fear of being rejected by her peers.

Shoplifter

We mentioned earlier that the self develops out of all our experiences. This relates to the next proposition: wholeness.

1.2.8 Proposition 3: Wholeness and unity

> *The organism reacts as an organised whole to this phenomenal field.*
>
> [Rogers 1987: 486]

As we said before, the self derives from all our experiences. Human beings have many different kinds of experiences, which will be discussed in more detail later in this chapter. All of these experiences also form part of the self, and none can be ignored when we try to understand the self of a person.

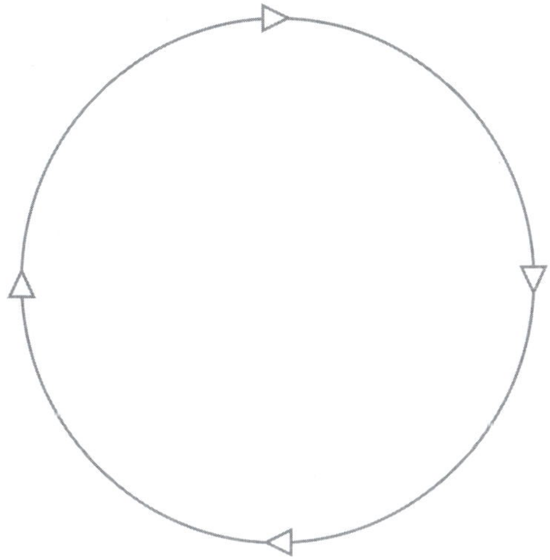

Wholeness and unity circle

Look at the illustration of the wholeness and unity circle. People, along with all their ideas, feelings, behaviour, needs, values and physical attributes, may be regarded as contained in the circle. Ask yourself where the human being begins and ends in this picture, or which part is not connected to every other part.

Do we act exclusively in terms of our perceptions, or in terms of our thoughts and feelings? Can these dimensions of the self be considered separate, or are they all integral to the person? Although we are not constantly aware of all these dimensions, they are always there, part of what we do and who we are.

Example 1.8

If you wanted to prepare a meal for your family, would you have to think about what the family members like and dislike, and then act on their thoughts and feelings to get the meal on the table?

The facilitator should therefore be open to all dimensions of human nature and not focus on just one aspect of a person.

Some people are under the misconception that person-centred theory deals only with emotions. When all the propositions have been explored, it becomes evident that this theory is far more comprehensive. Only one of the nineteen propositions deals specifically with emotions. The propositions examine needs, behaviour (Proposition 5), emotions (Proposition 6), the self (Proposition 8) and values (Proposition 10). All of this, together with the observations or perceptions discussed in Proposition 2, should be taken into account when attempting to understand people. For instance, the mother in our earlier example should be understood in terms of the way in which she experiences her self (Proposition 8), the values that she attaches to parenthood (Proposition 10), her needs as a mother and as an individual (Proposition 5), and how she expresses such needs (Proposition 5), how she feels about these needs (Proposition 6), and how she perceives herself and her daughter (Proposition 2). The same demands are made of the facilitator's understanding of the daughter and how she experiences all these aspects.

1.2.9 Proposition 9: The self and significant others

> *As a result of interaction with the environment, and particularly as a result of evaluational interaction with others, the structure of the self is formed (an organised, fluid, but consistent conceptual pattern of perceptions of characteristics and relationships of the 'I' or the 'me') together with values attached to the concepts.*

(For the sake of clarity and continuity, the description of the self given earlier is repeated here as originally formulated by Rogers.)

[Rogers 1987: 498]

This quotation tells us that one of the experiences that affects the self is our perception of our interactions, both with the environment and particularly with other people whom we see as important to us. It is a flexible yet organised picture of the attributes and relationships of the self, as well as the values attached to that picture.

No person lives in isolation. Everybody interacts with others, and our perceptions of these interactions become part of who we are (or see ourselves to be). So, for instance, we can hypothesise that a person usually experiences the self as a parent in relation to a child. In other words, a father or a mother can perceive him- or herself as a parent in relation to his or her own (or adopted or foster) child. This means that the 'I' or identity is defined in relation to the child, as in: 'I am the caretaker, protector, nurturer, educator and disciplinarian of this child', or any other perception a person might have about what it means to be a parent of a child. (However, this is not necessarily always the case, as someone might relate to a pet or a grandchild in a parental way, or see him- or herself as a parent in that relationship. On the other hand, if a person did not want to become a parent, the self might not change into a parent-self in the event of such a child.) The same hypothesis applies to the perceived self in any other interaction, for instance between a wife in relation to a husband (and vice versa), or an employer in relation to an employee.

What is of great significance here is that it is our perception of others, ourselves and our relationships that is relevant. As people are different and have different perceptions (see more on this in Proposition 1 and Proposition 2), each person's perception of him- or herself, other people and their relationship will differ. It is thus very important to listen to people sharing their perceptions with you, to understand their experiences and perceptions of themselves.

As other people are such a crucial part of the development of the self, clients often come to see a facilitator to talk about someone else. A mother might want to talk about her child, for example, a husband about his wife and so on. We might be tempted to discuss the other person, or try to understand, or even defend or explain the other person to our client. It requires a mental effort to keep in mind that we need to concentrate on how the speaker is being affected by his or her perception of the speaker's self, the other person and their relationship. This does not mean that we 'forbid' clients to speak about others, or subtly steer them away from doing so. Instead, we need to listen very carefully to them. We need to try to understand how they experience themselves and how they believe they are being affected by the person they are talking about. For example, when a mother speaks about her naughty child, she may experience herself as being a failure as a mother in relationship to the child. Remember that the theory guides our behaviour and thinking, not the behaviour and thinking of our clients. What is significant is what we do with what they tell us.

Theory is supposed to enable us to think and act in a professional manner. It is also intended to enable us to deal in a professional way with anything that clients talk about. It is only in interaction with our clients that we become professional facilitators. (In interaction with our clients, our selves as facilitators develop.) The way in which we see ourselves, our clients and the relationship between us is different from any other self or relationship. We determine how we perceive these elements and what we do with our perceptions in the professional relationship. (See also Proposition 4.)

Initially, your self as facilitator and the values attached to this self also develop in interaction with your lecturers and the authors you study. Proposition 10 teaches us more about values and the self.

1.2.10 Proposition 10: Values: Own and those adopted from other people

> *The values attached to experiences and the values that are a part of the self-structure in some instances are values experienced directly by the organism, and in some instances are values introjected or taken over from others, but perceived in distorted fashion as if they had been experienced directly.*
>
> [ROGERS 1987: 498]

Values attached to experiences and forming part of the self may be shaped by the individual's own experience, but they may also be taken over from others and assimilated into the self as if they had been experienced personally.

Initially, the child's self is shaped mainly by interaction with the parents. Later, the peer group and teachers also play a significant role. Other significant others (as illustrated in Proposition 9) become part of our lives as we grow older. It cannot be emphasised enough that the critical issue here is how the child (individual) perceives or experiences the interaction and the values of the significant others. Thus a mother may give both her children porridge for breakfast (she may value a healthy breakfast for her children). One of the children likes porridge and feels good about himself and his mother. The other child does not like porridge and might experience a sense of being punished, so that she feels less good about herself and her mother. Thus parents may have good intentions (values) that are not experienced as such by their children. (This also applies to children who want to give their parents a treat by bringing them breakfast in bed, but in the process turn the kitchen upside down.)

Children do not always experience the good intentions of their parents as positive.

A mother may encourage her son to take part in athletics because he is a good runner. She believes in his potential and wants the best for her child (her values include being a good and encouraging mother). The son, on the other hand, may feel that he is under pressure to achieve and may wonder whether he will still be accepted if he fails to achieve. (This is like the girl in our example who wondered whether she would be accepted if she did not produce presents for her friends.) Consequently, the boy may import the value that he has to achieve in order to be accepted. Then, if he fails to achieve, he may resort to steroids or drugs because he fears rejection if he were to fail.

Children do not always understand their parents' values.

In interaction with the facilitator, both the self of the client and the self of the facilitator are influenced. (As mentioned above, you are only a facilitator in relation to a client, and a client is only defined as such in relation to you). This can be seen as the motivation for our professional interaction with clients, that is, that their selves can change (be restructured) in interaction with a significant other. In this case, the facilitator becomes that significant other. Clients can therefore also be tempted to take over values from the facilitator. It is thus vital that a facilitator not praise (or condemn and criticise) a client. Since this is done in terms of the facilitator's values and frame of reference, clients may act in a particular manner simply to gain the facilitator's acceptance and not because this behaviour reflects their own values.

We will introduce you to some of the values that are associated with being a professional facilitator in Chapter 2. These values are introduced to you by the authors and your lecturers, and you could feel that you have to take them over from these people without making them your own. That is why you must think carefully about these values. You must see whether they fit with your (developing) professional self and whether you can really own them. If not, your behaviour might reflect this inconsistency. Experiences that are inconsistent with the self are discussed in more detail in Proposition 11 and Proposition 13.

Values attached to experiences and forming part of the self may therefore be shaped by the individual's own experience, but they may also be taken over from others and assimilated into the self as if they had been experienced personally.

Proposition 12 also refers to behaviour that fits with the self and with conscious experiences.

1.2.11 Proposition 12: Self and behaviour

> *Most of the ways of behaving that are adopted by the organism are those that are consistent with the concept of self.*
>
> [Rogers 1987: 507]

Behaviour motivated by symbolised experiences (that is, experiences that fit with the self and are therefore allowed into consciousness) is usually consistent with the individual's self-concept.

Here we see, once again, that the self plays a significant part in determining our behaviour. Behaviour is not merely directed at the satisfaction of needs (Proposition 5). It also has to agree with the individual's self-perception. In other words, we usually behave in ways that fit with our sense of who we are and we avoid behaviours that do not fit with our sense of self.

Consequently, behaviour can be viewed in terms of both needs and self-perception.

Example 1.9

All people eat (behaviour) when they are hungry (need). But how and what they eat depends on how the individual experiences his or her self and culture. Some people use a knife and fork. Other people use only a fork or only a knife. Some people eat with their hands or use chopsticks. In addition, people have preferences. However hungry people may be, not everyone likes the same kind of food. Person A may not like spinach (it is not to his or her taste), while person B adores spinach (it is to his or her taste). People and their tastes (in other words, what they believe to be in line with their selves) differ. Observe how people's taste in clothing differs. This applies to all human experience and behaviour.

Understanding the connection between the self and behaviour of people can enable the facilitator to understand how he or she views him- or herself and what behaviour he or she is comfortable with.

Example 1.10

If, during an interview, a client does not look directly at the facilitator, this may be an indication that looking directly at another person does not fit with the self of this client. It could indicate many different perceptions of self, such as that the client perceives him- or herself as a shy person, or a person who does not like confrontation. Whatever the case may be, it guides the facilitator in terms of what fits with his or her self and what does not. In order for a facilitator to show acceptance of this person, he or she has to accept this behaviour and self, rather than trying to force the client to make eye contact.

We have now explored all the different experiences from which the self develops that the person-centred theory emphasises. When considering all these experiences, we should remember that people determine their own selves and their experiences. This idea is expressed in Proposition 4.

1.2.12 Proposition 4: Self-determination

> *The organism has one basic tendency and striving – to actualise, maintain and enhance the experiencing organism.*
>
> [Rogers 1987: 487]

All human beings have one basic aim: to actualise, maintain and develop their total selves. This is an extremely important principle, but it is very difficult to put into practice, particularly when it comes to people in need.

We must keep in mind that this proposition refers to the self of the person as he or she experiences it. This self or identity might not be what an outsider sees as 'good'. However, we must remember that it is not the facilitator's experience of what is good or necessary that is at stake, but rather what the client sees as relevant to him- or herself. This is further complicated by unconscious experiences, which are dealt with under Proposition 11 [c and d] and Proposition 13.

Activity 1.5

Answering the following questions for yourself may help you to understand this proposition more clearly:

1 Why are you reading this book?

2 Do your efforts to achieve whatever it is you are trying to achieve by reading this book complicate your life?

3 Do these efforts create problems that you will need to overcome?

4 Do you accept these problems as the price to be paid for your striving for self-actualisation and self-development? Could these problems perhaps be regarded as part of your aspiration to become more of what you are as a person? For instance, if you are a facilitator of some kind, are you striving to become a better facilitator, thus enhancing your self as a facilitator?

5 Do you think that the poor also aspire to self-respect and the respect of others? Or are they only concerned about food and clothing? For instance, when people are poor, and believe that this is their lot in life, can they strive to be honest or clean 'poor' people?

6 If you had an accident and were left handicapped, would you still aspire to happiness? What would happiness be to you in those circumstances? Can you think of things to which your parents or family might aspire? (Ask them.)

7 Do you feel good when you do things for people, and they then thank you and tell you that they could never have managed without you? How would you feel if you were forever dependent on other people's favours?

Example 1.11

The client is a woman, married for the past eighteen years. She has two children and has never been employed outside the home. She left her parental home to move in with her husband. She sees herself as a homemaker, whose main aim in life is to provide a warm, caring, healthy environment for her family (husband and children). To enhance this self, she has attended various culinary and interior-decoration courses.

Her children have all left home to start careers of their own. They have started asking her why she does not have a career and why she relies on their father for money instead of earning her own income. She feels that all her efforts to be a good wife and mother have not been appreciated and that what she has spent her life trying to achieve is no longer valued.

>>

In interaction with her children, the self she has maintained and striven to enhance for the past eighteen years is being questioned and now she does not know what to strive for any more. Should she, for instance, as a good mother, do as the children think best and start thinking about a career outside the house? If yes, then the very effort to be a good mother as she understands a good mother to be will threaten her self as a homemaking mother and wife.

This kind of conflict can be very confusing and painful. Although the facilitator may have different ideas about motherhood, about how to be a career person and a homemaker that work for him or her, this does not entitle the facilitator to impose these ideas on the client. She has to define her own self, what she is, what she is becoming, and how to maintain and enhance that particular self.

In order to create the safe climate mentioned in Proposition 17, the facilitator needs to understand all clients' perceptions of everything, as they perceive it. This is explained in Proposition 7 below.

1.2.13 Proposition 7: Frame of reference

> *The best vantage point for understanding behaviour is from the internal frame of reference of the individual himself.*
>
> [ROGERS 1987: 494]

Example 1.12

A story is told in Malawi about a monkey that landed in a river. Eventually, after some struggle, the monkey managed to climb out of the water. When the monkey saw a fish splashing in the water, he assumed that it too needed to be rescued from the water. Obviously, this led to its death.

This frame of reference refers to people's perceptions (Proposition 2). Metaphorically speaking, it could be described as the picture of their whole reality as seen or created by people, framed by their experiences.

Look again at the illustrations on page 23 under Proposition 2. If a facilitator sees a picture of a vase, for instance, while his or her client sees two faces, the facilitator needs to let the client explain how he or she sees that picture, rather than trying to convince the client to see what the facilitator sees. What clients see is their reality or their frame of reference.

Since behaviour is motivated by needs and accompanied by emotion, these three dimensions (behaviour, needs and emotion) are also best understood in terms of the individual's frame of reference. As stated in Proposition 12, behaviour also mostly fits with the self. So the self and all the experiences that are part of it also need to be understood from the client's frame of reference.

Example 1.13

A woman described an incident that occurred when she was buying a birthday present for her mother. The present was a few fair-sized bushy trees for her mother's garden. In order to avoid damaging the trees, she let down the roof of her convertible car and transported them on the back seat. As a result, she was sitting under an umbrella of foliage as she drove along. While she was waiting at a red traffic light, the motorist in the adjoining lane stared at her in disbelief and called to her: 'Lady, wouldn't it be easier just to put up your roof if you want some shade?' Clearly, outsiders do not always understand our behaviour unless they enter into our world.

In all the examples already mentioned, each individual's behaviour needs to be understood in terms of his or her frame of reference. The behaviour of the mother and children, of the teenage girl who shoplifted and of any client you may encounter is best understood from within that individual's own frame of reference. Empathy accordingly means that while a facilitator recognises and retains his or her own frame of reference, the facilitator must also respect the right of a client to his or her own frame of reference and allow the client to express it.

The client's behaviour makes more sense if it is understood in terms of his or her own total frame of reference. (This also applies to the client's needs, which motivate behaviour, and emotions, which accompany and facilitate behaviour.) This may sound simple, but the facilitator may encounter several obstacles, which will be explored under the discussion of empathy in Chapter 3.

Once you understand the thirteen propositions discussed in this chapter, you might be able to create a mental picture of what it entails to understand your clients. Remember that you need to consider the whole person with all of his or her experiences. All of these experiences contribute to that person's frame of reference, from which the person creates his or her self or identity.

1.2.14 Exploring your self as a person and a facilitator

It is important to keep in mind that you are a whole person, with all your experiences. Your own identity develops in interaction with your significant others. You are also self-determined. Not only do you determine who you are and who your significant others are, but you also determine what you perceive, think, feel, do, and value about yourself and other people with whom you interact.

This can be a disturbing thought if you are used to thinking that others are to blame for who you are and for what you think, feel or do. Accepting that you are responsible for all this can be a heavy burden to bear.

Activity 1.6

1. When you wake up in the morning, how do you feel?
2. Is it always the same?
3. Are you always aware of why you are feeling the way you do?
4. Who is to blame for how you are feeling?
5. Who do you rely on to change what you are feeling?

Another way of looking at this belief or world view is to see it as empowering or liberating. If we have the ability to create our own thoughts, feelings and behaviour, we can create new experiences for ourselves, about ourselves and others.

We choose (not always consciously) to think, feel and do what fits with us. This also implies that if we do not accept any of what we think, feel or do, we have the ability or freedom to change it ourselves. We do not have to wait for someone else to do it for us or give us permission to do so. Of course, these kinds of changes have consequences with which we will have to live.

Example 1.14

If your boss told you to do something that went against what you believed in, you would have a difficult choice to make.

You could choose to do as he said, whilst feeling uncomfortable about it. This would suggest that you see yourself as a person who follows the rules and does not want to upset your boss. It could also mean that you need to keep the job, no matter what it costs you on a personal level.

If, however, you chose not to do as you were told, it might indicate that you valued your integrity or values more than your job. The manner in which you expressed your refusal might also be an indication of how you see yourself. For instance, you could be calm and diplomatic about it. You could explain why you like to work with your boss, but find it difficult to so in this instance. Or you could express your feelings in an angry way so as to show your boss how strongly you feel about the subject. (Maybe you see yourself as an honest person with strong views who never backs down.) So, how you deal with the situation depends not only on how you perceive the situation, but also on how you perceive yourself in that situation, as well as how you perceive your boss and your relationship. Of course, your boss will act in terms of how he or she perceives him- or herself and you, in your relationship and that particular interaction.

Are you ready to embrace the idea of your own self-determination? Can you take responsibility for your own thoughts, feelings, values and actions? It is so important, because what you think, feel, value and do is up to you. There is an important distinction to make here, though: the distinction between taking responsibility for yourself and taking responsibility for your clients. As all people are self-determined, your clients are responsible for themselves!

You need to explore how you see yourself as a facilitator so that you know what values and behaviour fit with your professional self. This will determine your interaction with your clients and the way in which you view your clients. In the next two chapters, we will discuss the professional values and the basic communication skills (in other words, the behaviour) that are required of a facilitator working from a person-centred perspective. You need to be aware of your perception of your self as we go along. If you read these sections and they do not fit with you when you read through them, you might not allow them into your conscious mind.

2 Professional values (Phase 1)

2.1 Introduction

Professional values refer to certain attitudes that the facilitator can adopt to help him or her to treat clients with respect. They are an integral and continual part of the process of facilitation. Without them, it would not be possible to create the safe space (Proposition 17) necessary for client self-exploration.

As facilitators, it is difficult for us to hide our genuine attitudes. The values that we hold are apparent in our whole attitude towards people, including our non-verbal behaviour. This is why it is so important for the facilitator to explore within him- or herself and establish what he or she believes. The facilitator must decide whether he or she genuinely believes in these attitudes or values, or if he or she has just adopted the ideas of his or her superiors or authors in the field in order to fulfil professional requirements (see Proposition 10).

We will now consider the four basic professional values without which facilitation is not possible: respect, individualisation, self-determination and confidentiality.

2.2 Respect

Rogers (1951: 24) describes the facilitator's basic hypothesis concerning humankind as respect and the belief '... that the individual has a sufficient capacity to deal constructively with all those aspects of his life that can potentially come into conscious awareness. This means ... a meaningful demonstration of the counsellor's acceptance of the client as a person who is competent to direct himself.'

This hypothesis reflects a belief that every person is worthy of our respect and esteem. If we refer to Proposition 1 and Proposition 2, and believe that all people create their own realities, including who they are, then we can respect all people. We can base this respect on the belief that people are creative and know what they have created within themselves, about themselves. They can then be respected as experts on themselves, their own experiences and their selves.

Without this respect, the facilitator will not be able to communicate empathetically or facilitate personal growth. He or she will not be able to create an atmosphere of acceptance and freedom in which clients can reveal their deepest, darkest and most painful experiences without fear of rejection (refer to Proposition 17). Boy and Pine (1983: 83) agree with this when they state that 'the creation of a liberating counselling relationship requires that the counsellor not only have a fundamental belief in the client's tendency toward health, but that the counsellor create a counselling atmosphere in which this tendency is nourished.'

Creating conditions in which growth can take place freely

In order to facilitate the client's self-exploration, it is necessary to believe in his or her potential for development and to create the conditions in which this can take place freely.

You might consider this attitude to be wishful thinking and believe that it is not possible in practice. You might think that it is easier said than done. How is it possible to respect a person who, for instance, has raped a child, committed murder, is very poor or is old and confused?

When a facilitator no longer believes in the client's striving for self-enhancement, the true purpose of any helping process may be questioned. Does the mission to help people to help themselves still remain plausible? This is a most important issue that the facilitator must resolve for him- or herself. As far back as 1964, Rogers (in Boy and Pine 1983: 80) addressed the dilemma of the facilitator developing his or her own value system.

> *Even more important, perhaps, is the fact that the modern individual is assailed from every angle by divergent and contradictory value claims. It is no longer possible, as it was in the not-too-distant historical past, to settle comfortably into*

the value system of one's forebears or one's community and live out one's life without ever examining the nature and the assumptions of that system. ’

Here are two ways in which a facilitator can implement respect in his or her practice.

2.2.1 Refrain from judgment

The facilitator is there to help his or her clients, not to judge them. It is not the facilitator's role to judge clients as good or bad, guilty or innocent, or to apportion blame. The facilitator's task is rather to understand clients and their pain, and to help them grow.

The concept of unconditional positive regard relates to a client's thoughts, needs, behaviour, feelings, self and values. The client must feel accepted by the facilitator, even when the client does not yet accept him- or herself. Thus, the facilitator must demonstrate consistent willingness to extend understanding, irrespective of the client's behaviour and of whether the facilitator approves of that behaviour or not. This does not mean that the facilitator gives up his or her own values, but that the values and pain of the client come first during the facilitation process. Putting the client first thus becomes one of the facilitator's own values or aims.

According to Hepworth and Larsen (1990: 53), the facilitator is confronted with the need to retain his or her own values without imposing them on others. The facilitator must also refrain from the tendency to condemn people whose behaviour is offensive to him or her. This is linked to the injunction to remain serene and imperturbable, and not to react with embarrassment, shock or disapproval when people discuss painful experiences. The facilitator will only be able to accept people whose behaviour conflicts with his or her personal values if the facilitator has developed openness and self-acceptance (see Proposition 18 and Proposition 19). Failure to do so may reduce his or her effectiveness, for it is impossible to hide negative feelings or to camouflage them so well that the client does not become aware of the facilitator's incongruence.

2.2.2 Enable the client to work through pain

The helping process is likely to be painful. The facilitator shows respect for the client by empathising with the pain rather than by avoiding it. This is done on the assumption that the client is prepared to pay the price for learning to live more effectively. So while the facilitator's respect is accompanied by the expectation that the process will be painful for the client, it comes with the assurance that the facilitator will be there with the client throughout the painful process. (See also Proposition 17.)

2.3 Individualisation

If a facilitator accepts the value of individualisation, then according to Rogers (1987: 29) he or she 'assumes the internal frame of reference of the client, to perceive the world sees it, to perceive the client himself as he is seen by himself, to lay aside all from the external frame of reference while doing so, and to communicate of this empathic understanding to the client.' This implies that the facilitator xperiential world of each client from the client's frame of reference.

In terms of Proposition 1 and Proposition 2, each person's experiences and perceptions of life and him- or herself are unique. This includes needs, behaviour (Proposition 5), emotions (Proposition 6), the self (Proposition 8) and values (Proposition 10).

It is not always easy to implement this idea or these values, especially when the facilitator is active in a specialised field. It is easy to generalise by seeing people as stereotypes and labelling them as such.

For instance, we could generalise and declare that all 'alcoholics' are the same. Yet people with a drinking problem differ in many ways. One person might drink one bottle of wine before losing control, whereas another person might be able to drink two bottles of alcohol before losing control. People also do not react in the same way when they are under the influence of alcohol. One person might become weepy and sad, another person might become angry at everyone around him or her, and a third person might become sleepy. If even the physical reaction to the same substance differs, why is it sometimes so hard to accept that the personal aspects will also differ? Similarly, everyone with such a problem will have a different perception of who they are and what needs are being satisfied by such behaviour. The person may not even be aware of these needs at a conscious level (see Proposition 11 and Proposition 13).

Saying that all alcoholics are the same is like saying that all women or all men are the same. Do you think that you are the same as all other people of the same gender? In spite of one similarity (your gender), you are unique in many other respects. In the same way, people with the same basic problem, such as alcohol dependency, differ considerably in other respects.

Ignoring or disregarding this uniqueness means that the unique potential, experiences and direction of the person you are dealing with are also being lost. Both the facilitator and the client may start believing that the client is just one more 'alcoholic', who will necessarily follow the same route as all others before. This may discourage both the facilitator and the client, and the facilitator's task will become tedious. The contrary is also true. The facilitator who approaches each client as a unique person will find a challenge in each new situation, like a lucky packet that simply has to be opened to reveal the surprise.

Surprise, surprise

Activity 2.1

If you already find yourself in practice (or have been in the past), consider the nature of your approach to clients.

1 How do you regard and treat your clients?

2 How do you experience the work you do? Do you still enjoy it?

3 Are you still confident that you and your clients will be able to achieve something? If you are no longer confident, why not? If you are still confident, to what would you attribute your optimism?

If you are still studying to be a facilitator, ask yourself the following questions.

1 How do you react to people who have transgressed the country's laws?

2 Are there any people you would truly never want to understand?

2.4 **Self-determination**

According to Angyal, as quoted by Rogers (1987: 489), 'Life is an autonomous dynamic event that takes place between the organism (client) and the environment. Life processes do not merely tend to preserve life but transcend the momentary status quo of the organism (client), expanding itself continually and imposing its autonomous determination upon an ever-increasing realm of events.'

Rogers (1987: 489) adds that the human organism (client) tends to move forward, or as the client will see it, in a direction of self-growth. A facilitator in the field of person-centred therapy must share this belief in growth and self-determination if he or she is to be of assistance to clients.

As we mentioned in the discussion of respect, the person-centred approach requires faith in humankind's pursuit of self-knowledge. This relates to Proposition 4. This pursuit needs to be viewed from the client's frame of reference (Proposition 7). The facilitator cannot decide what the client's goals should be, or what would be best for the client. (This would imply greater belief in and respect for him- or herself than for the client.)

Self-determination therefore means that a client determines for him- or herself:

- How the client experiences and perceives him- or herself and his or her world (Proposition 1, Proposition 2 and Proposition 8)
- How the client wishes to satisfy his or her needs in line with that which corresponds with his or her self (Proposition 5, Proposition 8 and Proposition 12)
- What the client's own values are and will be (Proposition 10 and Proposition 19)
- The direction in which to move in the exploration of painful experiences (Proposition 17 and Proposition 15)
- What the client needs to enhance, maintain and develop his or her self (Proposition 4).

Each person knows his or her self better than anyone else.

If we accept the principle that each person knows his or her self better than anyone else, and is therefore in the best position to explore, expose and understand the self, we see that counsellor direction of a counselling session is non-productive (Boy and Pine 1983: 9 and 10).

This implies that it is the client who directs the process of facilitation, in terms of:

- What he or she wishes to discuss
- How he or she wishes to discuss it
- Whether he or she wishes to discuss it (sometimes the client does not want to talk and remains silent).

This means that the facilitator is guided by his or her clients, and not the other way around. Clients guide us into their experiential world, taking us on a journey of exploration of themselves. Only they know how quickly or slowly we can travel.

2.5 **Confidentiality**

Confidentiality is a debatable and controversial issue. In this section, we will highlight some of the dilemmas for your consideration.

According to Proposition 17, the facilitator should create a climate within which the client feels completely safe. This allows the client consciously to acknowledge and explore painful experiences that have not been symbolised or that have been distorted because they threaten the self (Proposition 11 [c and d]). The facilitator therefore facilitates the acknowledgement of painful experiences by the client. This gives rise to two issues:

- What should we do with this knowledge?
- Will the client trust us with such knowledge if he or she is not entirely certain that it will not be repeated to others or used against him or her?

Would you share your deepest experiences with someone if you were not certain that these experiences would not be repeated to others? If you had discussed a sensitive issue with a person and then found that it had been repeated to someone else, how would you feel? Is there any reason why a client would not feel the same way or, even worse, should not be allowed to feel the same way? Even though people are unique, a negative reaction, such as disappointment, shame or anger, is virtually guaranteed if confidentiality is broken. It is also very unlikely that the client will ever again trust the facilitator.

According to Odendal et al. (1987: 1 273), trust includes believing in someone's honesty and loyalty. Confidentiality means that what has been said will remain private and will not be repeated to someone else. What are the practical implications of this confidentiality? Think about these scenarios:

- Having conducted an interview with a married woman, are you entitled to discuss with her husband what was said?
- Are you entitled to tell the wife about a conversation you had with her husband?
- Are you entitled to inform parents of conversations conducted with their child?

We often say: 'Yes' in the above situations, believing that breaking confidence is permissible if we believe that it is in the best interests of the client. But who should decide what is best, the facilitator or the client? How can we be sure that we know what is best? (See Proposition 1, Proposition 2 and Proposition 4.)

Now consider these scenarios:

- You are working where you have to share an office. Could you ensure confidentiality?
- Your organisation is a part of a small community where you also live. Clients know you on different levels, not just as a social worker. Could you ensure confidentiality?

Responsibility towards the community raises another dilemma. When we hear something that poses a threat to others, we have to make it known. Does your client know this? Could it be that he or she has a need to report something of this nature knowing that you will be obliged to take action? If the client has shared such information with a facilitator, it may be an indication that he or she can no longer keep things bottled up (even if this is only on an unconscious level).

The client is the key to solving this dilemma. A facilitator and his or her client are involved in a partnership, so the facilitator has to decide on any action together with the client. If you bear this in mind, it may be easier not to feel overwhelmed by the client or your own sense of responsibility. This will make it possible for you to respect the client. At the same time, it will enable clients to respect themselves and you.

This brief discussion of confidentiality has already suggested that it is not an easy value to uphold. You need to be continually aware of making it happen. In this sense, then, it is also a skill, something that you have to do to create the necessary conditions for effective facilitation. You might expect your future employer to make facilities available where confidentiality can easily be maintained, but this is not always the case. For instance, you might be expected to interview clients in an open-plan office, or one in which the doors cannot close, or cannot close completely. In any of these situations, your conversations might be overheard, which nullifies any possibility of confidentiality.

Activity 2.2

Imagine you found yourself in the situations mentioned above. In each case, describe what you could do to maintain or create a sense of confidentiality.

CHAPTER

3 Basic communication skills (Phase 1)

3.1 Introduction

Rogers (1951: 5 and 6) was not particularly concerned with the techniques or methods of rendering assistance. In his opinion, the facilitator's entire attitude and actions need to facilitate the growth of the client as a person. In time, the facilitator assimilates the theory and values, and is able to implement these aspects in his or her own unique way. (See Proposition 12 for a description of actions that fit with the facilitator's professional self.)

It is not easy at first to convert this theory into action. The theory focuses largely on understanding the client as a person, so a newcomer to the person-centred approach may get the impression that the facilitator is not being active. The theory defines clients as the experts on their own lives, so that clients are the ones who determine the direction and rate of the facilitation process. The facilitator's role is therefore non-directive. In other words, the facilitator does not decide on behalf of his or her clients what their experiences are or should be. This does not, however, mean that the facilitator is passive.

> *This misconception of the approach (that it is merely passive and has a laissez-faire policy) has led to considerable failure in counselling and for good reason. In the first place, the passivity and seeming lack of interest or involvement is experienced by the client as rejection, since indifference is in no real way the same as acceptance. In the second place, a laissez-faire attitude does not in any way indicate to the client that he is regarded as a person of worth. Thus, [with] the counsellor who plays a merely passive role, many clients will leave, both disappointed in their failure to receive help and disgusted with the counsellor for having nothing to offer.*
>
> [Rogers 1987: 27]

The inexperienced facilitator often has this kind of experience, as it can be hard to find the difference between doing nothing (being passive) and giving advice or solutions (suggestions) for a client's problems. Being actively non-directive is not easy. On the contrary, understanding clients and facilitating their personal growth requires intense concentration and considerable skill. For instance, if a client is unemployed, it might be easier to pick up the phone and arrange employment than to enable the client to find ways of earning an income. And yet it is the aim of the facilitation process to enable people to help themselves, therefore to facilitate a process whereby they can become all they can be.

One way of realising this objective is to implement the person-centred approach. The communication skills provide the basis for all forms of assistance and for the total facilitation process. The skills are applied not only during the initial contact, but continually, until the termination of the process.

We will discuss the following three communication skills in more detail below:

- Attentiveness
- Listening
- Empathy.

We hope that what you will learn here will enable you to use these skills in communicating with individuals within the framework of the person-centred approach.

Since you might not be familiar with the implementation of this theory, we will indicate the relationship between the propositions and their implementation in the discussion of each technique.

3.2 Attentiveness

As mentioned in the discussion of Proposition 17, if the facilitator wants to create a safe space, he or she must practise certain behaviours actively while avoiding other behaviours. Attentiveness is one of the behaviours that must be practised actively throughout the facilitation process.

When the facilitator is attentive, he or she enters the client's total life world, all the client's experiences and selfhood (Proposition 1–Proposition 8 and Proposition 10). The message to clients is that the facilitator is accessible to them as people.

We can describe attentiveness as the way in which the facilitator orientates him- or herself physically and psychologically towards the client so that the client feels sufficiently at ease to share his or her experiences, ideas and emotions. The message is thus conveyed to the client that the facilitator is open to him or her, that the client can trust the facilitator and drop his or her defences in discussions with the facilitator. This enables the facilitator to be 'with' the client and to maintain continual contact with him or her through attentive listening.

Shulman (1982: 86) points out that attentiveness is a two-directional process during which the facilitator attends to what he or she says, does and feels. This is the crux of attentiveness. On the other hand, the facilitator must attend verbally and non-verbally to the client.

On the personal level, the facilitator can ask him- or herself before an interview whether he or she is emotionally ready to communicate with another person. In other words, the facilitator can ask him- or herself if he or she is able to focus all his or her attention and energy on the client, or if there are any distractions that might impede this process. Distractions can be created by the physical setting, for example, when there is a high level of noise in the surroundings, or if the setting is too hot or too cold. Another example of a distraction is if the facilitator is still mentally 'with' a previous client whose world was entered into quite deeply. The facilitator has to 'clear the decks' metaphorically speaking by bringing his or her attention back from that client and focusing it on the client to come.

At another level, a distraction could be created by a personal issue in the facilitator's life. A sick child or spouse about whom the facilitator is concerned, for example, could cause his or her attention to stray.

It is important to use your body posture and facial expression to indicate that you are there for a client during facilitation. Remember that you communicate with your whole being (Proposition 3) and not just with your voice. The way in which you use your body will depend on what you are familiar and comfortable with. You also need to learn what your clients are comfortable with. You can do this by observing their posture. There are three important issues to consider here.

3.2.1 Arrangement of the physical setting

If you see the person in an office, how are the chairs arranged and how does the client respond to that arrangement?

- Is there a desk between you and the other person, and if so, why?
- Do you need to write notes while you are talking to the client? If so, can this be done in such a way that you remain respectful of and attentive to the client? Are there any other arrangements you can make, like tape recording the interview (with the client's permission) so that you can make notes afterwards?
- If you have two chairs arranged close to each another, does the client push the chair back a bit when sitting down? If so, what do you make of it? Do you feel rejected, perhaps, or compelled to move closer because you think it is necessary for the communication process? Can you allow clients to determine the most comfortable space for themselves and follow their lead?
- If you have to speak to clients in hospital, do you sit on the bed? If so, are they comfortable with this physical closeness? If not, can you arrange a different setting? Is there sufficient privacy for a personal discussion?

3.2.2 Eye contact

In some cultures, direct eye contact indicates attention and awareness of the other person. However, this is not always the case. There are cultures in which direct eye contact is seen as rude, a challenge or even as confrontational. Sometimes a younger person is not permitted to look directly at an older person. There is no rule that will hold true for every person you talk to. The client is usually the best guideline. Observe clients carefully. Be sensitive to their use of eye contact and what is comfortable for them. If you realise that they perceive direct eye contact as threatening, then avoid it, because you want to create an atmosphere where no threat to the client is perceived (Proposition 17).

3.2.3 Non-verbal communication (body language)

Non-verbal messages are important when you are interacting with clients. You can use your body deliberately as a means of communication by being aware of the signs and messages you receive and send out while in contact with clients. Consider conducting an interview with a child, an extremely tense person or a person who cannot maintain direct eye contact. Think about how you can physically adapt your communication. Middleman and Wood (1990: 49) point out that the facilitator can engage in the client's medium by doing what the client does. This will probably lead to verbal interaction. For example, an elderly lady sits reading a newspaper during the facilitator's visit. The facilitator also takes a newspaper and pages through it, which gives the client the opportunity to decide when or whether she will start speaking.

Linked to this is the choice of a communication medium that suits the client, based on indications of the person's interests and/or the facilitator's observation of what is acceptable to a particular person. For example, a child may find that it is easier and less threatening to communicate verbally while involved in an activity such as playing a ball game, stroking a pet or drawing a picture. Sometimes this also applies to an adult. For instance, if the facilitator walks with an adolescent while they drink cooldrinks, the adolescent may feel more relaxed and inclined to talk. This could be the beginning of an interaction that will bind the facilitator and client together.

3.3 Listening

In order to understand a client's experiential world (Proposition 1), his or her perceptions and realities (Proposition 2) and self (Proposition 8), we first need to listen carefully to what the client is experiencing and how he or she is experiencing it.

We need to listen to what the client is saying in relation to the total person (Proposition 3 and Proposition 8). In other words, we must listen in terms of his or her:

- Experiential world (Proposition 1)
- Perceptions and thoughts (Proposition 2)
- Needs (Proposition 5)
- Behaviour to satisfy needs (Proposition 5)
- Emotions accompanying needs and behaviour (Proposition 6)
- Self (who the client is as he or she experiences him- or herself) (Proposition 8)
- Interaction with others (which self developed in interaction with the significant others to whom the client refers) (Proposition 9)
- Values (those arising from the client's own experience and those adopted from others) (Proposition 10).

All these experiences should be heard and understood from within the client's own frame of reference (Proposition 7).

Active listening is closely related to active attentiveness. It is a process of observation and listening to both verbal and non-verbal communication. It is a prerequisite for all other communication skills and precedes all other skills. Listening may be regarded as the inverse of talking, and unfortunately we are all more inclined to talk than to listen.

Listening can be defined as the active process of receiving auditory stimuli, attaching meaning to what we hear and making sense of the raw vocal symbols we receive. It is a deliberate, selective process in which the hearer selects the sounds the speaker makes, and pays attention to, recognises, understands and makes sense of them (Kadushin 1990: 244). Listening forms a bridge between hearing and understanding a person. Listening is a complex process consisting of many different elements, which are discussed below.

3.3.1 Hearing

There is a difference between listening and hearing. Hearing is an automatic physiological process in which auditory stimuli are received. Problems can arise even at this stage if the hearer has a hearing defect and cannot hear or can only hear imperfectly, or if there is so much noise that hearing is not possible. The speed of speech can create a further problem. The hearer can process the message faster than the average speed of speech, with the result that the hearer's thoughts may begin to wander.

3.3.2 Understanding

During the process of understanding, meaning must be attached to the words that are heard. The meaning must correspond with the message intended by the sender. The message must be understood, which means that we must at least understand the language, the intention of the message (for example, serious or funny), the context of the message, the relationship with the person, the climate of the meeting and the subject of the message. According to Tubbs and Moss (1991: 180), the process of understanding involves the hearer associating the message with his or her previous experiences. At this stage, we are inclined to evaluate and judge the message, to approve or to disapprove, to accept or to reject. Such evaluation is regarded as one of the biggest stumbling blocks in interpersonal communication. The attitude should rather be to receive the message as it was intended by the person who sent it.

From the perspective of this theory, the facilitator also has to understand the person who is uttering the message. In other words, it is not just the message that should be understood (or the words or content of what is being said), but also what this conveys about the person who is uttering the message.

3.3.3 Remembering

Remembering takes place when information is stored for later retrieval. Part of the proof of how well we listen is how much we remember of what is said. Research shows that most people remember only 50% of what has just been said to them, and only 35% after eight hours. That is why it is so important to write a report as soon as possible after an interview with a client.

3.3.4 Listening to and understanding non-verbal behaviour

What constitutes non-verbal behaviour? Communication without using words is the most basic way of conveying information to another person. For example, long before a baby can speak, it expresses its dissatisfaction by crying and waving its arms around. Non-verbal communication comprises two-thirds of communication between people, which means that just one-third of all communication is verbal. Non-verbal communication is a continuous process that may or may not be accompanied by verbal communication. It is the most important way of conveying attitudes and feelings (Brill 1990: 64). Cormier and Cormier (1985: 66) show that many 'leakages', by which they mean messages that are valid, but were not sent intentionally, occur by means of non-verbal communication. They maintain that non-verbal messages often give a deeper, fuller picture of the client than verbal communication.

3.3.5 Body language

Body language is a type of non-verbal communication that relates to movements, gestures and attitude. It is constantly observed during an interview by both communicators. Shulman (1982: 88) makes the important point that the expression of feeling in particular occurs through body language and that the observant facilitator can perceive this in many ways. Equally, the client can gauge a facilitator's attitude by reading his or her body language. A tense body and a relaxed body send out different messages. An interviewer who is sitting bolt upright on the edge of the chair with his or her arms and legs crossed may convey a tense message.

3.3.6 The face

The face is the part of the body that provides most of the clues. Kadushin (1990: 284) says: 'The face is naked and so is open to observation.' Kadushin goes on to say: 'It is said that the most important thing we wear is the expression on our face.' The face is the part of the body that expresses the most automatic signs of tension, such as blushing, sweating and dry lips. Furthermore, the face is capable of thousands of different expressions. We can learn to adopt certain facial expressions that we perceive to be appropriate for certain occasions, for example, a funeral or a discussion with our boss. There are certain categories of 'primary affect displays' (intense emotions) (DeVito 1991: 161) such as joy, surprise, fear, anger, sadness and loathing, which find expression on the face. Often, the mixture of these emotions makes it more difficult to read them. Different parts of the face can manifest a certain emotion for a fraction of a second, followed by a reaction on another part of the face. It is only when we film facial expressions and play them back slowly that we can see the full extent of the variety of facial expressions.

Listening is an active process. It does not just happen; we have to make it happen. Kadushin (1990: 244) says that it is not an automatic process, but that '... we have to make a conscious, deliberate and continuing commitment to listen. It almost requires that we occasionally command ourselves to listen, stop to listen.' It demands energy and dedication. Listening is a vital skill for all forms of human communication (DeVito 1991: 70). It sounds easy, but from the cries of distress of so many people who say: 'You don't listen to me. You don't hear what I say', it is clear that listening is not so easy.

There are many reasons why listening is a fundamental skill:

- It shows respect for other people and demonstrates to clients that the facilitator values them enough to give them his or her full attention.

- Active listening removes the need to make assumptions about clients because they are giving the information. Because clients feel safe, they can remove the masks used to protect their selves.
- It bridges differences in age, gender and culture. How can the facilitator know what it is like to be old, male, female, Zulu, white, dying, hungry, raped and so on if he or she has not experienced the condition or is not one of these people? People with experiences that are different from yours can help you to understand them, if you listen well.

This was confirmed in a lecture presented by Carl Rogers in 1965.

> *I think I know why I'm satisfied to hear someone. When I can really hear someone, it puts me closely in touch with him. It enriches my life. It's also true that it's through hearing people that I have learnt all that I know about individuals, about personalities, about interpersonal relationships ...*
>
> [BARRET-LENNARD 1988: 415]

Different facial expressions

3.3.7 Minimal encouragers

Minimal encouragers are verbal and non-verbal messages that the facilitator uses to encourage clients to continue sharing their experiences. The facilitator listens and tries to understand the person, without interrupting him or her. This shows clients that the facilitator is 'with' them. They feel that the facilitator is paying attention and is interested in them.

Examples of non-verbal encouragers include the facilitator nodding his or her head, and using gentle hand and body gestures to keep the conversation flowing.

Even silence can be described as a non-verbal encourager, as it gives clients space and time to collect their thoughts without putting any pressure on them. They do not feel pressurised to keep on talking even if they are not yet ready to do so.

Examples of verbal encouragers include the facilitator saying things like: 'uh', 'uhm', 'uh-huh', 'I see', 'go on' and 'please continue'.

The facilitator can also use emphasis as a verbal encourager. This involves the facilitator repeating a word or phrase of the client's with an enquiring intonation. Consider this example.

> ***Example 3.1***
>
> Client: I am so scared.
>
> Facilitator: Scared?
>
> Client: Yes. I am scared of ... *(He continues with what scares him.)*
>
> Or:
>
> Client: I am completely alone in this world.
>
> Facilitator: Completely?

3.4 Basic empathy

> *This formulation would state that it is the counsellor's function to assume, in so far as he is able, the internal frame of reference of the client, to perceive the world as the client sees it, to perceive the client himself as he is seen by himself, to lay aside all perceptions from the external frame of reference while doing so and to communicate something of this empathic understanding to the client.*
>
> [ROGERS 1987: 29]

> *Empathy as a form of communication involves both listening to and understanding the client.*
>
> [EGAN 1994: 123 AND 124]

Empathy means being able to see what the client's world is like to him or her and how the client sees him- or herself. This means that the facilitator temporarily sets aside his or her own frame of reference. He or she then attempts, without prejudice or preconceived ideas, to hear and understand the client, and to convey this understanding to the client verbally and non-verbally. The latter is most important because it is of no benefit to the client if the facilitator understands him or her, but the client is unaware of it and cannot see or hear that he or she is being understood. The facilitator should therefore consciously endeavor to demonstrate to the client that he or she is being understood.

It is important to note that the understanding referred to here is not just of the content given by the client while talking to the facilitator, but more importantly, of the person who is being talked to. What does the content shared by the client tell the facilitator about the person who is talking? The question remains whether such understanding is possible. It is, in fact, contrary to Proposition 2 of this particular theory. Briefly, Proposition 2 states that each person's perception of the world is his or her own reality. It is a personal, subjective view. As a unique person, the facilitator also has his or her own frame of reference, which differs from that of the client (and of other people). It is not easy to enter another person's frame of reference. Here are some of the stumbling blocks that make it so difficult.

Both of these people, F (Facilitator) and C (Client), live in their own worlds, with their own experiences and selves, which they perceive from their own frames of reference.

What could happen between these people during the process of facilitation?

Does F see what is happening with C, and then try to pull C into her own world?

Or does F step up beside C, gently take her by the hand and try to guide C into F's world?

Or does F step up beside C, then try to push or shove C into her own world?

These kinds of actions on the part of the facilitator could be understandable. After all, the facilitator usually knows who he or she is, and is comfortable with who he or she is and with his or her experiences. The facilitator might believe that his or her clients would be happier if they lived in the same space as the facilitator does, saw themselves and their worlds in the same way the facilitator does, and felt, thought and acted as the facilitator does or wants them to.

The facilitator's own world is safe and familiar to him or her. The facilitator would probably be more comfortable working with clients in this world than making the effort to move out of his or her own comfort zone and into the experiential world of the stranger before him or her.

After all, the facilitator does not know where the client is going to take him or her. The facilitator does not know if he or she will be able to follow and stay with the client in this new and unfamiliar (maybe even dark and dangerous) experiential world.

That is what empathy entails: stepping out of our own comfort zones or frames of reference and into the experiential world of the other, the client, no matter what this new, strange world might hold (see the illustration on page 56).

The facilitator has to trust him- or herself. The facilitator has to trust that he or she will be able to get back into his or her own world and not get lost in the new world, or be overwhelmed by it. Entering the client's world also entails staying there as long as the client requires, without trying to change the client's experiential world.

If, for example, C is feeling depressed, F has to stay in that depression, exploring its depth and intensity, for as long as C needs to be there.

So, if a client is angry, the facilitator does not try to calm him or her down, but rather accepts, understands and explores the anger. The same goes for any other experience: hate, love, jealousy, mistrust, confusion, anger or frustration. If the facilitator tried to change the experience, he or she would be acting from his or her own frame of reference. The facilitator would be imposing his or her need for the client to be calm, composed or comfortable on the client.

Clients mostly come to see facilitators because they are not feeling all right, because they are upset and unhappy for some or other reason. During the initial stage, it does not matter why this is the case. It matters more to demonstrate acceptance of these experiences and the person experiencing them.

If the facilitator stays with and enables the client to explore these experiences, the reason for them will become clearer during the exploration process.

Activity 3.1

What do you think some of the stumbling blocks to demonstrating empathy would be for you?
Can you think of ways to deal with them?

Rogers (1987: 29) agrees that this is a difficult task. Note what he says in the quotation on page 52: '... in so far as he is able ...'. This implies that the facilitator is not able to enter into the client's life world fully. Egan (1994: 107, 115–116) makes provision for the problematic nature of total immersion in a client's life world by distinguishing between accurate and inaccurate empathy. Inaccurate empathy means that the facilitator has understood the client incorrectly, or not entirely correctly. In such a case, the facilitator must allow him- or herself to be corrected by the client. Bear in mind that the client knows best how he or she perceives his or her life world and self, and that it makes no sense to argue with the client about his or her experiences. It is the facilitator's task to become familiar with the client's view and to explore together with the client. (This does not mean, however, that the facilitator should adopt the client's perspective. Each person retains the right to his or her own ideas, but the facilitation process revolves around the client, and therefore his or her ideas, experiences and perceptions provide the material with which to work.)

In terms of Proposition 3 of the person-centred theory, a client should be seen in his or her totality. This means that we need to work with everything that the client provides. (In this section, we are dealing with empathy. The meaning of 'work' in this context is to communicate with empathic understanding.)

According to Proposition 7, a person's behaviour can be understood only from within the individual's own frame of reference. Therefore the client's behaviour (in and away from your presence) should be understood and this understanding should be communicated to the client.

Behaviour, however, relates to needs. In terms of Proposition 5, behaviour is aimed at satisfying needs, and needs are therefore also material for empathy.

Needs depend on the person's experiential world (Proposition 1), as he or she perceives it (Proposition 2). The client's experiences and perceptions should therefore also be treated with empathy. Emotions in turn accompany behaviour, and empathy is therefore also applicable to emotions.

A part of the total perceptual experiential field is gradually distinguished as the 'self', and, therefore, the self also becomes a subject of empathy. The self refers to the way in which the client experiences him- or herself, who he or she is. This may differ from the way in which the facilitator or even family members see the client, but during interviews, it is the client's experience of him- or herself that is relevant. When a mother has shared her perception of, for example, her son with you in an interview, it represents her frame of reference, not that of the child. When talking to the child, you should not listen with prejudice, attempting to ascertain whether his ideas are the same as those of the mother or thinking that the child is simply lying to you if his ideas differ from her ideas. Give the child the opportunity to share his story and his experiences with you. Try to understand how he experiences himself from his frame of reference and try to convey your understanding to him in his own language.

Values are attached to experience and form part of the self, and empathy therefore also applies to values. In this respect, empathy involves understanding of the distinction between values attached to own experiences and those adopted from others, as experienced by the individual him- or herself (Proposition 10).

Empathy is therefore a complex skill requiring a great deal of concentration, verbal and non-verbal communication skills, and mental skills. (Of course, the common misconception is that it consists of passive, uninvolved listening!).

We might wonder why the facilitator goes to all this trouble and what good it actually does the client. To answer this thought, we need to turn to the theory and process of facilitation once more. (It is theory that guides our professional opinions and actions.)

As at the beginning of this chapter, we can start with Proposition 17, which provides the facilitator with some indication of the most useful behaviour in enabling the client to explore the self. When the client experiences no threat to the self, he or she can start allowing into his or her consciousness those experiences that have been painful and have therefore not been allowed into his or her consciousness. The client can then face these experiences and start assimilating them. How does the facilitator create a situation in which the client experiences no threat?

Proposition 16 provides an indication of those things that the client does find threatening and that should be avoided, namely any experience that threatens the symbolised self (Proposition 8). A threatening experience will cause the person to protect the self and to deny the experience access to the consciousness. If the facilitator therefore says something that is contrary to the client's frame of reference, the client will protect him- or herself against the facilitator. (In the past, this was called 'resistance': the client resisted those actions of the facilitator that were contrary to the self.) The facilitator should show the client that he or she poses no threat, but understands and accepts the client. If the client is fully understood and accepted (and knows this), he or she can start restructuring the self in order to cope with those experiences (perceptions, needs, behaviour, emotions and values) that are in conflict with the self. Once again, the facilitator cannot decide how this should be done, or whether the client will accept such experiences or not.

Example 3.2

A young man had grown up in a home where premarital sex was not acceptable. He and his girlfriend had a close and intense relationship, although they were still struggling financially. He was not sure that he himself believed that premarital sex was wrong.

Depending on your own values, you may have some or other preferred solution to this problem, but that is your business, just as the young man needs to develop his own solution, his own values that will fit with his self! This is in fact the objective of person-centred theory, and empathy is one of the most important aids at the disposal of the facilitator in realising this objective.

Activity 3.2

Make a list of all the experiences of the client as a human being that are relevant to empathy.

There is a big difference between telling a client you are being empathic and actually demonstrating empathy. In the same way, there is a big difference between telling a client that you understand and actually demonstrating your understanding.

In the first place, telling the client means that the facilitator is operating from his or her own frame of reference. Secondly, it means that the facilitator expects the client to understand him or her, not the other way around.

So, instead of explaining the person-centred approach, just invite the client to start where he or she would like to, or to share whatever he or she wants to or feels ready to share.

Consider this example. If a client said: 'I am so angry at my son, I could strangle him!', it would not demonstrate understanding if the facilitator just said: 'I understand how you feel.' The client could respond with something like: 'How could you? Has your son ever used drugs?', or: 'Then tell me how I feel.'

However, if the facilitator responded with something like: 'I sense you are so furious right now, you could wring his neck!', it would show the client that she is being understood and accepted with her feelings and needs.

Here are some hints on how to demonstrate understanding (empathy) actively:

- Use keywords that have a particular meaning for the client, without repeating verbatim everything he or she says. Automatically repeating everything the client says may convey disinterest, lack of involvement and disrespect. It offers the client as little value as a conversation with a parrot.
- Try to feel an affinity with the intensity of the client's experiential world. For instance, if a client become angry, you should try to convey your understanding of his or her feelings with the same animation. Speaking softly may calm the client down,

but it will not encourage the client to share the full extent of his or her anger with you. If you demonstrate to your client, however, that you truly understand the depth of his or her experience, the client will feel a sense of acceptance. This will encourage the client to elaborate on his or her experiences. Remember, the facilitator's task in this instance is not to change the client, but to accept and understand him or her.

- Avoid the following question and statement: 'How do you feel?', and: 'I know how you feel.' In both instances, the client will be quite justified in saying to him- or herself, or to you: 'In that case, please tell me how I feel!' Furthermore, asking the client about his or her feelings is indicative of inadequate observation by the facilitator.
- Be tentative when feeling your way into the life world of the client. It is no easy task to enter another person's frame of reference and we should therefore respond in such a way that the client has the opportunity to correct us. Nevertheless, a somewhat inaccurate, tentative response is better than questions or clichés.
- Avoid confrontation and arguments with the client. These serve only as an indication that the facilitator is approaching the client from his or her own frame of reference, and might scare the client. The facilitator can ask him- or herself what he or she is experiencing that is creating the need to argue with the client.
- An accurate empathic response may encourage the client to delve deeper. If you are aware of this, such movement will not catch you unawares. It is very important to keep following the thread and intensity of the conversation. The client may find it stressful to delve deeper, and that is exactly when he or she will most need your understanding and acceptance.

Various stumbling blocks to effective empathy are described in the literature. Some of these, which are not very obvious, are discussed below.

3.4.1 Sympathy

There is a difference between empathy and sympathy. Sympathy stems from the facilitator's own experiential world, rather than from that of the client. (In other words: 'I [the facilitator] feel sorry for you.') Although his or her intentions may be good, a sympathetic facilitator will be burdening the client with his or her feelings. The client then has to cope with the facilitator's feelings, rather than the facilitator being there for the client, irrespective of the facilitator's own needs.

3.4.2 Advice, approval and disapproval

These aspects also imply ideas arising from the facilitator's frame of reference, rather than from the frame of reference of the client. A facilitator may believe that his or her solution will please the client (good intentions), but should rather consider:

- The client's self-determination (Proposition 4)
- That the client has his or her own values, and needs to develop a value system (Proposition 10 and Proposition 19)
- That we wish to enable the client to generate his or her own way forward, determined by the client's own perceptions, experiences, needs, self and values.

It is not always easy to refrain from giving advice. Clients often ask for advice because they do not have solutions of their own. This is, after all, why they consulted a facilitator. It is therefore what they need, and simply to refuse would be insensitive and contrary to the client's frame of reference, which is something that we wish to avoid. What should we do?

The propositions of the theory may provide the answer. Proposition 5 states that behaviour (the client's action of seeking help, and his or her verbal and non-verbal communication, which also constitute behaviour) indicates a particular need, accompanied by emotions (Proposition 6). What could the emotions be in this instance? (Remember that we are surmising and that the emotions will vary from one client to the next.) If we assume that the client is experiencing anxiety and uncertainty, we may respond as follows: 'You are asking me what to do and you sound uncertain', and/or: 'It appears that you have lost confidence in yourself/your own decisions.'

This shows your client that you understand him or her and provides the client with the opportunity to elaborate on him- or herself and his or her experiences or fears.

Activity 3.3

Write down a few responses that you could use as a facilitator with a client who does not know whether or not to get a divorce.

Read through these five interviews conducted with clients by different facilitators. As you will notice, each facilitator's response has its own unique style, but the principle of empathy as basic point of departure is maintained throughout. More accurately, an attempt is made to maintain empathy, but even these experienced facilitators do not always succeed. In some of the interviews this is indicated, in others it is not indicated. You could try to identify the less empathic responses yourself.

There are two reasons for presenting this variety of interviews:

- To provide a practical demonstration of the concept of empathy (it is, after all, not just a theoretical notion without any practical value)
- To demonstrate that each facilitator, as a unique person, has his or her own style of intervention (the theory serves only as a guideline to be implemented by each facilitator according to his or her own professional self).

Example 3.3

The case of a young female client demonstrates movement in the origin of her values. It seems fairly clear that during her earlier life, these values provided satisfactory guides to action. However, a sense of discrepancy (lack of fit with her self) has arisen, which is profoundly dissatisfying. She no longer wishes to abide by these values, but has nothing to use in their place.

>>

S102: It seems ... I don't know ... It probably goes all the way back to my childhood. I've ... for some reason I've ... my mother told me that I was the pet of my father. Although I never realised it – I mean, they never treated me as a pet at all. And other people always seemed to think I was sort of a privileged one in the family. But I never had any reason to think so. And as far as I can see looking back on it now, it's just that the family let the other kids get away with more than they usually did me. And it seems for some reason they held me to a more rigid standard than they did the other children.

C103: You're not so sure you were a pet in any sense, but more that the family situation seemed to hold you to pretty high standards.

S103: M-hm. That's just what has occurred to me; and that the other people could sorta make mistakes, or do things as children that were naughty, or 'that was just a boyish prank', or 'that was just what you might expect', but Alice wasn't supposed to do those things.

C104: M-hm. With somebody else it would just be just – oh, be a little naughtiness, but as far as you were concerned, it shouldn't be done.

S104: That's really the idea I've had. I think the whole business of my standards, or my values, is one that I need to think about rather carefully, since I've been doubting for a long time whether I even have any sincere ones.

C105: M-hm. Not sure whether you really have any deep values that you are sure of.

S105: M-hm. M-hm.

C106: You've been doubting that for some time.

S106: Well, I've experienced that before. Though one thing, when I make decisions I don't have – I don't think – it seems that some people have – have quite steady values that they can weigh things against when they want to make a decision. Well, I don't, and I haven't had, and I guess I'm an opportunist. *(Laughing)* I do what seems to be the best thing to do at the moment, and let it go at that.

C107: You have no certain measuring rods that you can use.

[From Rogers. *Client Centered Therapy: Its Current Practice, Implications and Theory.* © 1951 Houghton Mifflin, 1986 reprinting, London: Constable.]

Example 3.4

Most of the time, there is no way of knowing just how the child is reacting to the therapist's acceptance of his or her silence, but an occasional case is revealing. Here is an example from a play contact with a nine-year-old boy who has spent the entire hour painting in silence. Near the end, he asks the therapist about the time.

>>

Dick: How much time do I have left?

Therapist: Seven minutes, Dick.

Dick: I might as well go rock awhile. *(He goes and sits in the rocking-chair. He closes his eyes and quietly rocks.)* How much time do I have left now?

Therapist: Five more minutes, Dick.

Dick: *(Sighs very deeply)* Ah, five more minutes all to myself.

Therapist: *(Very softly)* Five more minutes all your own, Dick?

Dick: Yes! *(Said with much feeling. He rocks silently for the rest of the hour. His eyes are shut, in apparent enjoyment of peace.)*

Therapist: It feels good just to sit and rock?

Dick: *(Nods)*

Therapist: That's all the time we have for today, Dick.

Dick: OK. *(He gets up immediately and goes to the door with the therapist. They say goodbye, and he goes out. A minute later, he knocks at the door.)* I thought I'd get you some clean water.

Therapist: You want to help me, Dick?

Dick: Yes, I do. *(He gets the water. The therapist thanks him and he leaves, skipping down the hall. This is the first time that he has ever made any effort to clean up after his painting.)*

[FROM ROGERS. *CLIENT CENTERED THERAPY: ITS CURRENT PRACTICE, IMPLICATIONS AND THEORY.* © 1951 HOUGHTON MIFFLIN, 1986 REPRINTING, LONDON: CONSTABLE.]

Example 3.5

Although the therapy process need not involve a great deal of verbalisation on the child's part, an occasional case presents a striking contrast to 'the silent case'. An example is that of eleven-year-old Henry. His case indicates a child's capacity for sophisticated insights.

Henry was referred for therapy because of his 'nervousness'. He had an assortment of tics, including rapid and continuous blinking of the eyelids, twitching of the lips, mouth and jaw grimaces, shoulder-tossing, feet-kicking and gasping for breath. He suffered from constipation, wept easily, stuttered, was a social isolate and was failing in his schoolwork. In short, there seemed to be no area of his life that afforded him satisfaction. During his first therapy hour, he told of often running all the way home from school in order to escape the men waiting in alleys to kill him. He reported his life at home to be an endless round of quarrels, reprimands, hypodermic injections

>>

of sedatives, suppositories and nightmares. His father, a physician, threatened him with shock therapy if his 'shaking' did not cease. It seems that a psychiatrist had told Henry's parents that he shook in order to gain attention, and they were determined to end his 'nastiness'.

In the face of his many problems, Henry felt quite overwhelmed. His own words provide a vivid account of his psychological state during this first therapy hour. The excerpt is from the last half of the hour, and is reproduced from his therapist's notes.

Henry: One time, my mother said she'd take me to Baltimore. So I got up early, 7 o'clock, and I went into the living-room. It was empty. I should have gotten up at 6 o'clock. She took Michael *(Henry's older brother)* instead.

Therapist: They left you when you'd hoped to go?

Henry: *(Nods. He weeps again.)* Up until I was six years old, I had a nurse, Miss Palmer. She protected me from everybody, but now, now she's gone, and – *(Interrupts his story with tears)*

Therapist: You're all alone without anybody to protect you now?

Henry: Yes. They say Miss Palmer spoiled me, but I don't think so.

Therapist: You miss her?

Henry: Yes, I do. I have a cousin, Jean. Well, I happened to fall in love with her. Michael says: 'Jean doesn't care for you a bit.' He says Jean likes him better.

Therapist: He doesn't want you to be happy?

Henry: No. He doesn't. He does everything he can to make me miserable. My father always says Michael is right. If I try to stand up for my rights, my father gives me a hypo.

Therapist: Things seem to be going pretty badly at home.

Henry: Yes, oh yes! *(He weeps again. He goes on to relate other incidents. Then, he becomes very insistent on knowing how therapy can help. Earlier in the hour, the therapist had said that she was there to talk things over with him.)*

Henry: What good will it do to tell you about it? I don't understand.

Therapist: You mean, talking won't help?

Henry: Yes. What good will it do?

Therapist: Sometimes people feel better about things after talking them over. *(The therapist falls into the trap of answering an emotional question as if it were a mere request for information. It leads to difficulties.)*

Henry: Yes, but what good does it do to feel better about things if they still go on?

>>

Therapist: Sometimes boys and girls can understand the way they really feel about things, and it helps them to know what they really want to do about their situations. *(The therapist is still trying to 'sell' the therapy session to the child.)*

Henry: Yes, but after I tell you about it, what if it's still going on?

Therapist: I know you feel pretty hopeless, Henry. I can't change your parents. All I can do is to help you think through your own problems. *(Pause)* It's hard for you to see it now, I know, but sometimes it helps.

Henry: Well ... *(He goes on to relate several more incidents.)* I still don't understand. What good will it do to talk about it if they still keep on the same way?

Therapist: You mean, what can you do if they don't change?

Henry: Yes.

Therapist: I don't really know. But I hope that's something we can work out together, here, when you come to see me.

Henry: Suppose it lasts ten or fifteen years and they keep on?

Therapist: You just wonder how long you can bear it? *(This should have been the response earlier in the session.)*

Henry: Yes, oh yes. *(He weeps for several minutes.)*

Therapist: It all looks pretty black.

This first contact has been presented in some detail in order to indicate Henry's feeling of hopelessness about altering his situation. It is interesting to note that although he stated his inability to see any use in it, he made eager use of the therapist's presence. Despite his stuttering and gasping for breath, he spoke very rapidly, and was astonished when the hour was up. He did not even see the paints and other materials until the third therapy hour. Then he painted a boy in jail, behind heavy black bars – a perfect projection of his feelings. Like many adult clients, Henry began therapy with a view of his problems as existing outside himself, in the actions of other people. Hence, he avidly desired the punishment of his 'villains'. The tenth therapy hour brought some interesting changes, as may be seen in this excerpt.

Henry: Michael and I had a fight. I wanted the window shut, I felt cold. He yelled: 'Who shut the window?' I said: 'I did!' So he said I was a brat, and he opened it. So then I shut it again. He got up out of bed and opened it and then he hit me. So I threw a shoe at him, and it broke the lamp. He started to cry. He's such a baby, honestly! So then my father came in and he hit me. He always takes Michael's side. I told him: 'Dad, Michael's your favourite.' He says he has no favourites, and that I'm just a little snot. He was lying, though.

Therapist: You feel he's pretty unfair to you, is that it?

>>

Henry: And sometimes I get so mad!

Therapist: You really get sore at him.

Henry: I hate him!

Therapist: You despise him.

Henry: Yes. I'd love to pay him back, too.

Therapist: You'd like some revenge?

Henry: Yes. If only he weren't here.

Therapist: You'd like to be rid of him?

Henry: I'd like to kill him.

Therapist: You want him dead?

Henry: Uh-hm. That would be the end of my problems.

Therapist: With him dead, things would be OK with you?

Henry: That's right. *(Pause)* But would that end my problems? Supposing he were dead. I'd still be the same, I mean my shaking and all. Now if he'd have got killed earlier, that might have done me some good, but now it's too late for that. I am what I am already, and that's my problem. He's just a fool.

Therapist: So that, all in all, you've decided to let him live?

Henry: Yes. It wouldn't do any good to kill him, I'd still have my same problems, and I'd still have to figure them out. He's supposed to be a grown man, but honestly, he acts just like a baby.

[From Rogers. *Client Centered Therapy: Its Current Practice, Implications and Theory.* © 1951 Houghton Mifflin, 1986 reprinting, London: Constable.]

Example 3.6

This therapy session was conducted as a demonstration in front of a group of other therapists and counsellors at a workshop on therapy.

Client: My nervousness is mostly related to the group, I think. Sometimes I have a ... a hesitancy to volunteer because I ... I always want to jump into things all the time. And sometimes I talk too much, and it ... uh ... don't let other people have a chance. That's why I've been waiting. Mm-hm ...

Therapist: It's like there's some kind of ... uh ... enthusiasm or excitement to kind of get in there and get involved, but it's also a conflicting thing because part of you says: 'Hey, let's let some other people have the ... have some time.'

>>

Client: I have been told a lot, even as a facilitator, I step in too much ... and, um, ... I want ... I'm trying very hard not to do that ... I'm getting better at it, but I'm hesitant. Also, something that's coming up ... that I realised when I was sitting there was ... the problem that I have ... I can almost start crying about it right away because ... but I don't want to do that.

Therapist: Maybe right now you're doing some of that ... like you're coming on a little too fast for your own self ... and you're saying: 'I want to step back a little from this and ...'

Client: Well, it's something that I ... I've dealt with many therapists and I've gone through it a lot *(Voice breaks)* and, uh, being in a therapeutic setting with people who are doing it, I start to think about my problem. Whereas, you know, normally I can go through the day and not think about it ... (Mm-hm) ... and, uh, being around so many people who I know are good counsellors, part of me wants to talk to 'em about it, and ... and part of me says: 'I'm sick of talking about it.' (Mm-hm) ... It's, uh, well, I want to tell you what it is, so you won't just be responding to this vague problem and it ... the label for it was originally called 'anorexia nervosa'. And I don't know if you know what this is. (Mm-hm) ... I think the label upsets me.

Therapist: It's like you're having to live with some label ...

Client: *(Crying)* Sort of ... I don't think other people label me that any more, but it ... on the outside it looks like it's gone, but it's not ... on the inside of me it's always still there ... (Mm-hm) ... and, uh, I feel like it's ... You know what that is, don't you? (Mm-hm) I don't know if we should ...

Therapist: Do you want to say more about that? Maybe we ... it would be better if you just said something about it ...

Client: Well, uh ... it's something that happens to you that you don't realise is happening to you in the beginning and, um, it started with me a long time ago when I was in college *(Voice breaking)* ... and I just ... went on a diet, like a lot of other people go on diets, but I ... just, for some reason I couldn't stop doing it ... I ... It was almost like I had to have complete control ... but anyway, I didn't realise what I was doing, and I had some doctor, my doctor, you know, say to me, gave me this book to read about it, and I said: 'Naw, that's not me,' and eventually I realised it was me, but I still couldn't stop it ... and now, even though I've gained the weight back, I'm terrified by the idea every day ... It's, um, it seems like there was another person inside of me, always talking to me ... (Mm-hm) ... and I want to get rid of it so bad ... and I've talked to so many people, and I wasn't going to talk to anybody here because I've decided I can only get rid of it myself ... but I guess every little discussion about it makes it get a little better, so ... I volunteered ...

Therapist: Like there's still something compelling you to tell somebody else about it, and hopefully this time maybe ...

>>

Client: Somebody else who might ... who might be able to help me understand it a little better because I could go around and talk about it sometimes. Sometimes I can talk about it very ... like, therapist. And I've been asked to work with people who've had it, and ... and, and I can't do it because what happens is I get jealous of the patient ... *(Crying)* That's hard for me to admit. (Mm-hm)

Therapist: It's like that's something you don't like about yourself that you do that ...

Client: That I get jealous?

Therapist: Jealous of the patient.

Client: Yeah, I think, it's crazy ... but on the other hand, if I see someone who's really thin or working with someone, and I think: 'How come I can't do that?' ...and I used to have so much control, and I used to be able to not eat, and I used to be able to turn down certain things and stuff, and now I don't have that any more, and I get jealous of the, and I ... feel a little crazy ... now I can go around and have a normal life and no one would guess, there's a former anorexic walking the street, but it's ... it's still there, it causes a lot of problems in relationships ...

Therapist: Like you can disguise that from most of the world most of the time pretty effectively, but inside you know that it's still there ...

Client: I can't seem to exactly turn it off, my, uh, my behaviours are changed ... I'll sit down at the table and eat, but almost the entire time, I'm ... someone's talking to me ... it's like: 'You shouldn't eat that, you should eat that, this has that many calories, you can't eat the whole day if you eat that,' and I just want it, just: 'Shut up' ... I guess ...

Therapist: 'Shut up, leave me alone,' those voices just keep hounding you.

Example 3.7

The client is a black woman who is experiencing financial difficulties because the father of her eldest child is not paying maintenance. She is living with another man at present. The client said she had to report the father of her eldest child for not paying maintenance, but she feared him because he used witchcraft.

Facilitator: So you are uncertain whether to apply for maintenance, because you are afraid of losing your child through witchcraft.

Client: Yes, his family is very much into witchcraft. I am also afraid of losing my present boyfriend, if he does not like the idea of asking X for maintenance. The problem is, he does not like talking about it. He just says it is my business.

Facilitator: This seems to hurt and confuse you?

>>

Client: We fight if X comes around and I can't ask him for money for X's child. I want him to be happy.

Facilitator: You want to hurt nobody, not your first or your present boyfriend.

Client: I just want to keep the peace, it worries me, but I just keep quiet because I am used to being hurt.

Facilitator: You feel unhappy a lot, and unable to change anything about it.

Client: *(Crying)* I do not understand my position and I just walk around, to avoid thinking. I prefer to be alone.

Facilitator: You seem confused, alone and hurt. Also unable to believe that anyone can help you.

Client: I have never enjoyed myself, except when I was working and could look after my child.

Facilitator: You liked it when you were independent and could look after your child, who is very important to you.

Client: Yes, I cannot even ask my parents for help.

Facilitator: You find it difficult to ask for help, your parents, first boyfriend, your present boyfriend ... you trust only yourself?

Client: Yes, but now I am confused and don't know which way to turn.

Facilitator: Coming to ask me for help must have been difficult for you, as you prefer to be independent. I am a bit confused, because, on the one hand, you prefer to be alone and independent, but on the other hand you seem afraid of hurting both your previous and present boyfriends?

Client: I don't know ... what do I want from them? Why do I want to protect them and from what? Is it only the witchcraft, or something else?

Facilitator: You seem confused at this point. These are some issues that are important to you.

Client: Yes, I have to go and think about them, as I usually do.

Activity 3.4

1 Which of these interviews did you find most interesting?
2 Why is that the case?
3 Has reading these interviews made you think about your own style of interviewing?

Activity 3.5

Here are several excerpts from conversations. Develop your own interview style by formulating empathic responses.

1 A 50-year-old woman who is in the process of getting divorced says: 'My husband and I have decided to get divorced. *(She is speaking softly and slowly.)* I truly dread all the legal implications ... *(Pauses)* ... actually I dread the entire business. I do not know what to expect. *(Sighs)* I am middle-aged and don't think I'll get married again. I simply do not know what to expect.'

2 A married woman with two teenage daughters says: 'Why does my husband always blame me for his problems with the children? I am always caught in the middle. He always complains to me about them. They complain about him. *(Looks the facilitator in the eye.)* I feel like moving out and leaving them on their own!'

3 A seventeen-year-old girl in a reformatory says: *(She is very quiet and does not respond to the facilitator's greeting; then shakes her head and looks around.)* 'I don't know what I am doing here. You are the third, or maybe the fourth, person to whom they have sent me. It is simply a waste of time! Why do they keep sending me here? Let's end this here and now.'

4 A girl in high school says: 'My classmates do not like me and now I do not like them either! Why are they so mean? They tease me ... well, actually my clothes. But my parents cannot afford to buy me the uniform. Well, they do not have to like me, but they should stop teasing me!'

5 A 40-year-old woman talking to a facilitator after being raped says: 'It was very difficult for me to come here. A friend said I should call the police. But then I will become yet another story in the newspaper, like the ones you read every day! They will ask me all kinds of questions. Oh no! I would rather just forget about it all. I do not want to relive it over and over again!'

6 A factory worker explains: 'My work is fine. I earn good money, which my family and I enjoy very much. My wife and I both come from poor families and we have a much better life than when we were children. But the work I do is always the same, day after day. I may not be the smartest chap in the world, but I do believe that I have much more to offer than what the machines at work demand of me.'

7 A 50-year-old widow discussing her seventeen-year-old son says: 'He knows he can try his luck with me. If he stops talking to me, or becomes moody for a couple of days, I go out of my mind! He gets everything he wants and I know that I am the only one to blame. But I love him very much. After all, he lives with me and he is the man in the house. He is planning to go to the local university, which means that he will still be at home for quite a while.'

8 A mother says: 'My daughter of fifteen no longer listens to me and she goes out with friends of whom I do not approve.'

9 A woman who comes to consult you says: 'I am having problems with my husband. He works overtime a great deal these days and spends very little time at home.'

10 A 38-year-old man says: 'I am so angry I could explode! My employer gave me a talking to, my car is giving problems, and when I got home the children's toys were lying around in my way!'

CHAPTER

4 Exploring unsymbolised experiences (Phase 2)

4.1 Introduction

Once a safe climate has been created in which the client feels free to share all and any experiences with the facilitator, the client may be ready to move deeper and examine experiences that are unconscious. This could be described as the second stage of the facilitation process.

In this chapter, we will explore why some experiences are denied consciousness (Proposition 11 [c and d]). We will look at what happens to people when they have many unconscious experiences (Proposition 13, Proposition 14 and Proposition 16) from a theoretical point of view. Then we will discuss how the values relate to this deeper exploration. Finally, we will explore some of the advanced communication skills that can be used to facilitate this exploration.

4.2 Why are some experiences denied consciousness?

4.2.1 Proposition 11 [c and d]: Dealing with experiences at an unconscious level

The second half of this proposition explains why some experiences are not symbolised. It is very important to note that it relates to the self of clients. Only experiences that do not fit with the self are not allowed into the conscious mind.

> *As experiences occur in the life of the individual, they are either [c] denied symbolisation [d] given a distorted symbolisation because the experience is inconsistent with the structure of the self.*
>
> [Rogers 1987: 503]

Rogers distinguishes between differentiation of the symbols we attach to our experiences and the differentiation of the perception of our experiences.

> *One of the most characteristic and perhaps one of the most important changes in therapy is the bringing into awareness of experiences of which heretofore the client has not been conscious. What, psychologically, occurs when the individual*

> *thus deals with 'repressed' material? Our experience would indicate that it is best described in terms of greater differentiation of perception, and more adequate symbolisation.* ❞
>
> [ROGERS 1987: 147]

As this proposition indicates, some experiences (specifically those that do not fit with the self) are not conscious and therefore we cannot attach any symbols to them. This could be expressed in many ways, like clients saying: 'I don't know what is happening to me', or: 'I don't know why I am behaving like I do.'

Some experiences, though conscious, are too threatening to the self for us to allow ourselves a clear idea of what it is we are experiencing, that is, what exactly it is that we are seeing, thinking, attaching so much value to or wondering about. A client might, for instance, say something like: 'I don't really know why I am upset', or: 'I don't know why this upsets me so'.

Other experiences are threatening to the self, and then we cannot allow ourselves to attach the appropriate symbol to them. The symbol we do attach might serve as a protective measure, but because the symbol does not fit what we are experiencing, it creates discomfort and stress.

As mentioned above, any experience that is perceived as threatening to the self in any way may be blocked out, either consciously or unconsciously. The following response by a client illustrates the point:

> ❝ *Well, I feel very much like I'm cornered. 'Cause I think that I'm going to find out something about myself that I don't like. Something I'm not facing. You know, like I want to avoid a whole bunch of things, I think, around that and what that says about me ... something that isn't going to be some ... I want ... that I'm trying to be somebody I'm not, or something ...* ❞
>
> [MARTIN 1983: 144]

In addition, some experiences that cannot be symbolised or blocked out completely are distorted to fit in with the self. For instance, people who do not experience themselves as unduly aggressive may refer to intense feelings of aggression as tension or frustration, which are more acceptable to the self. (This is not dishonesty or manipulation, as an outsider may perceive it. It is the only 'reality' that such people can permit themselves to experience.)

Such distortion may also apply to positive experiences. For instance, someone who believes in modesty may find it difficult to say, after a successful examination or interview: 'I've done well and I can be proud of myself.' Instead, the experience might be distorted into something like: 'I was lucky', or: 'The examination (interview) was easy.'

To reiterate: only experiences that do not fit with the self of a person are denied conscious symbolisation or are distorted to fit with the self.

This proposition thus makes it clear that in order to understand the unconscious experiences, the facilitator needs to understand the self of each client. This will allow the facilitator to understand how that self is being threatened, or which experiences of the client do not fit with the image of his or her self that the client has created.

As the self develops in interaction with others, this understanding will also include the client's perceptions of his or her relationship with his or her significant others.

Thus, all the experiences (discussed in Chapter 1 under Proposition 3–Proposition 6) that fit with and do not fit with the self of the client need to be understood.

However, Rogers singles out one specific experience: the client's behaviour. He gives it special attention in Proposition 13.

4.3 What happens to people when they have many unconscious experiences?

4.3.1 Proposition 13: Behaviour and unconscious experiences

> *Behaviour may, in some instances, be brought about by organic experiences and needs that have not been symbolised. Such behaviour may be inconsistent with the structure of the self, but in such instances, the behaviour is not 'owned' by the individual.*
>
> [Rogers 1987: 509]

Unsymbolised experiences and needs, or experiences and needs that have been symbolised in a distorted way, may also motivate behaviour. If the behaviour does not correspond with the individual's self-concept, the person will deny the behaviour.

When an individual with a certain self-perception (of who he or she is and of what is consistent with his or her self) manifests behaviour (motivated by unsymbolised experience) inappropriate to that self, the individual will deny such behaviour rather than change his or her entire self-perception (the latter being a drastic and painful process). A husband who beats his wife, but cannot reconcile this behaviour with his self-image, for example, will deny that he is beating her. He is literally unable to believe that he is capable of doing such a thing. Confronting such a person with the behaviour will merely lead to further denial and defences (see Proposition 16 below). The person is, moreover, not aware of the needs and experiences motivating this behaviour, because if these experiences have been symbolised at all, they have been symbolised in a distorted way. A possible response in such a case would be: 'I am a decent guy. All my colleagues respect me and I can't believe that I would do such a thing. It's simply not me!'

This proposition enables the facilitator to understand that if clients deny behaviour, it is not about lying or manipulating the facilitator. Rather, it is about protecting the self, which we will discuss in more detail under Proposition 16 below.

It is thus very important to understand what is happening with the self of the client when behaviour is denied.

In terms of Proposition 12, namely that behaviour mostly fits with the self, it is always important to make the connection between self and behaviour.

Thus if a client says something like: 'I do not know what to do', it could imply uncertainty about the self and what behaviour would fit with the self, rather than ignorance.

If the facilitator then told the client what to do, it would not enable him or her to explore what creates this uncertainty around the self. Instead, in terms of Proposition 9, it could be that the client now develops a self of being incompetent in interaction with the facilitator. (In other words, the client could develop a dependent self, a self who does not feel able to do things for him- or herself.)

4.3.2 Proposition 14: Psychological tension

> *Psychological maladjustment exists when the organism denies to awareness significant sensory and visceral experiences, which consequently are not symbolised and organised into the gestalt of the self-structure. When this situation exists, there is a basic or potential psychological tension.*
>
> [Rogers 1987: 510]

When there are many experiences that cannot be allowed into conscious awareness, it creates psychological stress for the individual.

The psychological tension Rogers refers to in this proposition is not to be confused with everyday tensions and stress. This distinction needs to be clarified to avoid any confusion and possible misunderstanding. In terms of this theory, it can be explored by looking at the difference between emotional and/or symbolised tension or pain, conflict, fear and confusion, and unsymbolised experiences that create tension, and why this is the case. In the first instance, we are aware of the source of our tension, as it is symbolised, while in the latter case, we are unaware of the source, as it is not symbolised.

We can have symbolised emotions that, in everyday language are also called 'stress', or, as some people maintain, these experiences create tension or stress. Whichever way you look at it, this kind of tension deals with symbolised emotions. For example, if you are afraid that you will not pass the exams and are aware of this, we could say that you are 'stressing' about the exams.

However, confusingly, the way in which Rogers perceives tension is more psychological and has to do with the self. If you are experiencing any thought, need or emotion, that is, any kind of experience that does not fit with your symbolised self, then you may experience psychological tension. This implies inner conflict (in your psyche or self, as it were) on an unsymbolised level. This could also be explained as an inner war: different parts of the same person are at war with each other, in terms of who that person believes him- or herself to be. As this inner conflict is at some level unconscious, it creates tension, because the person is unaware of the source and nature of this conflict.

Let us link this concept to the example of a person stressing about the exams. If you have a self-concept that defines you as always doing well (or being perfect) and you think you will not be perfect this time, but cannot admit the thought as it does not fit with your self, you might, for instance, to protect your self, blame the lecturer for not helping enough. Now it is not just the tension of the exams that you are experiencing, but also the inner conflict of fearing failure, while not allowing your self to harbour such fears.

Let us consider another example.

Example 4.1

A man hears intruders in his house. He is afraid for his life and his possessions. This is at a symbolised level. He calls the police, but before they arrive, the intruders assault him and his family, and rob them of some of their possessions. This is a very painful (stressful?) experience for them all. They are aware of this and therefore the accompanying tension is experienced on a symbolised level.

However, a few months later, the man begins to experience undefined tension and stress that he cannot really explain. He says he just feels restless and depressed, not as strong and in control as he used to be. This last statement implies a person who perceives himself as strong and mostly in control. During the assault, this self was threatened. He now wonders whether he is or can still be this person. So, besides the physical threat, he also experienced a psychological threat to the self, of which he is unaware. After becoming aware of this inner conflict, he decides that he still is a strong person. He then takes various actions to make his home and neighbourhood safer for everybody. The locus of control reverts back to him, although he had believed that the intruders had taken it from him.

The person's behaviour attempts to satisfy needs of which he or she is unaware. The lack of symbolisation impedes the individual's conscious control of this behaviour. The husband who beats his wife may well promise, after an incident of abuse, that he will never do it again. However, the moment the needs or unsymbolised experiences surface again, the behaviour will most probably be repeated. Fear that this might happen exacerbates the sense of poor control and leads to further psychological tension. Because the man is not conscious of the exact nature of the motivating experiences, he cannot be on his guard against them or handle them in a different, less stressful way.

This proposition reminds us that if a client is very tense, it does not help to ask him or her why this is the case, as the tension is at an unconscious level. The facilitator should rather use the values (Chapter 2) and basic skills (Chapter 3) already discussed, as well as the advanced skills discussed in this chapter, to enable the client to explore his or her experiences and how these experiences relate to his or her self.

Besides creating internal conflict and stress, experiences that do not fit with the self have another consequence. Proposition 16 describes this consequence.

4.3.3 Proposition 16: Defence of self

> *Any experience that is inconsistent with the organisation or structure of self will be perceived as a threat, and the more of these perceptions there are, the more rigidly that self-structure is organised to maintain itself.*
>
> [Rogers 1987: 515]

Experiences that conflict with the individual's self-perception are considered threatening to the self. The greater the number of such experiences, the more intent the self-structure becomes on self-preservation.

A simple example serves to demonstrate this principle. A person threatened by a lion will act very promptly to protect his or her self by screaming, running away, climbing a tree or whatever is possible at that moment. No facilitator observing this or hearing about it would find it peculiar or deviant. Yet if a person becomes scared, angry, evasive or rebellious when his or her psychosocial self is under threat, the facilitator may tend to regard this behaviour as abnormal (describing it as resistance, poor prognosis or poor motivation). Of course, facilitators do not enjoy experiencing themselves as threatening (a roaring lion), yet this might be how some clients experience them. Facilitators are, in fact, threatening when they are perceived as behaving in a way that does not accord with the client's self.

Is this behaviour attack or defence?

This can be linked to Proposition 17, as described in Chapter 1. A safe environment where clients feel free to share their experiences with the facilitator can only be created if there is a complete absence of any kind of threat to their selves. This safe environment has to be maintained throughout the process. The facilitator cannot begin the process by being understanding, accepting, respectful and empathic, and then lay into the client in a confrontational or reprimanding manner. If a client experiences any threat to his or her self at any stage of the process, the client will immediately defend him- or herself from the experience. This is another reason why the values and basic skills discussed in earlier chapters are a part of the total process.

4.4 How do the values relate to this deeper exploration?

4.4.1 The self of the facilitator

The propositions discussed above explain why some experiences are not symbolised, and how these unconscious experiences can create tension and defensive behaviour in clients. The values and advanced skills discussed in this chapter are some of the ways in which the facilitator can deal with these experiences without threatening the client even more. However, every facilitator must explore whether he or she is ready to use these values and skills before attempting to do so.

The activity that follows may enable the developing facilitator to explore and clarify his or her own thoughts on the subject.

Activity 4.1

1 Does the idea of unconscious experiences and how they relate to the self fit with your own way of thinking?
2 Does the idea of enabling clients to explore these painful experiences scare you?
3 How would you know that you are ready to go deeper with a client?

4.4.2 Values

As mentioned in Chapter 2, the professional values are a permanent part of the whole facilitation process. Clients have to be treated with respect and dignity. They must be treated like unique individuals all the time. However, it can be quite challenging to maintain these values when encountering unsymbolised experiences.

Unconscious experiences can create confusion in a client. They can even create a sense of helplessness in the client, who might then ask for solutions to his or her problems. This could happen because the client does not know which behaviour fits with his or her self (see Proposition 13).

However, if the facilitator were then to give advice, it would circumvent the client's self-determination. This would prevent the client from exploring and determining which self is being threatened and in what direction he or she wants his or her self to develop.

Proposition 13 tells us that a client may behave in ways that do not fit his or her self. As a result, the client will deny the behavior. Just as the client cannot admit the behaviour to him- or herself, so the facilitator might find the behaviour hard to accept and understand. This could also tempt the facilitator to breach confidentiality, as he or she might feel the need to share his or her own experiences with another person.

Proposition 16 reminds us that clients may be experiencing a lot of psychological stress, which could be expressed in various ways. A client might shout at the facilitator, for example, or act in a silent manner, withdrawing totally into the self and feeling afraid to reveal his- or herself to the facilitator. This again demonstrates how important it is to be totally accepting of the client. The facilitator must avoid putting any pressure on the client to speak or to be quiet, or to behave in any other way.

It is thus very important to adopt the values of self-determination and confidentiality. The facilitator needs to convey respect, total acceptance and a non-judgmental attitude to the client. Only then will the client be able to share threatening experiences with the facilitator. The client will then be able to explore the experiences and how they threaten his or her self.

4.5 Advanced communication skills

In every encounter, the basic skills required of the facilitator are to observe and hear the client in order to understand him or her, and to communicate this understanding to the client. These skills remain unchanged, irrespective of the stage of your work with the client. In other words, the skills remain unchanged whether it is the first interview or the eighth interview, or Phase 1 or Phase 4. The only thing that changes is the kind of understanding required.

Initially, by using the basic skills, the facilitator shows understanding of the client's symbolised experiences and self. Once a safe climate has been created, the facilitator can use advanced skills to share his or her understanding of those experiences that threaten the client's self, and are therefore not symbolised or are symbolised in a distorted way.

If work is being done with a client's unsymbolised or distorted experiences, the facilitator usually also uses basic empathy because exploration of these experiences could be very painful. The facilitator should be careful to communicate his or her understanding of the pain to the client (rather than ignoring or trying to minimise it).

In the discussion of the advanced skills that follows, we will look at examples of advanced responses without first considering more basic empathic responses. This is only done to illustrate the advanced skills. It does not mean that the basic skills are ignored or not deemed important. During the process of facilitation, the basic skills are always used initially and continuously. We will assume that the facilitator has already responded with basic empathy.

e are some guidelines to remember when communicating advanced responses to

- As with basic empathy, be tentative in giving responses. Give the client the opportunity to correct you if you are not in line with his or her experiences. Do not insist that your ideas are correct. It could help to keep Proposition 2 and Proposition 7 in mind. You must work from the client's reality and frame of reference.
- Avoid any form of judgment, including blaming one person for the experiences of another. For instance, a mother might say: 'My son is so naughty, I worry about him becoming a delinquent.' If the facilitator said something like: 'Your son's behavior makes you …', it would imply that the son is responsible for what the mother is feeling. However, as the mother is self-determined, her feelings are determined by her self. Her self as a mother, which developed in interaction with her son, seems to be threatened.

If the advanced response (which includes the threat to the mother's self) fits, the facilitator could become excited and try to go on too quickly with the issue. This can and must be done, but not necessarily immediately, and not without recognising the associated experiences. If you do not show basic empathy here, the client might become fearful, feel threatened and anxious, begin to defend again (Proposition 16) and perhaps lose confidence in you.

If you realise that a client is feeling threatened, you should immediately show that you understand this and allow the client to move at his or her own pace. In this way, you demonstrate that you do not expect anything from the client for which he or she is not ready. Note that this must be demonstrated to the client, even if it is only by your choice of words. You could say, for instance: 'It seems that this issue hurts you very much/is painful/makes you anxious/makes you feel like hiding/running away', or something of this kind.

We will look at three advanced skills:

- Advanced empathy, which includes identifying implied messages, connecting islands and developing themes
- Exploring distortions
- Immediacy.

Although these skills are different ways of approaching the unsymbolised experiences, they can be used whenever the facilitator is ready and the client's experiences warrant them.

Here are some essential principles to remember when using the advanced skills:

- They deal with unsymbolised experiences.
- Only experiences that threaten the self of the client are not symbolised or are distorted.
- In order to use the advanced skills, the facilitator must understand how the client perceives his or her self.
- The facilitator must also understand which experiences threaten the client's self.

All unconscious experiences are connected to the self.

In the physical world, it is easy to see that no thought, feeling or behaviour can occur in isolation without the rest of the body. Yet in the psychological world, facilitators often focus on one experience (a behaviour, feeling or thought) at a time and try to change that experience on its own. We need to remember that all experiences are part of the person. Experiences are influenced by each other and the self, and in turn, they influence the self (see Proposition 3 and Proposition 8).

So with any unsymbolised (painful or bloody) experience, the facilitator has to ask him- or herself: 'How does this experience threaten the self?'

4.5.1 Advanced empathy

Advanced empathy involves the ability to:

> *... see clearly what clients only half see or hint at. This deeper kind of empathy involves 'sensing' meanings of which the client is scarcely aware.*
>
> [Rogers 1980: 142]

Advanced empathy therefore concerns the client's unsymbolised experiences as discussed under Proposition 11 [c and d] and Proposition 13. It is very important for the facilitator not to use his or her own frame of reference, but rather to build up the skill of understanding clients fully (regarding both their symbolised and unsymbolised experiences, and how the latter threaten the self). In a certain sense, the facilitator understands clients in ways in which clients do not consciously understand themselves. In this way, the facilitator enables clients to understand themselves more fully.

Martin (1983: 3) refers not only to empathy, but also to what he calls 'evocative empathy', which is 'communicated understanding of the other person's intended message'. Each word in this definition is important. It is not enough to understand what clients are saying. The facilitator must also hear what clients intend. In other words, the faclitator must understand the intended or implied message. In addition, the facilitator needs to react to the message by communicating this understanding to clients. This deeper understanding serves no purpose, however, if clients do not hear it, so it must be communicated to them in some way.

Visibly expressing your understanding

Identification and communication of implied messages

When clients talk to a facilitator, they are saying more than is expressed by the words they utter. There is always a hidden or implied meaning behind the words.

Can you find the cat, dog, hen and cow hidden in the picture?

When using advanced empathy, the facilitator thus also has to listen for the hidden meaning about the client's self so that he or she can communicate it to the client.

This means that the facilitator has to be able to hear more than just what the client is saying directly. The facilitator must also hear what is hinted at about the self and how it is being threatened. If the facilitator keeps in mind that the advanced skills deal with unconscious experiences, he or she will realise that clients cannot express these experiences directly, as they are not aware of them.

There is also usually more than one intended message encoded in the explicit message (which usually has only one meaning). A client might convey explicitly what he or she wants changed, but the self that the client does not want to change, the self that he or she wants to maintain as it is, will be implicit in the message, or vice versa. The facilitator must therefore search for the other or deeper messages that have been conveyed or that manifest in other forms. These forms include non-verbal behaviour, for example, the tone of voice or the facial expression.

In everyday life, we listen to people's implied messages all the time. For example, if someone says that he is tall, the implicit message is that he is not short. If we say that someone is thin, it implies that she is not fat. If someone says she is tired, it implies that she does not have a great deal of energy. If someone says he is worried about his child, it implies that he is concerned about the child and that he cares about what is happening to the child. It also says something about the father's self in relation to this child.

In our professional lives, we listen specifically for what clients' messages imply about their selves, as all the advanced skills deal with those experiences that threaten the self.

The implied message could be related to various aspects of the self, such as the client's perceptions, needs, behaviour, emotions, the self and the values of the individual.

Example 4.2

A woman says: 'My husband beats me and I do not know what to do.'

This short sentence contains more than one implied message:

- She is married, thus in interaction with her husband, she has developed a self of a married woman (see Proposition 9).
- The fact that he beats her, yet she does not want to leave him, could imply that she needs to maintain this married self.

Example 4.3

A 14-year-old boy says: 'My parents want me to play soccer, because it will help me make friends. But I don't want to do that. I would rather read a book about nature. I don't know what to do.'

This statement contains several implied messages:

- In interaction with his parents, he has developed a self of a son who usually obeys them.
- He does not want to be a bad son.
- He sees himself as a person who enjoys reading about nature on his own.
- His self as a good son and his self as a reader are now in a struggle with each other.

Please note that the boy's parents are not to blame for this inner struggle. It is a struggle in himself, about himself.

Example 4.4

A young mother says: 'My baby won't stop crying. My parents say I should ignore her and she will stop on her own, but I think that is cruel. What should I do?'

This example has four possible implied messages:

- In interaction with her parents, a self of a daughter has developed.
- In interaction with her baby, a self of a (new) mother is developing.
- The young mother is unsure whether she should take over the values of her parents as a new parent herself or whether she can develop her own value system.
- She does not see herself as a cruel person.

These examples illustrate that the facilitator needs to listen carefully to what clients say and imply about themselves. It does not require a lot of information to understand the person or the self of each individual. It does, however, require a great deal of understanding.

Your understanding of the implied message can be conveyed to the client in any manner that fits with your self and the self of the client. For example, in the case of the mother expressing concerns about her son earlier in this chapter (see page 79), the facilitator could say: 'You seem concerned about your son, and whether you, as his mother, can protect him from becoming a delinquent.'

Example 4.5

A mother comes to ask for your advice. She says: 'I would like to know what to do with my daughter. She suddenly wants to do exactly as she pleases, without asking me. We used to talk about everything, but now she spends most of her time in her room. What should I do?'

What could the implied message be in a case like this? It could be that she is uncertain about what to do, as she might be worried about her self as a mother, which developed in interaction with her daughter. In previous interactions with her daughter, she saw her self as a present, responsible and involved mother. Her behaviour would fit with this self. Now that this self is being threatened by the changes, she no longer knows how to behave. A new self needs to develop, and until she (not the facilitator) has symbolised a new self for herself, she might feel helpless and confused. The use of the words 'no longer' makes it sound as though the relationship has changed recently and she might be afraid of losing her daughter, which may threaten her self-structure as a mother even more.

A response could include one of the following: 'You feel as though the mother you were to your daughter is no longer good enough', or: 'You feel as though you no longer know this child of yours and this confuses you', or: 'What has always worked in the past in your relationship with your daughter no longer works, and now you do not know what to do, what kind of mother to be'.

The message could be conveyed in one of these ways or in a combination of these ways. What is particularly important is that the facilitator should see whether it links with the client's frame of reference and enables her to move deeper. If it does not succeed, the facilitator's intuition was wrong and the client will correct him or her. She might say something like: 'No, this child of mine has always been difficult and I'm getting tired of struggling with her disobedient behaviour.' In a case like this, the facilitator could first fall back on basic empathy, by saying something like: 'You are angry and discouraged, and you are in the mood to give up.' The fact that she has come to the facilitator for advice implies, however, that something is preventing her from just giving up, and so the facilitator could add: 'But something is preventing you from simply giving up.' This could enable the mother to explore her own experiences further. The 'sudden' change in the mother/daughter relationship may relate to life-span changes such as adolescence.

Also, if the facilitator wants to link with the client's frame of reference, he or she cannot ignore the client's request for advice. It could help the client more if the facilitator listened intently and enabled her to symbolise her fears. If the facilitator does give advice, he or she confirms the client's fear that she is not good enough or reliable enough to take decisions. In this way, her self-confidence is undermined still further. By enabling the mother to discover for herself what her fears are and to find behaviour that would be appropriate to any change in her self-structure, she is also enabled to handle herself in a way that suits her.

It would, however, not be accepting to say something like: 'I cannot tell you what to do. You have to figure it out for yourself.'

This would be responding from the facilitator's frame of reference and could threaten the self of the client. It also does nothing to help her explore her own unconscious experiences.

Our actions and responses should be guided by the thought that the goal of the process is to enable clients to become aware of their unsymbolised experiences. So an advanced response to this mother would include her doubt about herself, of being afraid to risk doing something that would threaten her self as a mother even more: 'I hear your uncertainty about your daughter. It seems that you are afraid of doing the wrong thing, thus risking losing her. She is very important to you and you want to be the best mother to her that you can be.'

Example 4.6

In a family where sexual molestation occurs, the mother could say something like: 'There are things in our family that we don't like, but we are still a close family.'

The facilitator can hear that the closeness of the family (Proposition 4) is very important to her and say something like: 'It is so important for you to maintain the family that you are prepared to endure a great deal of pain for it,' or: 'You would sacrifice many other things for the sake of your close family,' or: 'You are afraid that speaking about the things that are painful will be detrimental to the closeness of your family.'

For example, a mother says: 'I must punish my child regularly.' Her choice of words suggests that she believes that a significant other's values have to apply. The facilitator could say something like: 'It sounds as though someone is sitting on your shoulder and telling you what to do or what kind of mother to be,' or: 'The fact that you feel compelled to apply strict discipline as a mother makes it sound to me as though it is not entirely your own choice.'

Activity 4.2

Here are a few extracts from conversations. Identify the implied message(s) and formulate responses with which to reply to the clients.

1. A girl says: 'Perhaps it would be better if I didn't speak about these things.'
2. A couple feels that their new baby, whom they love very much, takes up a great deal of their time.
3. A child obtained 80% in a test. His parents say: 'It was probably just a fluke.'
4. A mother is discussing one of her children who has been referred to a doctor. The mother is angry with the school because she does not think that it is necessary.

5 The parents are upset because their daughter, who has just turned sixteen, suddenly wants to start wearing jeans.

Helping clients to make connections

If you were to look at the statements made by a single client in the course of one or even several interviews, they would look like separate entities to the facilitator and the client. Yet, in the light of Proposition 3 (the individual should be seen as a whole), the facilitator could wonder about the connections between seemingly separate statements. He or she might wonder how the statements connect to each other and to the self of the person. This can be compared to the figure of the different parts of the human body (page 80). The person only emerges when we put all the pieces together.

Who am I when I am complete?

This puzzle illustrates how the facilitator has to put together the different pieces of the client's experiences. Through this process, the facilitator is able to understand which self or identity emerges and is being threatened (see Proposition 3 and Proposition 8).

This skill, which we could call 'connecting islands', is related to the identification of themes. The facilitator, who is able to see these connections, can give feedback about them to the client. Egan (1994) uses the metaphor of connecting islands to illustrate clearly that the facilitator should not see the islands (statements, experiences, relationships, problems and self) as separate entities, but should try to determine which of the experiences that occur on island A are also found on islands B, C and D. This connection between islands could be horizontal, such as between the various contexts in which people live from day to day: their work, their home and their circle of friends. There could also be vertical islands, such as similar behaviour that is found among people in various generations. Particular patterns of behaviour, beliefs, values and experiences that are observed among different generations may be factors that eventually play a very important role in the perceptions or processes of the current family. For example, in certain families we often find very strong female figures in every generation, alcohol dependence, absent fathers or the idea that achievement is a very important prerequisite for acceptance (see Carter and McGoldrick 1989).

As Egan (1990: 219) points out, clients often speak about these islands as though they have nothing to do with each other. Even if the contents differ, the process that occurs may be the same. The facilitator enables the client to build a bridge between these islands. According to Egan (1990: 219), this bridge is built with empathy and is therefore part of advanced empathy, not merely an interpretation by the facilitator. The identification or connecting of islands (as in the case of identifying themes) is hypothetical and is not correct if it does not have significance for the client. If the client does not accept it, other connections should be sought and 'therefore it is extremely important to check advanced empathic statements with the client' (Egan 1990: 219). This checking of the meaning that the empathic statement has for the client can be done by making the statement tentative, as Martin (1983) illustrates, for instance:

- 'I do not know whether I am correct, but ...'
- 'Correct me if I heard the wrong thing ...'
- 'I might be completely wrong, but what I hear is the following ...'

The riddles below demonstrate how new symbolisation can occur if seemingly separate entities are connected.

- Which trees grow fingers? Palm trees.
- What do you call a painting of a bad-tempered woman? The Mona (moaner) Lisa.
- Did you hear about the ship transporting red paint that crashed on a brown rock? The crew was marooned.

[*You*, 23 March 1994]

To illustrate the necessity of connecting islands, let us consider the following example.

If we talked to a boy who runs away from home and then focused only on the behaviour of running away, it could be illustrated as follows:

Can behaviour be seen in isolation?

In the physical world, we would not even think of just looking at the legs alone, for they cannot move on their own. Yet in the psychosocial world, we could be tempted to focus on the running away and try to stop it, without looking at the whole person, the self, the needs and how the behaviour of running away relates to the total self. It could indicate some threat to the self, and the running away could be a way of protecting the self. The behaviour of running away from home also has to be connected to the interactions at home, in which the self developed and where the threat seems to be perceived.

The facilitator cannot, therefore, just focus on one island, the running (or the legs). He or she has to connect it to the whole person (or body, as the legs cannot move on their own). The facilitator has to ask him- or herself: 'How does the running away relate to his self and his interactions with his significant others at home, in interaction with whom the self is developed?'

Example 4.7

A mother of three young children says: 'I am so tired! I pick up after the children all day long, prepare their meals and wash their clothes. I am worried that I do not have enough energy to play with them when they want me to.'

If all the experiences (behaviour, feelings and needs) are linked together, it appears that she tries hard to be a good mother in interaction with her children. However, this mother-self seems threatened by the fear that she is not spending enough play time with them, thus not being the good mother she wants to be.

A possible response could be something like: 'You are really spending a lot of time taking care of your children, doing all you can do to provide for them and be the best mother you can be, yet you seem to worry that you are still not doing enough?'

In this example, all the experiences the mother shared with the facilitator evolved from the same self. However, this is not always the case. The threat or inner conflict could revolve around or between different selves, as the following example illustrates.

Example 4.8

Here are several statements made by an older woman over a period of time:

- 'I have always stayed at home to look after my family.'
- 'I have four children and I am so proud of each one of them. They are all working now and have their own families.'
- 'I cannot believe my husband left me! After so many years together, he has taken a younger woman.'
- 'I feel so alone and empty.'
- 'I do not know what the future has in store for me.'

If we connect all these statements or experiences to each other and the self, it seems as if she used to be a mother and wife (and woman to her husband). Her significant others have all left, so it might seem to her that these identities are no longer who she is now. She might feel that she does not know who she is or who she is becoming.

Activity 4.3

Try to formulate some examples that include the connected islands.

Identification of themes

When clients share their inner world of experience with us, they may talk as if these experiences are separate from each other. However, as we perceive each person as a whole and as the self is central in the person's experiences, these experiences are usually connected to each other and to the self in some way. There is often a main theme to the person's statements. This means that the sentences share the same or similar meanings (although this might not be obvious at first glance, and that is why we need to listen with a 'third ear'). We can ask ourselves what the shared experiences have in common and how they relate to the self. (We cannot ask the client, because we are dealing with unsymbolised experiences, which means the client is unaware of them.)

These themes are, therefore, not necessarily explicit or obvious in the (sometimes sensational) story of the client, but implicit. Although themes come to the fore repeatedly, only a good listener can hear them.

Egan (1994: 183) reminds us of the following guidelines:

- 'Make sure the themes you discover are based on the client's experience and are not just the artefacts of some psychological theory. Advanced empathy works because clients recognise themselves in what you say.'
- Clients themselves are often unaware of the fact that certain themes are inherent in their experiences. If these themes are pointed out to clients, it could help them to create new symbolisations and restructure their selves.
- The way in which these themes are picked up and conveyed to the client must give evidence of the facilitator's communication skills and must also be meaningful to the client.

The facilitator's identification of themes is still hypothetical until the themes have been confirmed by the client. The themes must therefore be conveyed in a tentative way to the client for him or her to confirm.

Activity 4.4

1 Indicate the themes for the groups listed below:
   a) Afrikaans, English, isiZulu, Setswana, Sesotho, Spanish, German
   b) Men, women, children
   c) Pears, peaches, apples
   d) Parents, brothers, sisters
   e) Shoes, earrings, twins
   f) Foetus, baby, toddler, teenager, adult
   g) Respect, individualisation, confidentiality
   h) Freud, Rogers, Skinner
   i) Love, hate, aggression, frustration
   j) Isolation, alone, lonely, exile
   k) Warm, snug, togetherness, closeness
2 Can you think of similar groups of words that create a theme?

Example 4.9

A male client says: 'I have never said this to anyone ... but I have thought for such a long time ... This is a terrible thing to say, but if I could just ... well ... (*Short, bitter laugh)* ... if I could just find some cause that I could give my life for I would be happy. I have never been successful in anything I do. My marriage has failed, my job is going nowhere. I have lost my faith. (*Sighs and is silent.*)

All the experiences he indicated point to a sense of failure. They all point to the fact that he perceives that he cannot be the person he wants to be and that he would rather be dead than be a failure.

It is important to note that although the facilitator may be tempted to cheer him up or reassure him that life is worth living, this would not be empathic. This reassurance would not be from the man's frame of reference, but would rather fulfil the need of the facilitator to save the man. It can sometimes be very difficult to stay in the client's frame of reference, and to explore his or her deepest and darkest fears and feelings.

Here is a possible response: 'You seem to be very down on yourself. You feel that there is no hope of you ever being able to be successful, of reaching the goals you set yourself.' Or: 'The road ahead seems to be going nowhere for you, and you wonder whether being dead is at least somewhere to go, and that you might find meaning along that road.'

Example 4.10

The client, a young woman, revealed during an interview that she was removed from her parents by child welfare when she was a young child. She was put into foster care twice. Each time, she was removed after a few months by child welfare and placed somewhere else, until she landed up in a children's home. She was not there long when she had to move again because she was too old for the home. She was in a place of safety for two months, and from there she was moved to various families for weekends and holidays. Each time she felt like an outsider and she still missed her own family. Child welfare informed her, however, that they did not know who her own family members were.

Activity 4.5

1 What theme can you identify from all of the young woman's experiences?
2 Formulate an advanced empathic response to her that includes your theme. You can give more than one formulation. (Remember that this is entirely hypothetical, since your responses cannot be confirmed with the client.)

4.5.2 Exploring distortions

The examples discussed under Proposition 11 [d] of Rogers' theory relate specifically to those experiences that are distorted because they threaten the self-structure for some or other reason. They are therefore part of the client's defences and should be handled cautiously.

> *The therapist perceives the client's self as the client has known it, and accepts it (basic empathy); he perceives the contradictory aspects that have been denied to awareness and accepts those too as being part of the client; and both of these acceptances have in them the same warmth and respect.*
>
> [Rogers 1987: 41]

In the warm, safe climate that the facilitator maintains, clients can explore these inner discrepancies or contradictory experiences of self and find some way of reorganising the self.

Note that these discrepancies refer to inner conflicts of the client's experiences, and not to differences between what the facilitator thinks or expects of the client and the client's own experiences.

One way in which the facilitator can 'hear' that the client cannot symbolise something is to listen to the contradictions or discrepancies between different experiences or statements. An example of this is when what the client says verbally differs from his or her non-verbal behaviour.

Example 4.11

A client says he is feeling well, but he is frowning.

The facilitator could say something like: 'I heard you saying that you are well, but unless I am mistaken, the expression on your face says something else?'

Example 4.12

The client says that he and his mother have always had a good relationship, but every time he mentions her, he frowns or clenches his fists.

In a case like this, the facilitator might wonder whether the client is not sending two different messages. The example could also be extended to a value conflict (Proposition 10). If the client has taken over the value that to be a good son, a man must have a good relationship with his mother, he will not feel free to symbolise any negative experiences about her. The facilitator could therefore begin by first maintaining the symbolised self: 'You see yourself as a good son, who loves his mother.' The facilitator could then add: 'You are afraid that your relationship will be destroyed', or: '... and it might therefore be difficult to allow yourself to be angry at her, sometimes?'

Example 4.13

The client says at some stage of the conversation: 'I do not like being told what to do.' Later he says: 'I am afraid that people will reject me if I do ...'

The first statement could mean that he needs to do his own thing, to be independent. The second statement, however, indicates a need for other people's approval. The question is, therefore, whether the client is aware of the discrepancy. Can these two seemingly conflicting experiences be integrated into one self?

The statements that clients make over a period of time should also naturally be related to each other. Refer also to the advanced empathy skill of linking of islands.

It is usually easier and more gentle to end such a response to the client with a question. If the client denies the discrepancy, the facilitator should not insist that it is correct.

The principles that were discussed at the beginning of the section on advanced skills are also applicable here. Clients know what they are experiencing and what they are yet ready for. Even if the facilitator's observation is correct, it could be that the client is not yet ready to examine the experience. The facilitator must therefore fall back on basic empathy, and listen and observe further, to see exactly what the client is experiencing and when he or she is ready to delve more deeply.

Exploring the discrepancy does not necessarily imply that one part of the discrepancy needs to be changed. It is therefore not a veiled form of criticism, but rather an effort to enable clients to symbolise themselves and their inner struggles more fully. There could, for example, be a conflict between two needs: a mother needs to be alone sometimes, but also to be a good mother who spends a great deal of time with her husband and children. If she is not aware of the two needs, they could confuse and immobilise her. If she is aware of the fact that both needs are important to her, she could accommodate both in some way in her self-structure and/or behaviour. The facilitator cannot predict or determine what she will do with her new symbolisation.

Activity 4.6

How would you respond to the following clients?

1. A wife says that it is very important to her to be a good wife to her husband, but at the same time she seems rather cross.
2. A woman says that she feels that her eldest child is becoming big and independent, but then she says that he is the only little boy in the home.

A special consideration: Differing frames of reference

It can happen that the facilitator has to deal with a client who has received some news about the self that does not fit with the symbolised self. This could pertain to medical information (like the diagnosis of an illness) or to some other event in the client's life. The person who imparts the information can become very frustrated if the client refuses to accept the given information. The person-centred facilitator can, in terms of the theory, understand the threat the information might have for the client. By exploring the 'what and how' of the threat, the facilitator could enable the client to also explore the nature of this threat.

Example 4.14

A mother of four children is admitted to hospital with a kidney problem. She is the breadwinner of the family and she has been strong, healthy and independent all her life. After many tests, the doctors inform her (from their frame of reference) that she is a chronic patient who will have to come in for dialysis three times a week. They try to convince her that she will always remain sick. They cannot understand that she refuses treatment and are amazed when she discharges herself from hospital.

Taking into account the earlier discussion of the self, how do you think this woman has always experienced herself? Do you agree that this self is now threatened? In addition to the fact that her self-structure is threatened, the children who are waiting for her at home and who need her also stand in the way of her symbolising the information about her illness.

In the following example, the information received was only a part of the overall process between a facilitator and the client (a girl in an institution). The facilitator also heard her fears – not only the symbolised fears, but also the unsymbolised or implied fears – and was not afraid to explore the girl's feelings openly. As a result, they could move together to new symbolisation and experiences.

Example 4.15

A girl is in a place of safety and is waiting to hear to which children's home she will be sent. She arrives early for the appointment with the social worker.

SW (social worker): You are early. I wonder whether it means that you are anxious?

C (client): Yes, I can't wait to hear where I am going. Isn't there anyone we can contact?

SW: You would like to know as soon as possible. *(She phones the Department, which informs her that M is going to X. She tells M. The girl's face falls and she looks worried.)*

SW: It seems that you feel that this is not good news?

C: I have heard a great deal about the place and very little of it is good. They say that it is a bad school that is full of gangs.

SW: You are uncertain – not just about the transfer, but also about your safety?

C: *(With tears in her eyes)* I will miss Pam and Selena *(Her friends)*. They cried when I told them I was being transferred.

SW: You feel unhappy because you have to leave your friends behind. You will miss them a great deal and you are also worried about them. They will miss you.

C: *(Sighs)* Yes, but still I am glad that I will be nearer to my mother, because she does not have the money to come and visit me here. I don't know why I am confused, because I knew from the beginning that I would not stay here forever.

SW: Are you surprised that you allowed yourself to become attached to the place and its people?

C: Yes – as I said before, it isn't easy for me to start relationships with people. And now look at me. *(Silence)* I wonder if I will also be able to make friends with the others at the new place?

SW: I am not quite sure what I'm hearing ... hope or uncertainty?

C: I don't know exactly. I will have to think about it and then we can talk again before I go.

Differences between implementing the basic and advanced skills

At the beginning of this section, we discussed the difference between the basic and advanced skills at a theoretical level. However, they also entail different actions or skills (implementation). This difference is not always easy to identify, as both are types of empathy, from the client's frame of reference, and deal with clients' experiences. It is the kind of experience that differs as well as what the facilitator does with clients' experiences. As we have now discussed all the different types of advanced skills (except immediacy, which is an advanced skill used only in a particular instance during the process), we can look at how the implementation of the advanced and basic skills differs.

> ***Example 4.16***
>
> The father of a 16-year-old boy says to the facilitator: 'My son does not listen to me any more. He comes and goes as he pleases, without asking or even telling me where he is going. I really don't know what to do.'

If the facilitator responds with something like: 'You seem concerned (or worried or frustrated) about the way your son is behaving', or: 'The change in your relationship with your son is really upsetting you', this demonstrates basic empathy.

Note that substituting one feeling word for another feeling word does not change basic empathy to advanced empathy, because you are still dealing with the same experience in the same way. However, if you move (advance) to the implied message, the implied threat to the self of the father in interaction with his son, this becomes advanced empathy. The facilitator can ask him- or herself why the father is so upset about the son's behaviour. How does this behaviour affect the father as a person?

Remember that it is the father's experiences we are dealing with here, not the experiences of the son. Only the son can know his own experiential world and he is not in the room to share it with us. The father is with us, and we need to understand his experiential world as influenced by his perception of his son, their relationship and himself. We need to take care not to become a 'ghost' voice, that is, not to speak for or about a person who is not physically present in the room.

The facilitator could respond with something like: 'You feel that your son does not respect you as his father, like he used to do. And now you could be wondering whether you are still his beloved and needed father figure.' Or you could say: 'Being a caring and responsible father appears to have been a big part of who you are, and now you seem to wonder how to deal with the possibility that you might not be needed quite as much as before.'

This example shows that the advanced response moves beyond the obvious experiences shared by the father to how these experiences affect him as a person, his self (identity) as a father.

It is important to note that although the basic and advanced skills differ, they are not used separately. In other words, the facilitator would not use the basic skills first, and then move on to the advanced skills, leaving out the basic skills. Instead, they complement each other. So, in the example above, the facilitator could start with the basic response, then give an advanced response at a later stage, or even combine the two.

Another way of highlighting the difference between the basic skills and the advanced skills is by exploring the difference between summarising and connecting islands, and developing a theme.

Example 4.17

A 29-year-old man who lost the use of his legs in an accident says: 'My girlfriend does not visit me here anymore. My family say that she is seeing someone else. I also don't know whether I can still go back to my old job. I wonder whether I will still be able to earn enough money to support my brothers and sisters. I am so frustrated at not being able to sort this out for myself.'

If, in his or her response, the facilitator just listed all the things that have happened to the man since the accident, the facilitator would be summarising, that is, demonstrating basic empathy. However, seeing a connection between these things and how they affect the self of the client as a person, and developing a theme from that connection, would be advanced empathy.

The theme can be identified by looking at what all the experiences he mentioned have in common. In this example, the theme seems to be one of loss: not just of his mobility, but also of the relationships he had before, for instance with his girlfriend and his family. The self that developed in interaction with his siblings was that of a strong provider, and he fears that this self will now be lost to him. He also fears the possible loss of his independent self.

For the facilitator's response to show advanced empathy, it needs to include something of this deeper understanding. He or she could say something like: 'You have lost so much through the accident. It seems as if you fear that you can no longer be the same strong, independent person who not only does things for himself, but also takes care of others.'

These examples illustrate that the advanced skills are used to express a much deeper understanding of the client, about himself and what is threatening him as a person. It goes beyond what he has expressed directly to what is only implied about what is really bothering him (threatening the self), but of which he is not consciously aware.

If it is accurate, the client might confirm it, if he feels safe and is ready to symbolise the experience. On the other hand, the facilitator might be wrong, and the client can then correct the incorrect understanding by exploring what does fit with him. It could open up a new path of exploration. As long as the facilitator remains tentative in his or her responses and allows the client to guide him or her, it is not so much the accuracy of the responses that matters, but the facilitator's genuine attempts at really understanding the client in depth and demonstrating this.

Here it is again important to remember what Rogers said about not being passive. The facilitator should rather actively attempt to share his or her deeper understanding with the client.

4.5.3 Immediacy

Immediacy is discussed separately from the other advanced skills because it has a very particular place in the facilitation process. It is often confused with basic empathy, as here too, the facilitator deals with the here and now. The difference is that immediacy deals with the here and now as it relates to the unfolding relationship between the client and the facilitator.

The word 'immediacy' brings to mind a sense of closeness. This is because it relates to the relationship between the facilitator and the client, in the here and now, that is, immediately. In other words, it relates to what is happening now, between the facilitator and the client, and how this affects the professional relationship they are trying to build. It is a skill used to understand and enhance this relationship, and to deal with any possible stumbling blocks that might damage the relationship.

For example, if a client says: 'I am angry with my husband', it calls for basic and advanced empathy. However, if a client says: 'I am angry with you (the facilitator)', it calls for immediacy.

Similarly, if a client says: 'I do not trust my husband', it calls for basic and advanced empathy, while if she says: 'I do not trust you (the facilitator)', it calls for immediacy.

Or, if a client says: 'I need to lean on my mother', it calls for basic and advanced empathy, while if she says: 'I need to lean on you (the facilitator)', it calls for immediacy.

If a client says: 'I do not believe in doctors', it calls for basic and advanced empathy, while if she says: 'I do not believe in you (the facilitator)', it calls for immediacy. It also suggests that the facilitator has a discrepancy to explore: she does not believe in the facilitator, yet she is here to see him or her.

These examples aim to illustrate that immediacy is used when the client expresses an experience regarding the facilitator and the relationship between them.

It is not always easy to build up trust and thus create a safe space for self-exploration. A client might be cautious about trusting the facilitator initially, but also later in the relationship when the facilitator is getting close to the painful experiences that the client has hidden from him- or herself. It is important to have empathy with this caution. Do not expect trust at any time, but always work on building it. Immediacy is one skill that can be used to do just that.

Remember that immediacy is used to develop the relationship, not to destroy it. This means that the facilitator cannot blame the client for his or her feelings or experiences. It is not an opening for the facilitator to confront a client or to give a client 'a piece of his or her mind'. The latter actions would imply behaviour from the facilitator's own frame of reference, whereas immediacy, like all the person-centred skills, is from the client's frame of reference. Also, to judge or criticise a client at any time will only threaten the client, who will then feel the need to defend him- or herself against the facilitator. This will destroy the relationship the facilitator has been trying so hard to establish.

This is not always easy to do. The facilitator might sometimes feel threatened by what a client says or does, and be tempted to defend him- or herself against the client, or to blame the client for his or her experiences. Here it is important to keep in mind that we, as human beings, are also self-determined. That is, we determine who we are, as facilitators, what our experiences are and which of these experiences threaten our selves.

So, if you feel any kind of emotion in interaction with the client, you need to understand yourself. You need to be able to access what is happening inside yourself and take responsibility, not only for what you are experiencing, but also for dealing with it. We cannot expect our clients to help us to deal with our own experiences. They are there to deal with their own experiences, not yours. Also, as we are unique people, we need to find ways of dealing with our experiences that fit with our selves as facilitators.

Some facilitators believe that to be congruent means to be honest with clients. We believe it means being honest with yourself. If you honestly want to be an effective facilitator, then it seems counterproductive to impose your own experiences (feelings, needs, values and expectations) from your own frame of reference on a client just to make yourself feel better. There are some exceptions, like setting certain limits for the therapeutic relationship. Examples include sexual and aggressive behaviour. It is, however, still important to accept and understand such behaviour in clients.

Example 4.18

C (client): I think emotionally I'm dying for sexual intercourse but I don't do anything about it ... The thing I want is to have sexual intercourse with you. I don't dare ask because I am afraid that you'd be non-directive.

F (facilitator): You have this awful tension, and want so much to have relations with me.

C: Can't we do something about it? This tension is awful! Can you give me a direct answer? I think it might help both of us.

F: *(Gently)* The answer would be no. I see that you desperately want this, but I could not do that.

C: *(Pause, sigh of relief)* I think that helps. It's only when I am upset that I feel like this. You have strength, and that gives me strength.

> *As in setting any limit in the therapeutic experience, this is something that is purely the responsibility of the therapist, and he (sic) takes that responsibility. Therapists should not attempt to evaluate (judge) the client's experience by a statement such as 'that really would not help you'. He simply takes responsibility for his own behaviour, at the same time indicating understanding and acceptance of the client's experiences.*
>
> [Rogers 1987: 211]

It can also be useful to provide a number of other outlets for expressing aggressive behaviour, like boxing gloves, a punch bag, hitting pillows or other breakable, non-injurious toys. (This can be used with both adults and children.)

Providing other means of expressing anger has a threefold purpose:

- It prevents breakages in the therapy room and injury to both the facilitator and the client, thereby also preventing the breakdown of the safe therapeutic relationship.
- It provides ways for the client to find new behaviour that fits with the self (Proposition 12).
- It communicates acceptance of the client's experiences and needs, while simultaneously providing a safe way of expressing them.

Here are some guidelines for the implementation of immediacy.

Self-based statements

Self-based statements involve comments that the facilitator makes on what the client is relating, or comments on certain processes that the facilitator identifies, which include the facilitator and their relationship, for example:

- The client asks the facilitator: 'How well are you qualified?' The facilitator responds by saying: 'I hear that you want to make sure that I am qualified enough to really be of assistance to you, otherwise you might find it hard to trust me.'
- The client asks the facilitator: 'Do you have children?' The facilitator can respond by saying: 'You seem worried about whether I will really be able to understand your concerns regarding you and your children, unless I myself have children?'

The following deductions can be made from the two examples:

- The facilitator includes him- or herself in the response. The personal questions are related to the client's needs and concerns about the facilitator, and their professional relationship. These concerns are usually implied, which is why immediacy is an advanced skill.
- Furthermore, these concerns are treated with respect and understood as part of the relationship-building process. It would not be useful to become defensive and try to convince the client of your ability to be of assistance. Rather, demonstrate this ability by the use of immediacy.
- The commentary must be sincere, otherwise the client will not accept it. If the remarks have significance for the client, this kind of immediacy could give him or her a different perspective on the process happening between him or her and the facilitator. The client might see something he or she has not seen for him- or herself (about him- or herself, you and your relationship).
- Immediacy can also lead to further exploration. The facilitator and the client become aware of any issue hampering the process, and have the opportunity to explore it.

Dealing with stumbling blocks in the professional relationship

This skill can also be used when the facilitator experiences that there is some kind of stumbling block that hampers the therapeutic relationship and there is no progress in the deepening of the relationship. This immediacy enables the facilitator to regain momentum in the interview by addressing the issue at hand. For example, the facilitator might say: 'It seems to me that what is happening between us at the moment does not fit with your expectations of where we are to go.'

Immediacy requires exceptional maturity from the facilitator to expose the facilitator–client relationship (and therefore him- or herself) to 'discussion'.

To promote this kind of immediacy, avoid any phraseology that might make the client feel that he or she is being blamed for any experience, such as: 'You make me...' This might sound as if the facilitator is blaming (and thus threatening) the client. It also denies the facilitator's self-determination.

The hypothetical (or tentative) nature of immediacy

Anchin and Kiesler (1982: 17) refer to the usefulness of the hypothetical explanation that the facilitator gives to the client. If what the facilitator conveys to the client has meaning and is useful, the client will accept it and expand on it. If not, the client can correct the facilitator.

As in the case of all the skills that have been discussed thus far, immediacy is also treated hypothetically. Because the facilitator could misunderstand the relationship or the interaction (as seen from his or her frame of reference), the immediacy is suggested hypothetically to the client. If the hypothetical response is significant to the client, it will create a certain momentum or heightened intensity in the interview and the relationship. If the facilitator's hypothesis is incorrect, the client will usually correct the facilitator by bringing up another issue.

Activity 4.7

Formulate immediacy responses to the following statements by various clients:

1 A female client says: 'I am angry with you today.'
2 A male client says: 'I do not trust you. I don't believe that you can help me.'
3 A female client says: 'I feel as if I cannot go it alone. I really need to lean on you.'
4 A couple look at each other and then the wife asks: 'Are you married and do you have children?'

CHAPTER

5 Reconstruction of the self (Phase 3)

5.1 Introduction

We have already discussed how to create a safe space in which clients can feel fully accepted and understood so that they can explore their unconscious experiences. In this chapter, we will explore what can happen to clients while they are exploring these unconscious experiences. As people are unique, this process is not predictable and does not always happen in the way the facilitator may hope. However, there usually is a sense of greater awareness of self as the process unfolds.

5.2 The third phase of the process – reorganisation of the self

5.2.1 Proposition 15: Reconstruction of self

> *Psychological adjustment exists when the concept of the self is such that all the sensory and visceral experiences of the organism are, or may be, assimilated on a symbolic level into a consistent relationship with the concept of self.*
>
> [Rogers 1987: 513]

'I can still express myself amidst painful changes.'

People become well adjusted (with concomitant reduction of tension) when all or a maximum of their experiences can be symbolised congruent with their self-perception.

The self-structure is now able to symbolise a wide range of experiences. Behaviour is no longer motivated by experiences that have not been symbolised (or that do not accord with the self-structure).

Such experiences include negative or painful experiences as well as positive ones that have been symbolised and integrated with the self. This enables individuals to express themselves in a more controlled way, as their experiences accord with their self-perception.

The self does not change so much that we become unrecognisable to ourselves. It is not as though clients become other people during the process of facilitation. When they get up in the morning and look in the mirror, they still recognise the person in the mirror. However, they may now have a different feeling or perception about that person (themselves).

When unsymbolised or distortedly symbolised experiences are allowed full symbolisation, various changes can occur:

- Clients can perceive the self in a broader way, as incorporating more and even contradictory experiences into the self, for example: 'Although I am a peace-loving person, I do sometimes get mad at others.' Or: 'Although I love my children, I can get mad at them sometimes, without it making me a bad mother.' Now these contradictory experiences no longer pose a threat to the self.
- Clients can reconcile different selves, like a woman who comes to realise she can be a dedicated wife to her husband as well as an individual in her own right. She no longer feels guilty for wanting a night out with her friends without her husband.
- Clients can expand their views of their selves, like being a father and a breadwinner.

Example 5.1

An example of a client perceiving him- or herself in a different way (first bulleted point above) would be a woman who has always seen herself as physically beautiful. Much of her sense of self had always been associated with her physical beauty. She had won many beauty contests and had worked as a model. She saw herself and her interactions with others in terms of these experiences. Then she was in an accident in which her face and body were badly scarred. She was very depressed and wanted to die. For her, the essential part of herself had in fact died.

During the facilitation process, she explored in greater depth her own belief or value that she was only alive or of worth if she was beautiful. She realised that much of this belief was taken over from her perception that she had to participate in beauty contests as a child in order to be accepted and loved, and her fear that if she did not win these competitions, she would also lose her parents' love.

She began to question these beliefs and was able to symbolise that she and her parents also had fun together when they were enjoying a picnic, even though her hair was full of sand and she stubbed her toes on the rocks at the seaside. She began to see herself also as a person who had fun and who could see the lighter side of life. This led to wondering whether she could share some of her vast experience about the world of beauty competitions and modelling with others who were struggling to survive. From this emerged a whole new career and sense of self.

Example 5.2

This example, which illustrates the last two kinds of change (last two bulleted points on page 102), can also be related to an accident. The client, a professional man, could not continue with his chosen profession after an accident. He too became very depressed and feared the loss of his family's love if he could not provide for them financially. When he explored this perception that he was only acceptable if he had money to give, he began to realise that his family loved and needed him for other things that he still could provide, like being there when they were afraid, lonely or confused. His self thus expanded to see himself also as a father and a protector, not just a provider. He could accept that he meant more to the family than a meal ticket, but he could not see himself as totally unoccupied and dependent on a maintenance grant from the state for his own income. He started exploring other possibilities for generating money and later went into business for himself.

Thus, he changed his behaviour (way of generating an income) to maintain the sense of self as an active member of society.

The facilitator cannot prescribe or predict what changes will occur in the client's world, but can only walk the road of exploration with him or her.

Although the theory hypothesises that people move towards self-development, it does not mean that the facilitator should expect all clients to be independent and strong. Rather, it tries to create a safe space where people can get to know themselves better, and be(come) all they can be.

So for instance, if a married woman says she feels she works too hard to please her husband because she does not want to lose him, the facilitator cannot expect her to become independent of her husband. She may come to realise that her fears of losing his love are unfounded and that she does not have to work so hard to please him. This could still be seen as a restructuring of the self, namely that she is a good wife and that she can trust herself in this regard. However, she still needs the husband to fulfil the wife self.

5.3 Discussion of the facilitation process

This phase aims to enable clients to explore all their experiences so that they can reconstruct their selves. All the theoretical principles discussed previously as well as all the professional values and skills are applicable during this phase.

Proposition 17 tells us that the safe conditions created and maintained by the facilitator permit the self to change, to allow more of a person's experiences into the conscious mind. What the person will do with these experiences is not predictable and cannot be determined by the facilitator. This is why it is so important to maintain the values of individuality, respect and self-determination. The facilitator has to believe that clients will be able to develop their own selves, in their own way, as determined by them and nobody else, including the facilitator. Holding on to this belief will help the facilitator to avoid the temptation to guide or nudge the client towards the way the facilitator wants him or her to move.

Each client needs to be seen as an individual and fully accepted, with all the different experiences he or she may share once trust has been built.

> ‘*The counsellor accepts and recognises the positive feelings that are expressed, in the same manner in which he has accepted and recognised the negative feelings. These positive feelings are not accepted with approbation or praise. Moralistic values do not enter into this type of therapy.*’
>
> [Rogers in Kirschenbaum and Henderson 1990: 72]

The idea of ‘moralistic’ values indicates the distinction between personal and professional values made in Chapter 2. During the process of facilitation, the professional values are at play. In his or her personal life, the facilitator uses his or her own, personal values.

As we are dealing with the whole person (Proposition 3), we know that it is not just the feelings that change as the self changes.

> ‘*Intermingled with this process of insight … is a process of clarification of possible courses of action. Often this is infused with a somewhat helpless attitude. Essentially the client is saying: ‘This is what I am, and I see that much more clearly. But how can I reorganise myself in any different fashion?’ The counsellor's function here is to help clarify the different choices that might be made, and to recognise the feelings of fear and lack of courage to go ahead that the individual is experiencing. It is not his function to urge a certain course of action or to give advice.*’
>
> [Rogers in Kirschenbaum and Henderson 1990: 74]

The client's behaviour now fits with his or her self. We can say that the client acts more in terms of Proposition 12 than Proposition 13.

Rogers warns here that the facilitator must resist the temptation to give advice in order to relieve the uncertainty. Giving advice would stem from the facilitator's own needs and be from his or her own frame of reference.

Rogers' warning indicates that the skills, both basic and advanced, are still very important. They enable the facilitator to stay with the client's experiences and frame of reference as this process of exploration of the self unfolds. There is no recipe for when to use which skills during this phase. The skills are used as the need arises, and the facilitator is guided by the client's experiences and level of symbolisation.

It is important to keep in mind that the facilitator does not ask for change of any kind. The facilitator trusts the self-actualising tendency of the client to provide the impetus for change, while the facilitator stays with the experiences expressed and implied by the client.

Rogers (1987: 135) also found that there was '…movement from symptom (problem) to self … from environment to self.' This means that the client can become more aware of him- or herself in relation to his or her problems. It also means that where previously the client sought control over his or her problems in the environment, now the client becomes more aware of the locus of control lying within him- or herself. (Compare Proposition 12 and Proposition 13 in this regard.)

The safe space that the facilitator has been working to create can also have a negative side. It could create an intimacy for the client and the facilitator where they can share anything. This intimacy could be confused with a relationship between friends or even lovers.

The facilitator must remember that it is and has to remain a professional relationship. It might be necessary to use immediacy to clarify any confusion arising in this regard.

This can also be linked with the issue of touching a client. Not all people are open to being touched. The issue is even more of a dilemma if the client and facilitator are of the opposite gender. Even if they are of the same gender, sexual complications can arise in this regard.

It may be safer to avoid touching a client. Instead, the facilitator can enter the client's world in other ways, including using metaphors, art or any other form of expression.

Although it is not expressly spelled out by the person-centred approach, the facilitator should remember that verbal communication is only a very small part of human expression. There are many other ways to communicate. The competent facilitator will develop his or her own ways of sharing the client's world.

CHAPTER

6 Ending the process (Phase 4)

6.1 Introduction

In this chapter, we will explore the last phase of the process: what usually happens when the client's self has been restructured.

6.2 The fourth and final phase of the facilitation process

The following propositions are just guidelines as to what is possible so that the facilitator can be prepared for the movement that may occur in clients and not be taken by surprise. However, if the process does not unfold as described here, the facilitator cannot push the client towards these goals. During each and every phase, the facilitator has to move with the client, at his or her pace, working with what the client is prepared to share and not expecting more than the client can deal with.

6.2.1 Proposition 18: Acceptance of others

> *When the individual perceives and accepts into one consistent and integrated system all his sensory and visceral experiences, then he is necessarily more understanding of others and is more accepting of others as separate individuals.*
>
> [Rogers 1987: 520]

When an individual is able to symbolise most of his or her experiences and to integrate them into a total self-concept, that individual will display greater understanding of others and be able to accept them as separate, unique individuals.

An individual who is conscious of most of his or her experiences and has integrated them into a self that contains no contradictions is not threatened by other people's experiences, even when these differ from the individual's own experiences. He or she is able to say: 'I know who I am' ('I'm OK', Proposition 15), and: 'I can allow you to be who you are' ('You're OK').

'We are both OK.'

If we take the example of the married woman discussed under Proposition 15 in Chapter 5, we can say that she now feels OK about herself as a wife and will no longer be threatened by other wives who differ from her. This proposition implies that the client's relationship with others will probably also change as the client's self changes.

Together, Proposition 18 and Proposition 19 present the long-term goal of person-centred therapy. However, these propositions presuppose that the facilitator has reached a stage in his or her life where he or she is able to permit and enable other people (especially clients) to be themselves, even though they differ from the facilitator.

The prospective facilitator may benefit by testing him- or herself against this thesis. Ask yourself:

- What do I experience when people differ from me?'
- What do I want to do with such people?'
- What will happen to me, in interaction with them, if the other parties do not change, and what will happen if they do change to become like me?'
- What will happen if they change in ways I do not agree with?

6.2.2 Proposition 19: Developing your own valuing process

> *As the individual perceives and accepts into his self-structure more of his organic experiences, he finds that he is replacing his present value system – based so largely upon introjections that have been distortedly symbolised – with a continuing organismic valuing process.*
>
> [Rogers 1987: 522]

As individuals come to perceive and symbolise more of their sensory experiences, integrating these experiences into their self-concepts, their value systems, which were perviously based mainly on distorted symbolisation of other people's values (Proposition 10), will make way for a process of determining their own values.

The first part of this proposition is linked to Proposition 15 and Proposition 18. The rest of it indicates another advantage of an integrated, symbolised self (the intended outcome of therapy). Individuals now decide for themselves what they consider to be important. They do not need to adopt other people's values (including those of the facilitator). It no longer matters all that much whether other people praise them and they become less dependent on others. Such individuals embark on a process of evaluation, continually testing and examining their values.

The married woman mentioned under Proposition 15 in Chapter 5 now feels OK about herself as a wife. She might have realised

Weighing up the good and bad for yourself

that the values she used to decide whether she was a good wife were taken over from her mother. However, she is now able to decide for herself from her own value system what it means to be a good wife.

6.3 Discussion of the facilitation process

These propositions indicate that many other changes may occur with the reconstruction of the self. This change can also be linked to the wholeness of people, namely that change in one part, the self in this case, can influence all the other experiences.

The client now knows and accepts him- or herself more, is able to relate to others without threat, and behaves in ways that not only accord with his or her self-perception, but also with values that the client has defined for him- or herself.

This indicates that the client may be ready to leave the relationship.

As with all the previous phases:

> *... there is neither compulsion on the client to leave, or attempt on the part of the counsellor to hold on to the client.*
>
> [Rogers in Kirschenbaum and Henderson 1990: 76]

Note that the values of the person-centred approach as well as all the skills used during the third phase (reconstruction of the self) are still being used in the last phase.

Allowing a client to decide when he or she is ready to terminate the process of facilitation takes respect for the client, and his or her individuality and self-determination. The client is not always able to express this message of readiness explicitly. This may be because the client still feels a little unsure, or fearful of offending the facilitator if he or she says so outright. So the client may say something like: 'I think I can manage on my own now', or: 'I wonder whether I still need to see you.'

The facilitator will require the advanced skills and even immediacy to understand what the client is implying about him- or herself and the relationship with the facilitator. The facilitator could respond with something like: 'I sense you might be ready to leave our relationship/terminate our association/end our journey together.'

It is not only the client who might have some difficulty in ending the relationship. As mentioned in Chapter 5, the client and the facilitator can become very close and comfortable with each other, like old friends, and one or both might not want to leave this comfortable relationship. If the facilitator finds it difficult to hear a message that the client is ready to end the relationship, he or she needs to explore not only what is happening in the process or with the client, but also with him- or herself.

SECTION

B

Group facilitation

In this section, we will consider how the person-centred theory, values and skills relate to working with groups.

Although the professional guidelines remain the same, utilising them in the group context creates some specific challenges that will be explored. In order to avoid duplication, the propositions, values and skills will not be repeated in great detail here. It is thus advisable for the reader to familiarise him- or herself with Section A, which lays the ground work for this section.

CHAPTER

7 Beginning the process (Phase 1)

7.1 Introduction

Dealing with diversity is a key aspect of working with more than one person, as is the case in group work. It requires that the facilitator be tolerant and accepting of different people and their experiences, at the same time.

Differences between people can be enriching. This is demonstrated by the colourful ceremonies and flags displayed during international events such as the Olympics and the World Cup Soccer. Here we see people from different cultures, ages and genders brought together by a common interest. In spite of their differences, they can work and play together.

On the other hand, differences between people can be perceived as threatening, to the point that these differences lead to violence. An example of this can be found in the Second World War, where Hitler wanted all people to look alike and was prepared to kill anybody who differed from his idea of the 'perfect' human being. (His idea was that all people should have blond hair and blue eyes.)

More recently in South Africa, there was a spate of xenophobic attacks and killings. Some South Africans experienced people from other African countries as different from themselves, and saw them as a threat to themselves. The fact that there is even a word ('xenophobe') for a person who hates or is very afraid of strangers illustrates that differences between people can create very strong emotions and reactions to those differences.

Activity 7.1

Explore your own attitude towards people who differ from you.

- If you discuss your religion with others and they hold opposing views, what do you do?
- If you discuss politics with others and they hold opposing views, what do you do?
- Are there any rituals or events in your own culture or religion that prohibit interaction (like marriage) with people from a different culture or religion?
- Can you describe any event at which you met people from a different culture or religion, which you found interesting, informative and/or enjoyable?

Another aspect that is a constant in group work is that the facilitator has to work on two levels all the time. He or she has to work on the level of the individual members who create the group, as well as on the group level, which in turn is created by the members of the group. This is represented by the movement between I/us, me/we or you/me.

During the process of facilitation, these elements are in constant interaction, as the members interact with each other and the facilitator. This process of interaction can enable members to learn more about themselves and each other.

Let us return to the example of people waving flags at a soccer match. Their behaviour implies that they are soccer fans who are loyal to their sport, their team and/or their country. They also seem eager to demonstrate this loyalty by waving their flags. However, if some people in the crowd do not wave their flags, it does not necessarily mean that they are not loyal fans. They may just have different ways of expressing themselves or be on the side of the losing team.

There may also be differences in how people react if the team they support is losing. Some people may go very quiet, whilst others may shout even louder to encourage their team.

This illustrates that people may differ, in their perceptions, behaviour and how they see themselves as people, even when they are brought together by the same interests or goals. The process of facilitation aims to create a climate or space in which people can get to know themselves better by sharing their ideas with each other and the facilitator in a non-threatening environment.

The theory, values and skills discussed in this chapter and the next two chapters are guidelines to help the facilitator create and maintain this safe space for the journey of self-exploration.

7.2 Conditions for facilitation

7.2.1 Proposition 17: Creating a safe space

> *Under certain conditions, involving primarily complete absence of any threat to the self-structure, experiences that are inconsistent with it may be perceived, and examined, and the structure of self revised to assimilate and include such experiences.*
>
> [Rogers 1987: 517]

This proposition may be regarded as a guideline for the group facilitator on how to treat group members during the process of facilitation. It is important that the group should hold no threat for any of its members. Members should not only feel safe (in other words, they should not feel threatened), but they should also feel that they are being accepted totally and unconditionally. To accept group members, the group facilitator needs to enter and deal with each and every member's experiential world, which also includes the member's internal frame of reference. The group facilitator needs to use the professional values as well as the communication skills to ensure that he or she treats members of the group within their own self-structure and frames of reference. If the group members experience that they are accepted, understood and respected in a genuine, open and honest way during the beginning phase of the group, an atmosphere that enhances self-exploration, among other things, may develop.

As the group consists of different people, they may not all agree on what 'safety' entails. Some might think it is safer not to talk too much, while others could want to talk a lot, without being interrupted. These differences can pose quite a challenge to the facilitator. It means that he or she has to be flexible and diverse in how he or she demonstrates acceptance and understanding to each member of the group.

The facilitator must be aware that he or she cannot side with one or more members of the group against another member. All of the members of the group are people who need to be accepted in their own right and for who they are. So for instance, with members who wish not to talk, it would not be safe to try to make them talk. There are other ways of communicating with silent members. These methods will be discussed in Chapter 9.

It would also not be safe to just silence the member who speaks a lot so that others can get an opportunity to speak. The speaker has to be shown that he or she is fully understood and accepted. This does not mean just listening to the content of what is being said, but more importantly, listening to what the person is saying or implying about him- or herself as a person.

Proposition 8, which follows, will explain in more detail what we mean when we say that all members of the group must be accepted as people.

7.2.2 Proposition 8: The self or identity of each member as a person

> ‘*A portion of the total perceptual field gradually becomes differentiated as the self.*’
>
> [Rogers 1987: 497]

On page 498, Rogers gives a more detailed description of the self as 'an organised, fluid, but consistent conceptual pattern of perceptions of characteristics and relationships of the "I" or the "me".'

This proposition relates to the group members as well as the group. Although members come to the group with a sense of self, a group identity is built up that both the individual and the group perceive as the self of the group. Both the individual self and the group self must be understood and respected by the group facilitator.

The point can be illustrated with an example from everyday life. If you eat a carrot, its colour, shape and taste tell you that it is a carrot. All these dimensions form part of the identity of the carrot.

The same can be said of a potato or a green bean. They all have their own identities, yet when they are put together in a group, this group now also has an identity, namely a group of vegetables. The group identity does not destroy the identity of the individual vegetables, but may indicate that in some way they have something in common.

Group identity = vegetables

In the same way, all of a person's experiences form part of his or her identity or self, which the person brings to the group. Together they then form a new identity, the group self.

However, the individual self of each group member still identifies each member as a specific and unique human being who is part of the group. Just as a carrot stays a carrot, Bob stays Bob, but now Bob is also part of a particular group, which he helped create by being part of it.

Consider these examples of the individual self of a member:

- The silent group member mentioned under Proposition 17 (page 112) could see him- or herself as a quiet person or an introvert, while the group member who talks a lot might see him- or herself as an outgoing and active person (self or identity). To challenge this self would thus pose a threat to the self and would negate the safe climate that the facilitator is trying to establish.
- Some elderly couples were complaining that they were becoming isolated. A group facilitator decided to start a group for the elderly in their neighborhood. During a visit to one particular couple, the elderly man mentioned that he did not want to belong to the group because he thought of himself as 'the one who helps other elderly people with their problems'. His wife was keen to join the group, but could not do so because of her husband's refusal, and she saw herself as a 'woman who stood by her man'. The group facilitator realised that both the husband and the wife could benefit from belonging to the group. Before the first group meeting, she again visited the couple and, using the old man's image of himself, asked him whether he would come along to help her because she could not facilitate the group on her own. The man agreed, and the facilitator made a point of including him in all decisions during the following few meetings. It was not until the fourth meeting that the man realised that the group could also be of value to him.

Proposition 17 reminds us that the facilitator has to accept and understand each member's self throughout the process of facilitation.

Example 7.1

In a group of young men discussing marriage, member B says: 'I would like to have at least three wives.' Member W reacts very strongly to this: 'How can you say that! It is not possible to give three wives the love and attention they deserve.'

The facilitator may react in different ways to these statements, depending on his or her own self and values. The facilitator might be tempted to agree with one member while disagreeing with the other. However, what is important is that both men indicated a sense of self by what they said, and it is important that both men should be understood and accepted for who they see themselves to be.

So the facilitator could say something like: 'B, I sense that you see yourself as a man who can share yourself with more than one woman, while you, W, see yourself more as a one-woman man.' In this way, both men can feel understood and accepted, so that there is no threat to the self, as indicated in Proposition 17.

There are many different kinds of groups in society, for example, friends getting together, church groups and people who work together at the same company. This grouping refers to the identity or self of the group. Have a look at this example of the self of a group as a whole.

Example 7.2

A group of women had been meeting for some sessions. During one such session, one woman said that her husband had asked about the group. She wondered about how much to share with him or whether she could invite him to the next meeting. The other members were quiet. On exploring the silence, it emerged that most of them saw it as a private group for women only.

The example that follows illustrates that members can have different perceptions about and experiences in the group self.

Example 7.3

The following statements were made by members of a group of unemployed men:

D: I have tried and tried so hard to find work. But nobody wants to hire me.

E: *(Nods his head)* I am also tired of going from place to place, only to be told they don't want or need me.

>>

J: *(Angry voice)* It is the government's fault. They should create more jobs for us.

K: At all the places where I have been, they say I am not skilled enough. *(Sighs)* It seems I don't have anything to offer. *(Turning to facilitator)* Do you have any ideas about what we can do? It seems we have all run out of ideas.

The individual self of the members is that of hardworking employed men, while the group self seems to be one of helplessness.

Not all the members have the same perceptions about themselves, the group or the facilitator. This is discussed in more detail in the next proposition.

7.2.3 Proposition 1

> *Every individual exists in a continually changing world of experience of which he is the centre.*
>
> [Rogers 1987: 483]

As members' experiences are unique and known only to themselves, the safe climate mentioned above is needed for them to feel able to share these experiences with each other and the facilitator.

The group facilitator, therefore, explores the nature of the experiential world of each individual and of the group as a whole. Often group facilitators refer to a session as 'difficult' because the members did not want to participate or listen to each other. This may, however, be because the facilitator did not listen to and understand the human experiences of each member.

Also, because each member's experiential world and the experiential world of the group as a whole may change in seconds, the group facilitator will find that long-term planning of the group is fraught with difficulties. In other words, the group facilitator may find that plans originally decided on are rejected at a later meeting. One of the reasons for this rejection may be that the experiential world of the members and the group has expanded or changed in the time between meetings. Such expansion may also have been stimulated indirectly by the previous group meeting. The group facilitator should, therefore, always be prepared to change any plans made by the group. This should not be too difficult if the facilitator accepts that a group belongs to its members, and that they themselves should decide on the functions of the group and the uncovering of their selves.

Even though members in traditional groups are brought together by a common concern, the facilitator must remember that, because of the uniqueness of each member's experiences and self, the members will have different needs and ways of behaving. No two group members or groups will therefore be the same.

This proposition refers to experiences that are conscious as well as experiences that are unconscious. What makes the difference? This is explained in Proposition 11. We will start with the first part of the proposition, which relates to conscious experiences.

7.2.4 Proposition 11 [a and b]: Conscious experiences are those that fit with the self

> *As experiences occur in the life of the individual, they are either [a] symbolised, perceived and organised into some relationship to the self [b] ignored because there is no perceived relationship to the self-structure ...*
>
> [Rogers 1987: 503]

When working with groups, this proposition refers to the self of each member as well as that of the group as a whole.

Conscious experiences are those experiences of which the members are aware, whether it is a feeling, a thought, a behaviour or a value. They are not aware of unconscious experiences. If they are not aware of an experience, they cannot talk about it.

Consequently, members will only be able to discuss freely those experiences that fit with their selves and are therefore consciously symbolised. They will ignore those experiences that they do not see as relevant to themselves. As each member is unique and has a unique self, it is possible that the members will differ as to which experiences are symbolised or not, as well as to what they find relevant.

In order to create and maintain the safe space mentioned above, it is important that the facilitator listen to each member, and respect and accept the experiences and self of each one.

Thus, if members indicate in any way that they do not want to discuss an experience, the facilitator should not press them to do so. If, on the other hand, some members seem bored during a discussion, it might indicate that the topic being discussed is not perceived as relevant by them.

It is therefore important to involve all members of the group in creating the group. This pertains to all aspects of the group, like when, where and how often to meet, as well as what is discussed and how this is done. In this way, members can indicate what they find relevant and what they do not feel is relevant to them. The only people who can ensure the usefulness of a group are the group members themselves.

As there are a number of people present during group work, this may pose quite a challenge. The facilitator might be tempted to side with some members of the group and ignore other members, especially if the facilitator deems certain members to be important or unimportant.

7.2.5 Proposition 2: Perceptions differ

> *The organism reacts to the field as it is experienced and perceived. This perceptual field is, for the individual, reality.*
>
> [Rogers 1987: 484]

The perceptions of each person or group member are unique and thus every group is unique. These perceptions become the members' reality, including their perceptions about themselves and other people. Their perceptions might differ from each other and the facilitator. For example, in one group some members may see one member as an angel, while other group members see him as a devil. To make this problem of perception even more difficult, members' perceptions may change during the group sessions.

It could, therefore, be threatening to some members if the discussion centred around only one member's perceptions. This dilemma is further aggravated when activities or discussions are planned according to the perceptions of the group facilitator, or the organisation or institution for which the facilitator works. The example that follows shows the danger of dealing with groups according to the perceptions of one or two people, or the perceptions of organisations and institutions such as schools.

Example 7.4

The management of a firm decided to instigate problem and growth-orientated groups for employees. The purpose of the groups was to give employees the opportunity to discuss anything that influenced their functioning in the work and social environments. One group consisted of five members: two adolescents, a married couple and a man who had recently been appointed as a control manager of 500 employees. The group decided that they wanted to discuss relationships. During the first meeting, it became clear that the members had different ideas about what relationships entailed. For example, the adolescents understood relationships to mean relationships with the opposite sex, while the manager thought it implied that attention would be paid to building up relationships with employees.

If the group facilitator had been unaware of these perceptions, the group sessions would have failed, despite the fact that attention had been paid to certain relationships. The group facilitator should be especially sensitive when raising broad concepts that could lead to different perceptions. He or she should always find out exactly what group members want and mean, and then identify shared experiences, perceptions or themes.

Activity 7.2

1. A group was asked to identify the element that did not fit into the following collection:
   Dog, cat and television.
   Which element would you choose?
   Answer: I do not know because I am not familiar with the group's perceptions. Should their perception focus, for instance, on animals, the answer would be 'television'. On the other hand, if their perception were focused on licences, the answer would be 'cat'. The group could even have a perception that indicated 'dog' as the correct answer.
2. A group consisted of seven couples with marital problems. One man and his wife, both immigrants, were not fluent in English. During the third session, the wife of the immigrant couple arrived late. She was also not accompanied by her husband. She excused herself by saying she had just poured boiling water on her husband.

How would you have perceived her statement? Do you think the other members of the group would have perceived it in the same way?

7.2.6 Proposition 5: Needs and behaviour

> *Behaviour is basically the goal-directed attempt of the organism to satisfy its needs as experienced in the field as perceived.*
>
> [Rogers 1987: 491]

This proposition emphasises the fact that the basic prerequisite that influences behaviour is the person's urge to meet his or her needs. All of the members of a group may have different needs, as well as different perceptions as to how to fulfil these needs. Even if members have the same need, they may have different ideas about how to meet the need in the group.

For instance, a group of teenage boys expressed the need to talk about leadership. Some members mentioned a video they had seen on the subject that they wanted to watch, while others wanted to talk about their own experiences. The facilitator explored both needs with the group until they agreed on a personal discussion, with the option of watching the video later if they still felt a need for it.

The metaphor of a choir can be useful in exploring this proposition. The members will all sing, but in different voices. These different voices create the richness of experiences that makes group work so rewarding. The behaviour of singing can express different needs (like joy or being part of a choir), just as attending the group can meet different needs of the members. Thus, exploring all the different needs and behaviours of all the members can enable the group to meet the needs of them all.

One group, many voices

Example 7.5

One of the boys in a group of teenagers showed the group the hunting knife he always carried. One of the other members asked him about the purpose of the knife. He replied that he carried it to defend himself, as he came from a rough neighbourhood where every man carried a knife to defend himself.

His behaviour meets his need, as he perceives it, to protect himself.

The behaviour of the group members in Example 7.3 indicates their need to be employed and to be useful.

7.2.7 Proposition 6: Emotions or feelings

> *Emotion accompanies and in general facilitates such goal-directed behaviour, the kind of emotion being related to the seeking versus the consummatory aspects of the behaviour, and the intensity of the emotion being related to the perceived significance of the behaviour for the maintenance and enhancement of the organism.*
>
> [Rogers 1987: 492]

When taking Proposition 6 into account, the group facilitator will also accept and understand all the different emotions expressed by the group members and the group as a whole. These feelings will be expressed both verbally and non-verbally. A member may, for instance, express emotions non-verbally by bringing a hand up to his or her mouth in an expression of surprise. Non-verbal behaviour may also be used to confirm verbal communication of emotions, for instance a group member may make agitated gestures while talking. The group facilitator will therefore have to listen to and observe the members in totality.

However, group members will only express or demonstrate their feelings if a safe climate of acceptance and trust prevails in the group. It is thus very important that all emotions expressed be accepted and understood by the facilitator.

In Example 7.3, some members had similar emotions, while others had different feelings. All felt despondent and helpless. Some were angry or frustrated. It is important for the facilitator to understand, accept and stay with these emotions. The facilitator might be tempted to make it better or to reassure them, by indicating that they are important or that everything will be all right. However, this is not what the members are experiencing. It would not enable them to explore the depth of their own emotions.

7.2.8 Proposition 3: Group wholeness

> *The organism reacts as an organised whole to this phenomenal field.*
>
> [Rogers 1987: 486]

In group work, the 'organism' refers to each individual member, as well as the group as a whole. As with Proposition 6, the group wholeness can be illustrated through the metaphor of a choir. There are many different voices in a choir, for example, bass, tenor, soprano and so on, yet put together, they create beautiful music. The music that they create together is different from all the individual voices, yet includes them all.

The identity of each member, for example, a soprano or a tenor, becomes part of the group whole or identity, namely the choir.

Not all the voices are heard as loudly as the others, or even as frequently, yet when they are singing, they become part of the music. They have to be there and they are part of the choir, even if they are not singing at a given moment in time. In the same way, the quieter members are there and they are an essential part of the group. When they wish to participate, their input forms part of the group.

When the facilitator hears and appreciates all the voices of all the members, it enriches the group experience for all of the members of the group.

Besides viewing the group as a whole, each member is also seen as a whole, including his or her identity.

In terms of this proposition, the facilitator should regard each individual and group as a whole and not concentrate only on one aspect, such as behaviour. All the experiences of all the members (such as their perceptions, needs, emotions, values and selves) have to be understood and accepted.

7.2.9 Proposition 9: Self and significant others

> *As a result of interaction with the environment, and particularly as a result of evaluational interaction with others, the structure of the self is formed (an organised, fluid, but consistent conceptual pattern of perceptions of characteristics and relationships of the 'I' or the 'me') together with values attached to the concepts.*

(For the sake of clarity and continuity, the description of the self given earlier is repeated here as originally formulated by Rogers.)

[Rogers 1987: 498]

People do not live in isolation. They are always interacting with other people, from before birth until death.

Their perceptions of these interactions influence the way they see themselves and the other people with whom they interact.

Thus in group work, the members' interaction with each other, as well as with the facilitator, will influence their selves as well as the self of the group as a whole (and the self of the facilitator).

When applying the metaphor of the carrot, potato and green bean mentioned before to this proposition, we can say that each one has an identity, but they only become vegetables in interaction with the group. Thus the group identify or self is defined in relation to all the members.

The metaphor of the choir is also applicable here. The people who sing in the choir create the choir (or group) in interaction with each other. Here they become members of the choir. They can also be members of a family and of a group of friends. Their identity can thus be influenced by their significant others, including the group.

So, if we return to the types of groups mentioned above, people interacting in a group as friends would perceive themselves, the other people and their interaction in a different way from the way in which they perceive their interaction with colleagues at work.

Also, not all working groups require a facilitator. Groups like AA (Alcoholics Anonymous) may have a group leader who is not necessarily a trained professional. Thus the facilitator only becomes a facilitator in interaction with a facilitation group. The facilitator has other identities, like being a wife to her husband or a mother to her child. Those are different interactions in which different selves develop. The facilitator cannot be a facilitator to her husband or child, just as a facilitator cannot be a parent or teacher in relationship to a facilitation group.

7.2.10 Proposition 10: Values

> *The values attached to experiences, and the values that are a part of the self-structure, in some instances are values experienced directly by the organism, and in some instances are values introjected or taken over from others, but perceived in distorted fashion as if they had been experienced directly.*
>
> [Rogers 1987: 498]

The metaphor of the choir can again serve as an illustration. If member J of the choir grew up with a family where it was accepted that all good Christians sing in the church choir, J might have taken over this value from his parents, rather than believing it for himself.

It is very important that the facilitator does not expect the members of the group to take over his or her own values. In the example of the boy with the knife, the facilitator might have expected the boy to give up the knife if the facilitator did not believe in violence as a means of self-protection.

Members can also not be expected to take over each other's values. In the case of the two young men with different values about marrying one or more women, neither has to take over the values of the other. During the process of facilitation, they are able to explore their own values without any judgment from the facilitator.

7.2.11 Proposition 12: Behaviour that fits with the self

> *Most of the ways of behaving that are adopted by the organism are those that are consistent with the concept of self.*
>
> [Rogers 1987: 507]

The metaphor of the choir can also serve as an illustration of this proposition. If a woman perceives herself to be a singer, but not necessarily a solo performer, then her behaviour of joining the choir, and then singing with the choir, would fit with her perception of her own self and the group self.

For example, if a family gathered together to celebrate a birthday, they might laugh a lot, enjoy loud music and even dance to the music. On the other hand, if they gathered at the funeral of a family member, this behaviour might not fit with their sense of self as grieving family members of a family group. However, some families, with different values and selves, might celebrate the death with singing and music. It depends on the self and values of each person and the group as a whole.

In the example of the boy who brought a knife to the group, his behaviour fitted with his self as a man who can protect himself.

In the example of the unemployed men, their behaviour of continually trying to find a job fits with their selves as hardworking, employed men. The facilitator might not agree with this sense of self, but the self is not up to the facilitator, but rather the client, as explained in the next proposition.

7.2.12 Proposition 4: Self-determination

> *The organism has one basic tendency and striving – to actualise, maintain and enhance the experiencing organism.*
>
> [Rogers 1987: 487]

This proposition relates to the self of each group member, as well as the group as a whole. The facilitator cannot determine who the members are or who they must become. The same goes for the group itself.

Let us return to the metaphor of the choir. If the members and the group as a whole see themselves as a church choir, the conductor cannot turn them into a rock-and-roll band. The choir strives to improve its performance by regular practice sessions, even though these sessions take time and effort. There might be different perceptions about how much training is needed or what form it should take. In a similar way, group members might differ in their perceptions about when the group should meet, how regularly the group should meet and what should be done during the meetings. If the facilitator trusts the members' self-determination and their need to enhance their selves (the selves of the individual members as well as the self of the group as a whole), he or she will let the group make these decisions.

The member who sees herself as a quiet person cannot be forced to become talkative. She will determine whether and when she will join in the discussion. Similarly, the man who would like to have three wives determines his self as much as the man who sees himself as having only one wife.

It may be easier for the facilitator to accept the selves of members who are most like what he or she wants them to be. It is those members who differ from the facilitator or from the social norm of the society to which the facilitator belongs that most often pose a challenge to the facilitator.

The way members determine themselves is expressed through their frames of reference. This is spelled out in the next proposition.

7.2.13 Proposition 7: Frame of reference

> *The best vantage point for understanding behaviour is from the internal frame of reference of the individual himself.*
>
> [Rogers 1987: 494]

Each member of the group has his or her own experiences, as described in Proposition 1. This includes the person's perceptions, needs, emotions, behaviour, values and self. When people speak about anything, they are expressing their experiences as they perceive them. In other words, they are expressing their experiences from their own frames of reference.

It is important to keep in mind that when members speak about anything, it is their frames of reference or experiences they are sharing. Thus, as explained in Proposition 2, it is their reality and not the reality of anyone else. This is especially important in group work, as members sometimes speak for or about another member.

For instance, in the example of the two men who disagreed about the number of wives they wanted, if W had said: 'I think B is wrong to want three wives', it would have indicated W's values and perceptions. It would not have been an indication of how B sees himself or of his values. Each man has his own reality or frame of reference, which the facilitator needs to hear, understand and accept.

The theoretical principles spelled out in this chapter are a way of thinking about the people whom the facilitator may encounter when working with groups. However, the attitude of the facilitator towards these people and towards group work itself is also very important for creating a safe climate or environment in which the process of facilitation can take place. We will discuss this further in the next chapter.

CHAPTER

8 Professional values (Phase 1)

8.1 Introduction

In this chapter, we will look at the meaning of values and the role they play in the process of rendering assistance. We will define the values of respect, individualisation, self-determination and confidentiality. We will also explain how these values are implemented when working with groups.

Although specific values have been identified, they are all inter-related. Values reflect the facilitator's entire attitude towards humankind. Professional values more particularly reflect the attitudes of facilitators towards their clients, the people in need with whom they are involved. Such values are applied (or implemented) in practice and form the basis of the total process of rendering assistance. This is an important principle, as the values are not just applied in the beginning phase and then forgotten. They have to be in operation during the whole process of facilitation.

The value basis may not be conscious, yet it still influences the facilitator's behavior. It is, therefore, important for all facilitators to try to examine their own values in terms of the people with whom they are involved. For instance, many people (including facilitators) feel awkward when reference is made to people in need – mixed feelings of pity and superiority are often experienced towards people who cannot cope with their situations or with life. It is somewhat peculiar that such sentiments are felt particularly towards people in psychosocial need. For example, when people experience problems with the plumbing in their home, it makes sense for them to call in the services of a qualified plumber. People who cannot cut and style their hair themselves visit a qualified hairdresser and people who are physically ill see a qualified physician. We do not pity them or think less of them for asking for help. Why should it be any different for people who are experiencing psychosocial problems to consult a qualified facilitator?

Activity 8.1

Analyse (as honestly as possible and for your own edification only) your attitude towards your clients.

1 Do you respect them?

2 Do you believe in their potential to grow and to function independently? If not, why not?
3 If you do believe in their potential, how do you demonstrate these sentiments to your clients?

In practice, the facilitator faces many obstacles that may hamper the application of professional values. These obstacles are discussed in detail by Boy and Pine (1983: 93–95) and can be summarised as follows:

- The values that facilitators internalise in a programme of studies do not seem operable in the real world.
- All groups that pressure the facilitator to do more and to do different things are well intended. They identify certain needs.
- Groups insist that the facilitator is in the best position to meet their needs.

According to Boy and Pine (1983: 95), the problem is that institutions and pressure groups that influence the organisational behaviour of institutions often identify human needs that are not the actual needs of clients within a community. Such institutions and groups often identify needs that are politically expedient, needs that flow into the interests and competencies of staff, needs that are aligned with the interests of funding agencies, needs that have a certain ethical or moral bias and needs that have become popularised by the mass communications media. According to Boy and Pine (1983: 94), such demands and pressures not only place a heavy burden on the facilitator's time and energy, but they create a psychological burden for the facilitator. The pressured and harassed facilitator becomes easily confused regarding his or her professional identity, mission and role. The question is whether you as facilitator attach sufficient importance to the issue of professional values, and whether you still have the energy to take a stand and even to take on the authorities and other professions on this issue.

What exactly are these values and how do they relate to the person-centred approach? Authors such as Glassman and Kates (1990: 21) place such emphasis on the value of the human being that they refer not merely to values, but speak of human values. They furthermore emphasise aspects such as support, cooperation, voluntary participation and respect for the differences between people.

> *The person-centred approach is not a psychology, a philosophy, a school, a movement, not many other things frequently imagined. It is merely what its name suggests, an approach.*
>
> [Wood 1995: 18]

Therefore it is a psychological posture, a 'way of being' – a way of being towards all people, also in groups. This 'way of being' is realised through 'living out' the values of the approach. The values should become part of the facilitator's value system and not something that we apply when necessary or needed. It is a way of being when moving alongside the individuals in the group as well as the group as a whole.

8.2 **Respect**

According to Gordon (in Rogers 1987: 338), group facilitators show respect when they accept the values of group members and they also accept the differences in their values. Group facilitators also realise that they cannot use (abuse) influence or lead members to achieve their own objectives or values. Gordon (in Rogers 1987: 338) also mentions that group members are people who do not want someone with superior qualifications and values to prescribe to them. The group-centred facilitator sees the group as an organisation that exists for its members. It offers members the opportunity to express themselves and to satisfy their needs. The group facilitator furthermore believes that the group itself should indicate the direction of the group work.

Moreover, Gordon (in Rogers 1987: 338) gives group facilitators guidelines according to which they can determine for themselves whether they have respect for the group and its members or not. The questions that they have to answer are the following:

- Do I trust the capacities of the group and of the individuals in the group to meet the problems with which we are faced, or do I basically trust myself?
- Do I free the group for creative discussion by being willing to understand, accept and respect all attitudes, or do I find myself trying subtly to manipulate group discussion so that it comes out my way?
- Am I willing to be responsible for those aspects of action that the group has delegated to me?
- Do I trust the individual (group member) to do his or her job?
- When tensions occur, do I try to make it possible for them to be brought out into the open?

Respect is present in a group when:

- The group facilitator listens carefully to what the members are saying. Experience has shown that group facilitators are generally good listeners.
- The group facilitator tries to understand the group members. This means that the facilitator views that which group members say within the appropriate context or in terms of the group members' selves and frames of reference.
- The group facilitator accepts members in totality.
- The group facilitator communicates a non-evaluative attitude.
- The group facilitator communicates and demonstrates empathy.

Example 8.1

In a group where the members were discussing what respect means in practical terms, one of the members said it means that a person has to stand in the shoes of the other person. Another member was not satisfied with this explanation, and said that a better example would be that a person has to stand on the shoes of the other person while that person is still wearing them. The group members and facilitator were sur-

>>

prised and asked the member to explain his metaphor. The member explained that people often listen until they hear what they want to hear and then follow their own trains of thought. If the facilitator were wearing a member's shoes, the facilitator could easily follow his or her own train of thought. However, if a person were to stand on the shoes that the other person was wearing, he or she wouldn't be able to move if the person wearing the shoes was not prepared to move.

The implication of this example is that the facilitator will not be able to change the pattern of thought or anything else in a group, as members are the only ones who can change, in a safe climate that makes this possible.

Here is an example of group work where the facilitator did not show respect for the group.

Example 8.2

The group facilitator working with a mixed group of teenagers (boys and girls) decided at one of the meetings that group members should work together in pairs. She also decided that each pair should consist of a boy and a girl. This decision caused moans and groans in the group. However, the facilitator insisted that the pairs consist of a boy and girl. The result of her insistence was that one of the girls decided to leave the group and the other members lost trust in the facilitator.

Another example of respect is respecting people's values, traditions and customs. Even disregarding a less-obvious aspect such as the venue in which groups meet may cause problems in the communication process.

Example 8.3

The facilitator working with a group of traditional Zulu people did not take into account their culture and traditions, and both young Zulu women and elderly Zulu men were included in the same group. Communication proved to be a problem from the outset because, traditionally, a Zulu woman is not permitted to contradict a Zulu male. Furthermore, a young person is required to respect older people, and one of the ways of showing such respect would be not to contradict them. The facilitator could clearly see that some of the Zulu women were not happy with events in the group, but they had to keep quiet because of their age and gender. The women only started participating in the group after special support from the facilitator. Comments such as: 'I notice that you are smiling' by the facilitator, and later by other group members, helped them to communicate.

If the facilitator respects the group and each individual group member, the members will experience the facilitator as real, caring, understanding and flexible in his or her approach. This is a prerequisite for the creation of a safe climate that will help the members to communicate freely, to focus on themselves and to take risks when needed in the group.

Activity 8.2

You are facilitating a group of elderly people to function independently within their community. A visit by a group of community leaders and the Minister of Health has been planned for the next meeting. The group has decided to serve tea and cake for the visitors. They have arranged who will bring what. You as facilitator are aware that some of the members have short memories and may forget to bring cake or tea. Discuss how you will ensure that those members meet their obligations without creating a threat to their selves or showing disrespect in the group.

8.3 **Individualisation**

It is interesting that, although Rogers emphasised the uniqueness of individuals, he also mentioned a few basic abilities that each individual human being possesses. These abilities are that human beings are basically:

- Rational
- Responsible
- Realistic
- Have the potential to grow (Farber et al. 1996: 6).

Rennie put these abilities in person-centred language with the following quote:

> *We are human beings. As human beings we have the ability to*
> - *Think about ourselves*
> - *Think about our thinking*
> - *Treat ourselves as objects of our attention*
> - *Use what we find there as a point of departure in deciding what to do next.*
>
> [Rennie 1998: 2]

Although each individual possesses these abilities, we must remember that everyone uses them in his or her own unique way.

Individualisation of group members and the group is stressed by virtually each and every author on groups.

- According to Douglas (1976: 26), one of the basic principles that can be formulated from the philosophy and knowledge of group work is 'a genuine acceptance of each individual with his unique strengths and weaknesses.'

- Corey (1990: 201) states that 'thoughts, feelings, beliefs, convictions, attitudes and actions are all expressions of the uniqueness of the person.'
- Glassman and Kates (1990: 114) are of the opinion that interaction showing respect for differences between group members is a prerequisite for a democratic communal help system such as a group. Glassman and Kates (1990: 114) add that 'this interaction is reflected in the members' abilities to listen to, to respond to and to incorporate different opinions, values, cultures and personalities without requiring adherence to a narrow ideology or to a narrow spectrum of permissible behaviours. Veiled reactions or avoidance of differences is brought to the members' attention.'
- Konopka (1972: 67) says that 'he (the group facilitator) must realise that each member is different from everyone else or from any other group, in past, present and future.' According to Konopka, no teenager is 'just another teenager'. Similarly, an elderly person is not 'just another elderly person'. Both are unique individuals with specific behaviour, needs and so on. Konopka (1972: 68) explains that group facilitators are inclined to be inflexible in their application of theoretical knowledge and to cling to the average characteristics for a group of people. This does not imply that we should ignore knowledge or theory because it does present a framework of possible human behaviour as well as possible explanations for such behaviour. However, theoretical knowledge should be applied circumspectly because certain theories can only reflect the average and general behaviour and explanations of individuals and groups.

In group work, facilitators should bear in mind that they cannot apply generalisations, but should work with the specific identity, behaviour, emotions, values and needs of each individual or group, in other words, individualisation. It is the task of the group facilitator to identify and acknowledge the uniqueness and specific nature of each member and group. According to Konopka (1972: 126–127), the group facilitator needs to possess certain skills in order to see individuals and groups in their totality and in the light of their individuality. How individualisation is manifested in groups is illustrated in the next three examples.

Example 8.4

In a group of bulimia sufferers, the group facilitator established that one of the girls had been moved to a boarding school. According to the facilitator, the bulimia may have been caused by the fact that the girl had to leave her parents' home. The facilitator consequently planned a group session dealing with the feelings and consequences associated with leaving home. The particular girl was very passive during the meeting. At subsequent meetings, it transpired that the girl's problem was not that she had to leave her home, but that she did not know how to cope with anger. The culture within which she had been raised dictated that anger could not be expressed. What was required, therefore, was for the group to focus on coping with anger rather than on dealing with the feelings associated with leaving home.

Example 8.5

When a member always arrives late for group meetings, it may be a sign that he or she is threatened by the group, but it may also be that the member has other responsibilities that make it impossible for him or her to be on time.

Example 8.6

The behaviour of a group of teenage girls attending a group meeting in sloppy clothes may be attributed to various factors. It may be a sign of rebellion against their mothers and the community, rejection of the existing values and norms of the community, rebellion against the group or facilitator, or even a case of the group wanting to look the same.

Activity 8.3

Various programmes have been constructed for groups. Taking individualisation as a value into account, would you use such programmes in your group? If so, explain how. If not, substantiate your answer.

8.4 **Self-determination**

In the human sciences, clients are often portrayed as passive, isolated and unable to help themselves. In the person-centred approach, however, it is believed that human beings are experts on themselves, and they are more aware of their own needs and abilities than any facilitator could ever be. Therefore, if people are allowed to speak for themselves, social science can reveal rather than mask the members' realities. In working with groups, it is possible that we as facilitators too often 'mask' the reality of the group members because we ignore the important value of self-determination or apply it incorrectly.

According to the existentialists, self-determination means that people have the freedom to choose between two possibilities (Corey 1990: 261). People are therefore responsible for the pattern that their lives follow. Rogers (in Corey 1985: 250) also believes in the group and group members' right to self-determination: 'The group will move – of this I am confident – but it would be presumptuous to think that I can or should direct that movement toward a specific group goal.' However, it is not necessary to wait passively for the group to move. By using the communication process and empathy with comments such as: 'You're angry about …', or: 'You're confused by …' , or: 'You think you're bad because …', it may be possible for the members to develop and to move in a direction that is still their own.

Glassman and Kates (1990: 176) agree with Rogers that group members cannot be forced to change their behaviour or to participate in a group programme that does not interest them. Members' right to self-determination and to make their own decisions must always be taken into account during group sessions.

Peggy Natiello (Farber et al. 1996: 132) found that since Rogers' death, 'the commitment to, and trust in, the self-determination of the client is at risk in the ranks of the client-centered therapists. It (self-determination) is the radical aspect of the approach and the most difficult to practise in a world where lures of expertise and authority are so pervasive.' If we want to respect self-determination, we must remember, as Rogers said (Farber et al. 1996: 131), that 'the therapist becomes the "midwife" of change and not its originator.' The group facilitator will therefore not:

- Take control away from the group members
- Interpret facts and behaviour to the group members
- Guide or manipulate the group members
- Change the direction of the session on his or her own.

Activity 8.4

A group of mothers said that they would like to discuss the disciplining of children at the next meeting. The facilitator had an American programme on discipline at her disposal and decided to present this programme. The meeting was a failure. In view of self-determination as a value and the group facilitator listening selectively as a hindrance, explain why the group did not succeed.

Activity 8.5

In a group of teenage girls, the facilitator focused on the development of social skills with strong emphasis on self-determination. The group had to decide for itself which issues were to be discussed. For the sixth session, the members decided to discuss relationships with boys. The facilitator established that seven of the ten girls were sexually active. During the session, the three girls who had not been sexually active decided to start experimenting with sex. The group had been presented under the auspices of a school that had conservative values about standards of behaviour between boys and girls.

1 Which factors would you take into account in further dealings with the group?
2 How would you handle the situation by taking into account the value of self-determination?

8.5 Confidentiality

To maintain confidentiality in a group, the group facilitator and the group members must be confidants. In other words, they must have the ability to keep the information that has been shared inside the group. To maintain confidentiality, it is necessary to believe in the worthiness of group members as human beings and to respect them.

Even group facilitators who do respect group members sometimes unconsciously breach confidentiality by:

- Using the names of group members in reports
- Asking members to reveal personal information to other members
- Not obtaining members' consent to make reports available to other institutions

- Not obtaining members' consent for discussing their actions in the group with other professionals, such as a case facilitator
- Passing on group information on minors to the parents without the consent of such minors
- Not obtaining a member's consent to reveal certain information to a group (it often happens, for instance, that a group member provides the group facilitator with information between two meetings; the group facilitator has to explore with the member whether this information is open to all the members)
- Making audio and video recordings of groups without the consent of members.

Example 8.7

During the first meeting, Agnes was one of the most outspoken members in the group. Owing to illness, she could not attend the second group meeting, during which the members consented to an audio recording being made of the third meeting. At the third meeting, Agnes was very quiet and did not participate in the group discussion. The group facilitator noticed this and asked whether she was still feeling ill. She placed her left index finger on her mouth and pointed to the tape recorder with her right hand.

This example, which actually happened, clearly shows how important it is that group facilitators take into account the confidentiality of the group as well as the confidentiality of each individual group member at all times. In the example, the group facilitator should first have obtained the consent of members who had been absent from the second meeting before starting the third session.

Example 8.8

In a group consisting of women experiencing marital problems, the group facilitator expected members to discuss their marital problems as early as the second meeting. One of the members suggested that the group should rather discuss the behaviour of a well-known person who was experiencing problems in her marriage.

In the example, the facilitator tried to direct the process and expected the group members to reveal personal information that they did not want to discuss. Because the particular member wished to remain in the group, she made a counter-proposal that she did not find too personal. A member who did not attach much value to the group would simply have left.

Confidentiality can be difficult to maintain, especially in certain group situations, for instance:

- Where the group members are in regular contact with each other outside the group
- Where people are in institutions, where the release of confidential information may be misused not only by other residents, but also by the staff of the institution

- Where the group occurs in a work situation where management may use confidential information against the facilitators or group members.

Activity 8.6

Consider how you would deal with the situation described in Example 8.8 on page 132.

8.5.1 Developing confidentiality in the group

Some group facilitators (such as Van der Kolk 1985: 190) experience no difficulty with confidentiality. According to these group facilitators, the group members know exactly how much to say without exposing themselves or the other group members. Van der Kolk (1985: 15) points out that if group members and facilitators share a mutual trust, this improves the group's functioning. However, Konopka (1972: 89) cautions that confidentiality should not be forced on members, but should develop from 'a voluntary effort on the part of the group members'. Confidentiality, even when as part of a contract, may therefore never be enforced by the group facilitator.

Van der Kolk (1985: 15) states that confidentiality should receive attention as early as in the pregroup phase. During this phase, the group members could be asked whether they would like to discuss the exact meaning of confidentiality in the group, how confidentiality will be applied, why confidentiality is important to the group, and also how difficult it will be to apply confidentiality at all times and to strengthen mutual trust. Corey (1990: 30) agrees that confidentiality should be negotiated in the group.

Confidentiality and trust are reinforced when group facilitators show that they are serious about confidentiality. The facilitator can do so, for instance, when a member asks for permission to share something that has happened in the group with his or her spouse. It would be easy to grant permission, but if the facilitator takes confidentiality and self-determination seriously, and wants the group to assume responsibility for maintaining confidentiality, the group should be allowed to decide.

Establishing confidentiality is not a single event, but it forms part of the total group process. That is why members should be reminded of confidentiality from time to time as the process develops. They should continue to think about it as the climate becomes more open, and members become prepared to divulge personal and confidential information more easily.

8.5.2 Is confidentiality a myth?

In the discussion so far, it has largely been assumed that confidentiality should be maintained at all times. Schwartz and Zalba (1971: 20) point out that it is more difficult to control confidentiality when working with groups than when working with individuals. Group members themselves often tell their friends, parents and spouses what happened in the group. Schwartz and Zalba (1971: 20) quote a group facilitator who said that confidentiality is a myth.

Although various group facilitators have said that confidentiality must be maintained at all costs, Corey (1990: 31) also feels that the group facilitator may breach confidentiality under certain circumstances. For example, if a member's behaviour poses a danger to him- or herself or to the community, the group facilitator may release information for the protection of the community. This information may, however, only be revealed after consultation with, and with the consent of, the group member and the group as a whole.

Activity 8.7

What would you do if the group member refused to give consent in the situation described above?

Information may be released to the parents who have consented to their children attending group sessions. According to Corey (1990: 32), however, such information may never be released without the consent of the child, and the child should also be present when the information is conveyed to the parents. Parents should also be informed during consultation that group facilitators intend telling the children what is said during telephone conversations. This is of significance to confidentiality, but may also prevent parents from providing children with inaccurate information about telephone conversations.

Activity 8.8

How would you act in each of the situations described below, taking confidentiality into account? Substantiate your answers.

1 The headmaster of a high school asks the group facilitator to provide him with the names of group members who may be using drugs. The headmaster needs the names in order to take disciplinary steps against the learners.
2 A probation officer calls and asks the group facilitator to evaluate a group member. The information will be used to determine whether the group member needs to continue serving a jail sentence.
3 A group member admitted to the group that his parents were supplying him with drugs. He then sells some of the drugs to other children.

If the values of respect, individualisation and self-determination are handled correctly by the facilitator in the group, confidentiality may not really become an issue. We believe that this is the reason why books on the person-centred approach seldom refer specifically to confidentiality.

The thinking and attitude of the facilitator play an important part in creating the safe climate necessary for the process of facilitation. However, if these thoughts and attitudes are not put into action, the group members may not perceive them. In the next chapter, we will look at the skills that can be used to put theory and values into practice.

CHAPTER

9 Basic communication skills (Phase 1)

9.1 Introduction

Groups consist of individual people. A group does not exist without the people who create it. Thus the principles and skills of the person-centred approach still apply.

The basic skills are an integral part of creating the safe space discussed under Proposition 17. Although the facilitator is working with a group, every member of that group remains an individual, who needs to feel safe. The values already discussed and the skills that follow are essential in creating this safe space for all the members of the group.

In order to avoid duplication, the basic skills, which were discussed in Chapter 3 of Section A, will not be covered here in great detail. Only a few aspects that need special consideration in group work will be explored.

9.2 Attending

It is important that the venue be big enough to accommodate the group without anyone feeling cramped. Children need enough space to move around for physical activities.

The venue should also allow for uninterrupted communication and provide for confidentiality.

The facilitator must be mentally prepared to deal with a group of people, not just an individual. In some organisations, facilitators work with individuals, groups and communities, so it can be hard for them to keep track of what event they are going to attend to next.

As the facilitator cannot verbally attend to all members at the same time, it is important to use non-verbal behavior to indicate to each member that he or she is being attended to. The facilitator can use intermittent eye contact, smiles, body posture and hand gestures to indicate to all members that the facilitator is aware of and appreciates their presence.

During group work, there is constant interaction between the members of the group, and between those members and the facilitator. This group process occurs continuously and the facilitator also needs to attend to it. It is important to be aware of who is talking to whom, who is silent, who agrees with whom, who disagrees and so on.

9.3 Listening

In order to create the safe space required for facilitation, it is very important that the facilitator accept, listen to and understand each member as a unique, whole person.

As discussed above, this includes the members' selves and all their experiences, from their own frames of reference. Listening includes attending to the content of what each member says, but also understanding what this content tells us about the person who is saying it.

In the example of the boy who carried a knife in Chapter 7, the facilitator could be shocked and even frightened when hearing the content or the word 'knife'. But if the facilitator listened to the person, it would be easier for him or her to understand that the boy saw himself as a man who needs to protect himself and was afraid not to carry the knife.

The facilitator also has to listen to the group as a whole. This includes the members' non-verbal behavior.

Example 9.1

When the facilitator arrived at the third group session with a group of teenage boys, all the group members were standing outside the venue. During the previous sessions, they had always waited for her in the group-work room. Noticing this change in behaviour, the facilitator commented that there must be something important they wanted to tell her. They said: 'Yes' and explained that because it was school holidays, they would like a more informal session. The facilitator asked them what they would like to do. They said that instead of talking inside, they would prefer to go to the beach. The facilitator agreed and together with the group members changed the venue, yet it was still possible to continue with the facilitation process.

This example indicates that listening is part of the whole facilitation process. It is not something that only happens during the beginning phase.

There are some additional challenges that the facilitator may face when working with groups.

The facilitator might be tempted to treat the members equally, by giving each one the same amount of time to talk. This could create an unnatural process in which nobody gets the opportunity to express themselves fully, while some group members are forced to participate against their will.

Not all members necessarily have the same needs at the same time. Some members of the group might be busy thinking about what is being said, while others might prefer not to talk at that time. So the facilitator needs to give a speaker his or her full attention while that person is speaking. It would also not be wise to invite comments on what the speaker said, as this would not indicate to the speaker that the facilitator had understood and accepted him or her.

If, however, another member responds spontaneously, the facilitator can allow the communication to unfold. It is, nonetheless, possible that a discussion between the members could turn into an argument.

Activity 9.1

What would you think, feel and want to do if a discussion between members of a group turned into an argument?

This can be a difficult situation for the facilitator to deal with. He or she might be tempted to side with one member against another member if he or she agrees with one of the parties. However, this would negate the creation of a safe space that the facilitator is working towards.

The principles of the person-centred approach can be of great assistance here, as they remind us that we need to listen to, accept and understand each member as a person from his or her own frame of reference.

Example 9.2

In a group of teenage boys referred because they use drugs, the members say:

J: It makes me feel strong, as if I can handle anything!

L: I feel it takes me away to a better place, where there are no worries.

N: When I use, I feel relaxed among my friends and we can just hang out together.

S: I don't need it. I can stop any time. I just don't want to. You are all making this out to be some kind of cure-all. It is not. It is just a way to show our parents we can do as we please.

N: I do not have a problem with my parents! It is my friends I find it hard to talk to when I am not high.

L: I do worry about my parents, but I do not want to hurt them.

S: *(In an angry voice)* I do not believe you. You are just saying so to irritate me.

Facilitator: *(Speaking to S)* I sense it really upsets you that the others do not agree with you. It seems very important to you that we understand that you have to show your parents who is boss, or that you need make some decisions on your own.

The reaction of S to the comments by the other members of the group indicated that he was no longer feeling safe (accepted and understood), so the facilitator had to demonstrate her acceptance to him by using empathy.

9.4 Empathy

Example 9.2 illustrates how important it is that all members of the group feel accepted and understood in the group. Empathy is a very useful way of demonstrating this to the members.

It is not enough to tell people you understand. In Example 9.2, if the facilitator had said only: 'I understand how you feel', S may well have reacted with more anger: 'How can you? You are not in my shoes!'

Empathy is therefore used to show the members of the group that the facilitator understands them as people. He or she understands their selves and all their experiences (refer to Proposition 3 in this regard).

Empathy is also used to build trust. Again, it is not enough to tell members they can trust you. Why should they? How do they know you are worthy of trust?

Example 9.3

Member P: I am not sure I can speak freely. *(Looks very worried)*

The facilitator may be tempted to reassure him that it is all right to speak up, but that would be from the facilitator's own frame of reference and would not show P that he is accepted along with his doubts. So, instead, the facilitator might say something like: 'It seems a great risk to you to allow yourself to open up in this group.'

P: How do I know you will not laugh at me?

Facilitator: You are not sure whether we will take you seriously.

The facilitator thus demonstrated total acceptance and understanding of P to him, thereby showing that the facilitator is worthy of his trust.

It is important for the facilitator not to blame one member of a group for another member's experiences (even if the members do so). This does not mean that the facilitator stops members of the group from doing so, but rather that the skill of empathy is used to demonstrate understanding of each member's frame of reference.

Example 9.4

The following comments were made in a group of teenage girls:

Ann: I think that Joan is angry with me, but I don't know why.

Joan: *(Looks confused)* I am not. Why would you think so?

Ann: When I was talking about you, you frowned at me as if I made you angry.

>>

Joan: *(Upset)* How can you tell what I was thinking? You are not a mind reader.

(Ann is silent and looks worried.)

Facilitator: *(To Ann)* You care about what Joan feels and do not want her to be angry with you.

Ann: Yes, I like to be on good terms with people.

Facilitator: So you are on the lookout for any signs that this might not be the case.

Ann: *(Slowly nods her head)* Maybe I did overreact. *(To Joan)* I am sorry.

Joan: *(Sighs)* It's all right. I was just surprised by what you said. Maybe I did frown, because I was thinking ...

(The conversation continues.)

The content of what was being discussed has been left out to illustrate that the facilitator needs to demonstrate his or her understanding of what the teenage girls are experiencing, inside themselves, about themselves and the other members of the group during their interaction, not what they are talking about.

During the initial phase of the group-work process, members might feel uncertain, not knowing what to expect from themselves, the other members or the facilitator. This might tempt the facilitator to give the group direction in order to relieve the members' anxiety. However, this would be from the facilitator's own frame of reference and would not enable group members to feel understood and accepted, or to express and explore their own uncertainty and fear.

Being non-directive does create structure: a structure where the facilitator does not give direction, but rather follows the lead of the group members.

When a member becomes angry, it could be tempting for the facilitator to calm him down. However, that would be from the facilitator's own frame of reference, and would not demonstrate acceptance and understanding of the group member and his or her experiences.

Example 9.5

Member B: *(Shouts very loudly, while banging his fist on the table)* I do not agree with the others. Why can you not pay attention to me?

Facilitator: It feels as if your voice cannot be heard unless you raise it above those of the others. It seems to you that only the voices of agreement are heard or accepted here.

This example illustrates how important it is to hear each member from his or her own frame of reference.

Example 9.6

Single mothers in a group were discussing their difficulties with their children.

V: I do not want to be too strict with Joan *(Her daughter)*. I want to let her know I trust her, so I do not check up on who she goes out with or where they go, but I worry, as she comes home so late.

D: You are too soft. You let her walk all over you. You should really sit her down and tell her what is what.

The facilitator needs to express understanding of each member to that member. He or she may not take sides. This might be difficult, especially if the facilitator has values that conflict with what one member says. In Example 9.6, a facilitator might believe that strict discipline is a necessity and thus be tempted to agree with D, but the members have to explore their own values and find what works for them.

Activity 9.2

Formulate your own empathic response to each group member in Example 9.6.

CHAPTER

10 Exploring unconscious experiences (Phase 2)

10.1 Introduction

Proposition 1 indicates that people have both conscious and unconscious experiences. The conscious experiences were discussed in Chapter 7 (Phase 1). We also looked at the ways in which the facilitator can demonstrate his or her understanding and acceptance of people and their experiences.

In the second phase, we will explore the unconscious experiences. We will consider why some experiences are conscious while other experiences are unconscious.

Note that the safe climate mentioned in Proposition 17 must be maintained throughout this phase.

10.2 What are unconscious experiences?

We need to explore what is meant by unconscious experiences. It may sound incomprehensible that people could have experiences (perceptions, needs, behaviour, emotions and values) of which they are not aware. If a person thinks or feels something, or behaves in a certain way, surely he or she must be aware of it? However, this is not always the case. We can compare it to being asleep. If a mosquito bites you while you are asleep, you might not be aware of it. You may wake up in the morning and find a swelling on your arm where it bit you. If you had not been asleep, you would probably have felt (experienced) a stinging sensation when the mosquito bit you.

Unconscious experiences can also be compared to a visit to a doctor. The patient experiences pain (a problem), but is not aware of what this pain implies in terms of the physical self being under threat. For instance, a pain in the patient's throat could imply that his or her tonsils are under threat, it could be a sinus problem or it could even be an ear infection.

In the same way, a behavioral or emotional problem or pain is an indication that the psychological self is under threat. The person is not aware of exactly how this self is being threatened. He or she needs to explore the self and where it hurts during the process of facilitation. This idea is spelled out in the next proposition.

10.2.1 Proposition 11 [c and d]: Dealing with experiences at an unconscious level

> *As experiences occur in the life of the individual, they are either [c] denied symbolisation [d] given a distorted symbolisation because the experience is inconsistent with the structure of the self.*
>
> [Rogers 1987: 503]

This proposition indicates that whether an experience is symbolised or not (conscious or unconscious) depends on whether the experience fits with or is consistent with the self.

As discussed under Proposition 11 [a and b], experiences that fit with the self (or identity) of a person pose no threat to that person. However, if a person experiences something that does not accord with his or her self, it creates a problem concerning how that person views him- or herself. In other words, if the person were to allow that experience into his or her conscious mind, it could destroy the person's sense of self, the sense of who the person thinks he or she is, and thus the person cannot allow the experience to become conscious.

For example, if a woman sees herself as an honest person, and then experiences a need to steal, she will have to deny that urge, or if it becomes conscious, decide whether she is now a dishonest person. That would mean creating a totally different self or identity, which she might not be able to live with. So rather than admitting this need into her consciousness, she will deny ever having had it, or distort it so that it can fit with her sense of self. She might say that she only wanted to 'borrow' the stolen object and would have returned it at some stage.

A metaphor could be the experience of hearing an unfamiliar noise that indicates that something is wrong when you are driving a car. You hear the noise, but you are not aware what it is (what part of the car may be about to cause the car to break down and stop being a reliable car).

The pain of unconscious experiences can be illustrated by a metaphor concerning clothing. If you try to wear something that does not fit your physical self or body because it is too tight, it will literally cut off your breath and pinch you so painfully that you just cannot bear to wear it.

In the same way, people cannot bear to make visible to themselves those experiences that do not fit with their psychological selves, as it would be too painful. Thus, if a woman who sees herself as slim gains so much weight that her clothes no longer fit, she might say that the clothes shrunk in the wash rather than admit that she has gained weight, as this would threaten her 'slim' self.

Think of the example of the group of men seeking employment in Chapter 7. The men see themselves as hardworking, so it would be very hard for them to symbolise that they are not seen as good enough for the work they want, which is what the continual rejections seem to imply. If they were to symbolise that nobody wants to hire them, would that mean that they are useless? Would it mean that they are failures and that they should just give up trying?

Symbolising such experiences would seriously threaten their selves as hardworking men. They fear the total loss of their selves, of becoming strangers to themselves.

In group work, the self refers to each member's self, as well as the self of the group as a whole. The experiences that are denied consciousness can be from within the group as well as from outside the group. In other words, group members can have denied experiences when they enter the group or they can deny experiences they have while attending the group itself.

Think of the example of the choir in Chapter 7. It could be that a member of that choir who does not see herself as a solo singer is asked to sing a solo. This does not fit with her self, so she might say that she has a sore throat to avoid having to sing the solo or admitting that she cannot do so and risking being rejected as a choir member (her self as a choir member is threatened).

This example indicates that people have different selves. The woman sees herself as a choir member rather than a solo singer. So singing solo does not fit, but neither does being kicked out of the choir (no longer being a choir member).

10.2.2 Proposition 13: Behaviour and unconscious experiences

> *Behaviour may, in some instances, be brought about by organic experiences and needs that have not been symbolised. Such behaviour may be inconsistent with the structure of the self, but in such instances, the behaviour is not 'owned' by the individual.*
>
> [Rogers 1987: 50]

In contrast with Proposition 12, where people are seen as behaving in ways that fit with their selves, here we see that people sometimes behave from unconscious motivations. Thus they are not aware of why they are doing what they are doing. As the behaviour does not fit with the person's self, he or she has to deny it because it is a risk or threat to the self.

So if members of a group deny certain behaviours, it is not because they are liars or are trying to manipulate the facilitator. They can literally not admit, even to themselves, that they are behaving in this way. Here again, unconditional acceptance and understanding of the person and what is happening inside that person is imperative.

The choir member who does not see herself as a solo performer and says she has a sore throat, while speaking in a normal voice, might deny that her throat is not really hurting when asked about this discrepancy. The woman who denies gaining weight does not own eating too much.

This proposition enables the facilitator to understand that if a group member behaves in a way that seems strange to the facilitator and/or the rest of group, that behaviour is meaningful and implies something about a threat to the person's self. This makes understanding and accepting the member as a whole person, with all of his or her experiences and behaviour, easier to do.

10.2.3 Proposition 14: Psychological tension

> *Psychological maladjustment exists when the organism denies to awareness significant sensory and visceral experiences, which consequently are not*

> *symbolised and organised into the gestalt of the self-structure. When this situation exists, there is a basic or potential psychological tension.* ’
>
> [Rogers 1987: 510]

This tension occurs when members of the group have to contend with an inner struggle. This involves a struggle between what the person experiences and how the person views his or her self, if these two are not in line with each other. It is a struggle to maintain the self while having experiences that contradict that self.

Proposition 4 can help to make this clear. Rogers believes that people have a basic striving to maintain their selves. They strive to be and become who they think they are. Thus any experiences a person has that hamper this process create a problem for the person, as well as psychological tension.

So in the example of the group of unemployed men, their efforts to maintain their selves as hardworking men while experiencing rejection create inner tension about who they are. Can they still see themselves as hardworking men, or are they failures for not having or finding work?

Also, in the example of the choir, the girl who does not want to sing solo, but also does not want to lose the self as a choir member experiences inner tension about how to maintain all of her self without losing a part of her self.

In group work, it is important to remember that disagreements between group members could cause them to experience stress, but on a conscious level. The disagreement would only create psychological tension if it threatened the selves of members.

10.2.4 Proposition 16: Defence of self

> ‘ *Any experience that is inconsistent with the organisation or structure of self will be perceived as a threat, and the more of these perceptions there are, the more rigidly that self-structure is organised to maintain itself.* ’
>
> [Rogers 1987: 515]

In group work, the self refers to both the individual self of each member and the self of the group as a whole.

This proposition emphasises the importance of continuously creating a safe space for all the members of the group. Unless the facilitator demonstrates unconditional acceptance and understanding of each group member, the facilitator risks being perceived as a threat to the selves of the members.

The proposition (together with Proposition 13) also enables the facilitator to understand that behaviour that he or she does not understand may be utilised as a defence of the member's self. This knowledge will help the facilitator to have a better understanding of members of the group.

Example 10.1

The members of a group for bereaved people mourning the loss of a loved one were discussing the intense pain of their loss. Later in the discussion, member S made a joke. Member P started crying. When exploring this behaviour, she said she did not really know what had happened. She was not crying for her loved one.

The facilitator said: 'So something else that happened in the group upset you deeply?'

She was silent for a while and then said: 'Yes. I thought this was a serious group and we are busy with very serious matters. I am afraid my pain will not be taken seriously.'

The crying of member P indicated a defence to the threat to her self as a grieving person, but it also indicated that the self of the group as she perceived it was threatened.

Example 10.2

In a group of students, member N was very quiet while J was active. H then said to J: 'You have to give N a chance to participate.' N just looked down at the floor during the silence that followed.

J: I want to make the most of this opportunity. We are here to learn and just waiting for someone to ask a question or make a comment seems like a waste of time to me.

H: Not all of us are so sure of ourselves or the group. I am not sure that I can say anything I want without you laughing at me.

Facilitator: H, you are saying the group is not a safe place to learn, to risk exposing yourself without risking being perceived as ignorant.

N: I do not want to sound stupid.

Facilitator: So not knowing the material means for you that you are stupid, rather than that you are a student who needs to learn something new?

In this example, N's silence was a defence of her self as a person who is not 'stupid'.

In the example of the group of unemployed men, their continuing efforts to apply for jobs even though they were always turned away can be seen as an effort to maintain and defend their selves as hardworking men.

The propositions discussed above explain how members of a group can struggle with experiences that do not fit with their selves. Threatening experiences can lead to inner tension (Proposition 14) as well as denied behaviour (Proposition 13). It might also prompt members to defend their selves (Proposition 16).

If a safe environment as described in Phase 1 has been created, it will be possible for the facilitator to accompany group members on a journey of self-discovery. During this journey, the members can explore those experiences that they dare not allow into their conscious minds lest the experiences destroy their senses of their selves.

The professional values and advanced skills discussed below can be of use to the facilitator on this journey.

10.3 Values

The values discussed in Chapter 2 of Section A must be expressed and maintained throughout this phase. Members of the group who are dealing with their unsymbolised experiences need to be accepted, no matter what painful revelations they make.

Group members may seem very vulnerable and helpless in the face of this exploration of themselves. The facilitator may be tempted to give sympathy or advice to alleviate their pain. This is when keeping a respectful attitude is important. The facilitator must believe in the members' ability to endure the suffering and come through it wiser about themselves.

The pain of every group member has to be seen as uniquely his or hers and must not be generalised. In a group where members have similar problems, it is especially important to understand each member's struggle with his or her own issues and self.

Each group also has to be treated as unique. All groups work at different tempos. Just because one group reached Phase 2 in two sessions, for example, it does not mean all groups will do so. For some groups, it may take four or five sessions, while other groups will start this process in the first session.

This is also why the facilitator cannot plan a programme ahead of time. No preset programme can meet the unique needs of the members of different groups. The group members have to decide what is important for them, as well as how and when it will be discussed. The facilitator thus needs to trust and respect members to find their own way forward on their journeys of self-discovery.

10.4 Advanced communication skills

All the skills discussed in Chapter 3 of Section A are also relevant in group work. The members of the group are all individual people, with selves that can be threatened, so the use of the basic and advanced skills will be required.

There are, however, some special considerations that rate further thought when working with groups.

One of the challenges with groups is that there is always more than one person present. So the requirement of Proposition 7 that the facilitator work from the client's frame of reference might be more difficult to put into practice.

Example 10.3

The facilitator is working with a group of parents.

P: I don't know what to do with my son. He stays out late at night and does as he pleases. It feels as if he has become a stranger to me, but I don't want to confront him.

R: I say lock him in his room! You are too soft on him. Children need a firm hand, otherwise they go off the rails.

The facilitator might be tempted to take sides, agreeing with either P or R. However, it is not what R thinks about P that is important when he responds, but what he reveals about himself through his response. He seems to see himself as a father who disciplines his children in an effort to protect them from 'going off the rails'. P is more concerned about not being too strict as a mother and risking alienating her son even more.

The facilitator needs to understand the self of each speaker and respond accordingly.

Members could also discuss people who are not in the room.

Example 10.4

The facilitator is working with a group of married women,

B: My husband expects me to have unprotected sex. I am afraid he will infect me.

J: My husband expects me to work all day, and then cook and clean at night. I am so tired of his demands.

H: Men! They are all so selfish. Yet I don't think I can live without mine.

Activity 10.1

1 Can you get to know the husbands of these women by what they are saying about them?
2 Whose frames of reference and selves are being expressed?

It is thus very important that the facilitator listen to the experiences and self of the speaker when making advanced responses.

As the selves of the members are so important when using the advanced skills, we believe the role of the self bears repeating here. The role of the self can be depicted as follows:

Conscious (symbolised) part of self (explore with basic skills)

Unconscious (threatened or hidden) part of self

The unconscious experiences are the hidden or threatening experiences of which the members themselves are unaware. This is why advanced skills are needed to enable members to access these experiences.

As people are seen as a whole (refer to Proposition 3 in this regard), they will express both kinds of experiences during any discussion. Thus the basic skills and all the values remain a part of the process, even when the advanced skills are being used.

This idea could be explained using the metaphor of cleaning a car. We clean both the inside (unconscious experiences) and the outside (conscious experiences) of a car. We use different methods to clean the inside and outside of a car. For instance, a vacuum cleaner would be helpful to remove dirt inside a car, but it would be less helpful when trying to get dirt off the outside of a car.

As these skills deal with a threat to the selves of members, the facilitator could be reluctant to communicate his or her understanding of these messages to group members, as the facilitator might fear that his or her understanding would hurt the members.

The facilitator could use this fear as a reminder that his or her response should be tentative so that group members can disagree if the response does not fit with them. It could also act as a reminder to the facilitator not to insist that what he or she senses is a threat to a member of the group is indeed a threat, even if the member denies this.

However, the facilitator should guard against being immobilised by his or her fears, as this could hamper the exploration of painful experiences. The facilitator needs to keep in mind that members of the group are already wrestling with these experiences, and that to face the experiences might bring them a sense of relief.

This could be compared metaphorically to an open wound that has become infected. Cleaning this wound would probably be painful, but if the wound is not cleaned, it could fester and get much worse. So while cleaning the wound is painful, it enables the wound to heal.

The advanced skills can be divided into three categories:

- Advanced empathy
- Exploring distortions
- Immediacy.

10.4.1 Advanced empathy

This skill can, in turn, be divided into four sub-sections: exploring implied messages, connecting islands, developing themes and exploring discrepancies.

Exploring implied messages

As the advanced skills deal with those experiences that threaten the self, it follows that implied messages refer to messages about how the self is being threatened. Since these experiences are unconscious, they cannot be expressed directly by members of the group, but they will be implied in what they share about themselves.

In group work, the perceived threat could be to the self of a member, but it could also be to the group self as perceived by members of the group. It is important to keep Proposition 7 in mind here. The self as well as the threat must be seen from the frames of reference of the group members, and not from the facilitator's frame of reference.

The comments of the women in Example 10.4 serve as an illustration here. The facilitator might think that the unprotected sex is the biggest threat to member B, as it could cause her death, but is that really what is threatening her psychological self? If she is afraid of getting an infection, why does she not just say: 'No' to him? Which self (developed in interaction with her husband) is she trying to maintain? This self would be threatened if she said: 'No.'

Activity 10.2

Which self of all the group members in Example 10.4 is being threatened?

Let us revisit the example of the unemployed men from Chapter 7.

Example 10.5

Look at the responses made by the facilitator to the comments of the men.

D: I have tried and tried so hard to find work. But nobody wants to hire me.

Facilitator: You work hard at getting a job, but it is not happening. It seems that you believe no employer wants you.

E: *(Nods his head)* I am also tired of going from place to place, only to be told they don't want or need me.

Facilitator: You too make every effort to find a job, but now you seem afraid that you might not be needed?

J: *(Angry voice)* It is the government's fault. They should create more jobs for us.

Facilitator: You seem angry at the government for not providing a job for you, as if you do not believe you can get a job on your own.

(J nods his head.)

K: At all the places where I have been, they say I am not skilled enough. *(Sighs)* It seems I don't have anything to offer. *(Turning to facilitator)* Do you have any ideas about what we can do? It seems we have all run out of ideas.

Facilitator: You all seem to feel quite hopeless and even helpless, as if none of you believes you have anything to offer anybody.

Their selves as hardworking men are being threatened by the rejection they have been experiencing to the point that they have lost faith in themselves as worthy human beings who have something to offer.

Connecting islands

The experiences that each member of the group shares are connected to his or her individual self and/or the group self. This links to Proposition 3 and Proposition 8. The self is created from all our experiences. So to be able to understand the self and the threat to the self, members' experiences have to be connected to how they see themselves as people.

Consider the metaphor of a car again. If all the different parts of a car were lying in a heap, it would not be clear that it was a car. To be able to see the identity, we have to put the parts together in such a way that they all fit with each other.

Another metaphor could be that of the human face: all people have a face consisting of eyes, nose, lips, cheekbones, forehead and so on, yet when these parts of a particular face are put together in a certain way, a unique identity emerges.

In the same way, the different experiences expressed and implied by members of the group are put or linked together to enable the members to see which identity or self emerges.

Example 10.6

Consider these comments made by members of a group of newly divorced women.

N: I find it hard to cope without my husband. I am not used to working out the family budget or taking the car for a service and things like that.

K: I just am so worried because there is not enough money to pay the children's school fees and cover all the household expenses.

S: I just find it hard to discipline the children. It feels as if I have to be mom and dad to them.

B: I feel I am stuck at home. All our friends are married and I do not want to go out alone.

Everything they say connects to their selves as newly divorced women.

Although they speak about money, children and friends, it all implies that they feel the loss of their husbands, or rather, the loss of their married selves.

It is important for the facilitator not to try to direct the woman in any way towards how they should deal with this loss, or which self can develop once each woman has symbolised this loss of her married self.

Developing themes

Through connecting islands, themes can be developed. When developing themes, we look for similar experiences. These experiences all relate to each other and threaten the self in some way.

We use themes every day of our lives. For instance, when we talk about fruit and vegetables, we are using themes (which identify the objects to which we are referring).

When we say we are getting dressed, we are referring to a theme for putting on our clothes (which identifies what we are doing).

In the same way, the facilitator tries to identify themes around the selves of who the members and the group are.

> ***Example 10.7***
>
> Look at the comments made by members of a group of women who have all survived some kind of violent trauma.
>
> M: After the hijacking, I am afraid to drive my own car on my own. I hate to have to depend on others to get around.
>
> S: After the rape, I cannot sleep alone at home. I now seem to need someone around all the time. *(Sighs)*
>
> V: *(The bank where she works was robbed)* I cannot face going back to work. I used to love working at the bank. I was promoted only last month, but now I freeze up inside when I think of going back there.
>
> D: *(Single mom who was robbed at home)* I worry about keeping my children safe. I want to move away from the neighborhood into a housing estate because it feels as if all the good we had there has been ripped away, but the children love their schools and have many friends in the neighborhood. I feel so trapped.

What they say about their fears implies a threat to their selves as independent and hard-working women and/or mothers. The theme is that they were robbed of their sense of self, not just of their possessions.

Exploring discrepancies

Discrepancies refer to a conflict between the symbolised self and an experience that does not fit with that self. In other words, there is a discrepancy between the self and an experience. In group work, this can refer to the self of each individual member as well as to the self of the group as a whole.

Who does not fit?

Activity 10.3

Look at the illustration. What do you see as not fitting in with the rest of the group?

In the group of divorced women, one member of the group says: 'I do not care any more. He can go and jump in the lake and I will say good riddance.' Later in the session, she says: 'I wonder whether he is seeing someone else.'

These statements indicate that her ideal self is one of not caring about her ex-husband any more, while a part of her still does care. She is not sure who she is at this moment in time.

The discrepancies have to be explored tentatively and gently. It can happen in groups that members confront each other directly and thus threaten each other.

Example 10.8

Read the comments of a group of young men who use drugs.

L: I know people say I have to give it up, but I know I can control it.

W: I tried that, but it does not work. For a week I was using a small amount, but then I began adding a bit more every day.

L: You are just weak. I know I am stronger than that.

W: If you are so strong, why use drugs at all?

L: *(In an angry voice)* I just want to, because I enjoy it.

When a member of the group challenged the discrepancy in what L was saying, L experienced it in a threatening way. The facilitator cannot take sides, but needs to understand both members. A response could be: 'It seems you two disagree on this. You, W, believe that it is not possible to control the use of drugs, while you, L, believe in your ability to do so. Both of you are looking for ways of dealing with the abuse of drugs.'

10.4.2 Immediacy

This is a skill that is used specifically to address any issues that might arise in the relationship between the facilitator and a member of the group, some of the members or the group as a whole. As it is still based on the person-centred approach, it is done from the members' frames of reference.

This can pose quite a challenge to the facilitator, as he or she is a human being with his or her own experiences. It would seem natural for the facilitator to lash out in anger at a member of the group who says or does something that triggers anger in the facilitator, or even to lash out at the group.

However, such a reaction would be from the facilitator's frame of reference. It would also destroy the safe environment and trusting relationship the facilitator is trying to create. The particular member of the group and the whole group would now see that the facilitator does not accept them unconditionally. So for the facilitator to lash out in anger would be like shooting him- or herself in the foot. It would hinder the facilitator's professional efforts instead of helping them.

In terms of Proposition 4 (all people, including facilitators, are self-determined) the facilitator is responsible for all of his or her experiences and self. So the facilitator needs to become aware of his or her own self and what triggers his or her anger. The facilitator must deal with this issue without involving the members. The facilitator's role is to deal with the anger and experiences of the group members. It would not be in the interests of either the facilitator or the members to burden members with the facilitator's experiences. The members of the group cannot be expected to help the facilitator deal with these experiences.

So if the facilitator feels overwhelmed by his or her own experiences, he or she has to find a way to deal with them. For instance, the facilitator could ask the group's permission to take some time out to be able to deal with his or her experiences. It is more useful for the facilitator to take five or ten minutes to overcome a feeling of anger than to sit through the rest of the session stewing inside. The facilitator will be unable to relate to the group members because he or she is occupied with his or her own inner struggle.

Example 10.9

A female facilitator is dealing for the first time with a group of men in prison.

P: *(Looking at the other members)* I cannot believe they sent this young woman to do our group.

Facilitator: *(Looking at P)* You seem disappointed and angry, both at my gender and my age?

P: *(Looking uncomfortable)* Yes. How can someone like you know what men like us need?

Facilitator: You are spot on. I do not know what men like you need, and I hope you can show me. I am willing to learn from and about you.

R: Maybe you will not like what we show you.

Facilitator: I sense you are afraid that I will reject you once I get to know you?

R: *(Nodding his head)* We are hard men and what we have been through could turn your stomach.

Facilitator: You see yourselves as tough men, who can endure a lot of pain, which would destroy a lesser person.

O: Yes, just yesterday ...

He goes on to relate his experiences. The others then join in.

The age and gender of the facilitator was no longer an issue for two reasons:

- She was not intimated or threatened by the initial doubts of the members.
- She stayed with all their experiences from their frames of reference, while not ignoring their doubts about her.

This example also illustrates that immediacy can be used during the first phase of the facilitation process. Although immediacy is an advanced skill, it might be necessary to use it to build the relationship and safe climate at the beginning of the process. The example also indicates that the phases cannot be treated as separate entities, but as part of an unfolding process.

CHAPTER

11 Exploring the self (Phase 3)

11.1 Introduction

During this phase, both conscious and unconscious experiences are explored in relationship to the group members' selves. This enables members to become more aware of who they are (becoming).

11.2 Reconstructing the self

Once members become aware of all their experiences, they are able to symbolise them and decide how they can become part of their selves, or whether their selves need to be changed. This is explained in the next proposition.

11.2.1 Proposition 15: Reconstruction of self

> *Psychological adjustment exists when the concept of the self is such that all the sensory and visceral experiences of the organism are, or may be, assimilated on a symbolic level into a consistent relationship with the concept of self.*
>
> [Rogers 1987: 513]

This proposition indicates why so much emphasis is placed on the self of each member and the group in most of the nineteen propositions. It indicates that the process of facilitation, from a person-centred perspective, is not about providing new information (as in talks given by so-called experts) or about learning a new skill (as is the goal with some life-skills programmes). Rather, the purpose of facilitation is for each member of the group to learn more about his or her self. Each group member should have the opportunity to discover who he or she is, what he or she is not, who he or she wants to become and which experiences stand in his or her way.

The process of reconstruction is not predictable or easy. It can be painful, as group members might fear losing themselves totally. Even believing that you have to give up a part of yourself can be frightening. If you compared the experience with losing a physical part of your body, you would agree that to have an arm or a leg removed would be very painful. It would be so painful that it would have to be done under anaesthesia. In the psychological world, no such assistance is possible. Group members have to be aware and allow those painful and threatening experiences into awareness. They have to be able to look at their selves and decide who they want to be in the future.

The facilitator needs to use both the basic and the advanced skills to help members explore all their experiences and how they relate to their selves, past, present and future. It is imperative that the facilitator not try to influence or guide members in any direction. The self that is developing has to be the group member's own self. He or she has to live with it, believe in it and act in terms of it.

This implies that the values of individuality, respect (believing in each group member's ability to work through the pain towards reconstruction of his or her self) and self-determination (determining what the reconstructed self will entail) must be upheld at this phase as much as at any other time.

The new self will never be completely different from the old. Group members will still be able to recognise themselves and each other. The new self may, however, seem new and strange to them at the time of exploration.

In the example of the church choir, member S may realise that he not only wants to sing church music, but that he is also interested in rock-and-roll music. So now his self might expand to include rock and roll. He might thus see himself as a member of a church choir as well as a member of a rock-and-roll band. The self as a rock-and-roll singer might seem totally new to him, although it is still being a singer.

In the example of the unemployed men, they could risk exploring their unsymbolised experiences of feeling useless and unwanted, and their fear of being people who are worthless in the safe climate created within the group. The conversation that follows took place during an in-depth exploration of their feelings of worthlessness.

Example 11.1

D: I like to keep busy. I work hard at home, making repairs as needed. I also love telling my children bedtime stories that I make up myself. They always ask for more.

E: I don't just do nothing while I don't have work. *(Sounds indignant)* I have a small garden in which I plant enough vegetables and fruit to feed my family.

J: I keep busy too. I cannot afford a new car, but I keep the old one we have in good shape. I do all the work on it myself. I actually enjoy it.

K: There are a lot of children who are alone in the afternoon in my neighborhood. I worry about them so I invite them home and help them with their homework.

Facilitator: You all, in your own unique way, contribute to your family and your community, even without having paying jobs.

(They nod their heads in a thoughtful way.)

K: Yes. We are doing things. We are not just wasting time.

Facilitator: Yet you do not seem to believe these efforts of yours are worth anything?

>>

E: Not in the job market, not for earning an income, so what good are they really?

J: They make me feel good, as if, in spite of everything, I still have something to offer.

K: Yes, giving to others is well worth it.

E: Maybe we can do more, as we have the time?

D: Yes! *(Excited)* I can tell stories to the children in the hospital. It is just down the road from where I live. My sister works there and she is always telling me how sad the children are. Maybe it will cheer them up a bit.

J: I know the place. I used to visit my mother when she was there. I can help with their vehicles. I know they are always short of money and are struggling to keep them in working order.

E: *(Laughs)* I am feeling all excited. I would like to join you. I can bring some fresh fruit. I am sure they will enjoy it and it would be good for their health. I could even plant flowers for them.

K: I might as well join you. I am sure they can use my help. While you *(Looks at D)* tell some children stories, other children may need help to keep up with their homework while they are in hospital.

Facilitator: *(Speaking to K)* You seem very interested in the children's homework, as if educating children interests you.

K: Yes. *(Seems thoughtful)* Maybe I could become a teacher. I wonder what that would require.

D: My children are always talking about their teacher. They like her very much. Maybe we could ask her?

K: You know, I think it would be better to ask the head of the school. I will go there tomorrow and try to get an appointment with him.

These statements indicate that the men are beginning to reconstruct their selves as useful people who are able to make a contribution even though they are not formally employed.

In later sessions, they shared how these new activities also led to new employment opportunities. From seeing themselves as a group of helpless men, they reconstructed the group self to such an extent that they no longer needed the facilitator. They did, however, stay friends, so it became a group of friends.

D enrolled in a programme at the hospital to become a male nurse, while J enrolled in a course to become a mechanic. K started to study part-time at a teachers' training college. E got a small business loan and started his own nursery.

Through exploring who they are, they found new self-worth, but also new directions for their working selves.

If the facilitator had just tried to get jobs for these men, he or she would not have enabled them to get to know themselves, and thus find the direction in life they really wanted.

The group self can also be reconstructed. The group of young men who used drugs (Example 10.8) was able to start meeting without the facilitator. The men also decided to make it an open group. In other words, the group was open to other people who had not been part of the original group, but who needed support in dealing with their drug use. Thus the group reconstructed itself from a closed facilitation group to an open support group.

The final phase, the idea of a new life after reconstruction of the self, is explored in more detail in Chapter 12.

CHAPTER

12 Ending the relationship (Phase 4)

12.1 Introduction

Towards the end of the facilitation process, certain experiences are possible. However, facilitators should keep in mind that all human beings are unique and so outcomes are never predictable. If the process does not unfold as described below, group members cannot be blamed for it or pushed towards it. The values and skills discussed in the previous chapters must be maintained until members are ready to end the relationship.

12.2 Recognising the final phase

One of the outcomes of the person-centred facilitation process is that members might feel less threatened by other people.

12.2.1 Proposition 18: Acceptance of self and others

> *When the individual perceives and accepts into one consistent and integrated system all his sensory and visceral experiences, then he is necessarily more understanding of others and is more accepting of others as separate individuals.*
>
> [Rogers 1987: 520]

As members are now aware of most of their experiences as they fit with the (reconstructed) self, they will probably not be threatened by others, even if these others differ from them.

The members of the church choir first mentioned in Chapter 7 might initially have been threatened by the new self and behaviour of member S, but if they accept themselves, they will be able to accept member S as different, yet still part of the choir.

So for instance, in the discussion on marriage and number of wives in Example 7.1, the members would agree to disagree.

Previously, member B said: 'I would like to have at least three wives.' Member W reacted very strongly to this: 'How can you say that! It is not possible to give three wives the love and attention they deserve.'

Member W is now able to say: 'You (B) see yourself as the head of a big family, with many wives. I, on the other hand, prefer a smaller family and know I will be happier with one wife.'

Another outcome of the facilitation process is that members are now ready to decide on their own values.

12.2.2 **Proposition 19: Developing your own valuing process**

> *As the individual perceives and accepts into his self-structure more of his organic experiences, he finds that he is replacing his present value system – based so largely upon introjections that have been distortedly symbolised – with a continuing organismic valuing process.*
>
> [Rogers 1987: 522]

In the example of the church choir, member S realised that his value of believing that rock-and-roll music is a sin was taken over from his parents. He now believes that he can be a Christian and also like rock-and-roll music. His own value system allows for both kinds of music.

In the group of young men who used drugs (Example 10.8), some members realised that they were using drugs because their peer group was using drugs and they wanted to be 'with it'. They decided that to be their own people, they did not need to keep up with the peer group any more and that using drugs was no longer part of their own value system.

Activity 12.1

If members of a group for which you were the facilitator developed values contrary to your values, what would you do?

As with the reconstruction of the self, the values that members develop have to be their own. These values have to fit with the reconstructed self, otherwise they will be perceived as threatening.

In the example of the unemployed men, the facilitator might have thought that to volunteer at a hospital was a waste of time, as the facilitator might have wanted to see the men employed. However, the men discovered the value of helping others, which in turn gave them a sense of self-worth.

Once members of the group have reconstructed their selves and developed their own valuing systems, they might be ready to leave the group. This can be a difficult time for members and facilitators alike.

Activity 12.2

How would you know that the members of the group and you, the facilitator, are ready to end the relationship?

The facilitator might find it hard to let the group go. One problem with the person-centred approach is that, after working so hard to create a safe space for everyone, getting involved with members' pain and getting to know them as people, the facilitator is expected to be able to leave this safe environment. For the members of the group, leaving the group could feel like leaving a warm and safe nest, and taking on the unpredictable world on their own.

The facilitator may feel abandoned and no longer needed, which could constitute a threat to his or her self as a facilitator. After all, most of us are in the profession to help others, in other words, to be needed by others. If the facilitator is not aware of this need and self, it could create unconscious behaviour as described in Proposition 13.

This unconscious behaviour could include giving advice so that members have to depend on the facilitator for solutions, rather than finding their own selves, and then finding values and behaviour to fit with these selves.

The facilitator might be tempted to identify more issues for the group to work on. Members might in fact, have more needs, as the process of facilitation does not guarantee instant or eternal happiness. Members might still be uncertain of their new selves. This just means that all the skills and values mentioned before still have to be maintained. The uncertainty can be explored, as well as the implied messages that group members may find it hard to trust these new-found selves and inner freedom from tension.

SECTION

C

Person-centred facilitation in communities

Rogers' ideas as described in Section A and Section B are so powerful and universally applicable that they have found their way into disciplines well beyond psychotherapy and counselling.

Rogers (1990:32) indicated that workers in the field of community development draw upon the person-centred approach and practice to facilitate the growth of communities. Rogers and Meador (1973) also confirmed that the person-centred approach is theoretically applicable to any relationship where people want to understand each other and be understood, where people are willing to reveal themselves to some degree and where people wish to enhance their growth. These characteristics are present in a wide variety of relationships. Consequently, the principles of the person-centred approach are being used in more and more situations.

The Department of Social Work at Unisa has now been implementing the person-centred approach when working with communities for several years. As a result of our interaction with people in communities, we have learnt how powerful this approach can be. We have seen how important it is to respect and value people, to learn from them, to appreciate them, to plan with them, to facilitate the implementation of their own plans and to celebrate with them.

This section is an attempt to give a brief description of the application of the person-centred approach when working with communities.

CHAPTER

13 An overview of person-centred facilitation in communities

13.1 Introduction

The person-centred approach was developed by Carl Rogers in the course of his work with individuals and groups. However, it can be used very effectively when working with people living in and as communities. While reading Section A and Section B, you probably noticed that the person-centred approach puts the person at the centre, instead of putting the problem or the project at the centre. If as a facilitator you think in a person-centred way, you will always act in a person-centred manner, whatever the context. You will ask yourself: 'How does the person think about this?', or: 'How does the person feel about this?, or: 'How does the person perceive the situation?', or: 'How does the person experience the situation?'. You will not ask: 'What is the problem here?', or: 'Who was responsible for this?', or: 'Who is at fault?'. You will not try to get an explanation or find the cause of the problem. You will focus on the symbolised (aware) and unsymbolised (unaware) experiences, perceptions and feelings of the person or people.

This attitude or way we think about people determines the way in which we work with them. We listen to them and work from their frames of reference. We attempt to understand their worlds and facilitate their journeys to healing or change. The person-centred approach becomes a way of being, and a way of thinking, believing and acting in all contexts.

We have emphasised the words 'person' and 'people' in the first two paragraphs because communities consist of people: people with different cultural and life experiences and perceptions, individuals, families of different kinds and groups of people. Working with people from the person-centred approach implies that people are the focus of our thinking and actions, as will be described in the chapters that follow. In order to act professionally, be accountable and take responsibility for our actions, we need to know both ourselves and the theory of the person-centred approach very well.

In this section, we will focus on the person-centred approach in order to guide your thinking about people and actions when working with communities. We will discuss the process of facilitating the relationship and the course of change. However, we will not deal with the technical facilitation of a development project since information on this subject can be found in many books.

We will also refer to the knowledge of person-centred thinkers like Paolo Freire, a Brazilian educationalist. He developed his way of thinking while observing the poor and oppressed people of Chile during the regime of Pinochet. He was branded a revolutionary and banned from Brazil. Rogers made comparisons between himself and Freire, saying that although Freire's thinking was considered to be revolutionary, he (Rogers) can be regarded as a 'silent revolutionary'.

We will not repeat the nineteen propositions outlined by Rogers here. If you need to be reminded of their content when we refer to them, consult the descriptions of the propositions in the Introduction (pages 4–7).

Similarly, if you need to refresh your memory about the meaning of the concepts 'symbolised experience' and 'unsymbolised experience', turn to pages 20–21 in Chapter 1.

13.2 The influence of other thinking on the person-centred approach

David Rennie (1994) said that the most significant quality of 'human beingness' is our ability to think about or reflect on ourselves, our actions and our thinking processes in an attempt to understand what is happening in our own world. In this section, you will be shown how to think and work as a person-centred facilitator with people in communities. You will be shown how to value the people in those communities. The theory of the person-centred approach will influence how you think about and relate to people in all contexts, including your family, your friends and your colleagues. The propositions and values of the person-centred approach will hopefully become your guiding light in everything you do.

According to Tolan (2003: 1), theory is the map that guides us through unknown territory. Of course the facilitator does not only use his or her chosen theory (for example, the person-centred approach) as a guide. The facilitator is also guided by his or her other beliefs, theories, experiences and perceptions. It is important to develop an awareness (symbolised experiences) of your own thinking processes, as these will determine how you facilitate processes, help people or simply provide people with handouts. This will determine if you will work top down or bottom up when working with communities. It will determine if you hold on to the power and the responsibility, or if you facilitate the process in a way that allows the people of the community to take responsibility. The use of the person-centred approach in communities requires a person-centred view of communities, a person-centred view of change, a person-centred facilitator and a person-centred process.

Even if you are an adherent of the person-centred approach, it is important to read widely and add the thinking of other approaches to the mix where you feel that it is valid. The ideas of person-centred authors like Paolo Freire, Manfred Max-Neef and Robert Chambers, as well as asset-based or strength-based thinkers, will add value to your way of thinking when working with people in communities.

Although Carl Rogers died in 1989, other person-centred authors have added to the body of knowledge that he established. The theory continues to develop, but the basis of the theory stays the same. For example, Peggy Nattiello (a well-known person-centred thinker and author) wrote that she uses theories like critical theory and chaos theory to try to understand certain group processes. You might also find the work of some post-modern or constructivist authors interesting. It is however, important to ensure that the values of the theories are compatible with each other.

13.3 Guiding principles of the person-centred approach

There are two important points to remember when working from the person-centred approach:

- We have to ask ourselves how we think about and value people and communities. We have to know what will guide our actions. We want to act professionally and be accountable for our actions. In short, we take responsibility for our way of working with people.
- We have to reflect on ourselves and understand ourselves. The person-centered facilitator reflects on his or her theory, perceptions and experiences. He or she asks questions like: 'Why do I get involved with poor/disabled/young people?', or: 'Why am I in this profession? What do I want to gain from this?', or: 'Am I comfortable that I have the role of facilitator and do not have a position of authority and power?', or: 'Does this theory really work for me?'

Activity 13.1

To assist you with your symbolisation (awareness) process of becoming conscious of your own ways of thinking, buy yourself a small notebook (not an electronic notebook!) that you can carry in your handbag, pocket or briefcase.

As you read through this section and other literature or theories, make notes of the aspects that have particular relevance for you. Make notes of the points that you agree with and those that you do not agree with. By doing this, you will develop an awareness (symbolisation) of your own thinking.

13.4 The concept 'community' seen from a person-centred perspective

Section A looked at the person-centred approach and how it is used when working with individuals. Section B addressed the use of the approach with groups. Now we will start thinking about how the person-centred approach should be applied when working with a community.

Professionals working for state departments, NGOs (non-governmental organisations) or NPOs (non-profit organisations) are usually allocated to render services in certain geographical areas or to certain groups of people, for example, foster parents, refugees, abused women and children, the elderly, disabled people, orphans and vulnerable children, the youth or men.

The word 'community' is usually defined as a noun. We speak of the community of [the name of a place or groups of people]. It is usually understood and defined as a geographical community (an area, town, area in a city, suburb or school) or a functional community (for example, a group of mothers, interested bikers, hikers, soccer players or people with a disability). The concept 'community' has been debated at length. It is an elusive, imprecise, contradictory and controversial concept (Burkitt 2001: 235). According to the person-centred approach, the concept 'community' cannot be described as a noun. The ideas about the concept 'community' are what have been deduced from the theory and are of course open to debate and discussion. Many people subscribe to the post-modern theory as it is based on the notion that realities, perceptions and experiences differ and change (Proposition 2 and Proposition 7), and will change continually (Proposition 1).

Burkitt argues that we should see the word 'community' as a verb – a doing word – and not as a noun. As a noun, 'community' is interpreted as an object or an end in and of itself.

> *Approaching 'community' as a verb rather than a noun reflects the notion that 'community' is not an object, rather it is a perception, experiences with on-going processes. It becomes a 'processual creation' rather than a fixed description. From this perspective, 'community' would not be a given – it would never be interpreted as fixed or stable – rather it would be considered a constantly shifting and changing process.*
>
> [Burkitt 2001: 235]

A community is a perception and an experience. Shriver (1995) refers to 'community of mind'. Ask yourself if you see yourself as part of a community. Do you experience 'community'? To know a community involves immersing the self in a subjective and intensely practical expression of how people experience living in a particular social reality or realities at a given period in time. Community becomes an experience and an expression of subjective everyday practices (Burkitt 2001: 238). Communities are created by people's perceptions and experiences. You can see yourself as being part of a community or not being part of a community. Even when we share a geographical locality, we may not experience ourselves as being part of that particular geographical community. If you ask migrant workers or day labourers where they live or where home is, the answer will usually be the place where their families live. If a day labourer is looking for work in a particular city, the labourer may not regard him- or herself as part of the community where the workers stand to wait for employment, but if the day labourers plan to act together to negotiate for water and toilets with the municipality at a particular hiring site, they may become a community of day labourers. Nell (2008) conducted research in which she interviewed the people affected by hundreds of day labourers who stand on the pavements in front of their houses every day. Business in the area is also affected. Churches provide food to the day labourers and the metro police do clean-up sessions. The police use the day labourers as informants to prevent criminal activities in the area. We may see them as a community, interlinked and in interaction. But will all of the role players agree? Do they perceive themselves to be a community?

The earlier description of the word 'community' as a verb challenges us to see community in places and spaces that have not previously been considered as sites for the development of 'authentic' community. Communities are therefore a perception or experience that is 'made' or constructed and not 'found' in a particular place. They can be physical (as we know them), but they can also be 'virtual'.

> *This community is not necessarily a site at which practice occurs, rather, it becomes a frame of reference that is neither map nor territory, but an orientation that emphasises the relationality and contextuality of human practice.*
>
> [Rogers 1989]

If the social development officer from a local metropolitan council called a meeting with all the people affected by the day labourers in the particular street, they might then have considered themselves to be a community of concerned people about the effect day labourers have on their neighbourhood.

Activity 13.2

1 It is important to understand the concept 'community' from a person-centred perspective. Write down a definition or explanation of the concept in your own words.
2 Think for a moment how many communities you are part of and make a list of them. Which of the communities listed below do you belong to?
   - Geographical communities
   - Religious communities
   - University, school or work communities
   - Extended family communities
   - Facebook (Internet) communities
   - Recreational communities
   - Other communities.

If we think of the processes that take place all the time in our world today, for example, migration, globalisation, Internet communities, movements and refugees, we will understand that communities are continually being created or constructed, experienced, and perceived and dismantled. Communities exist or develop in the minds of people.

Activity 13.3

How do we look at people living in the same geographical community? Debate the following question with other students or colleagues: 'Is a geographical community necessarily a community? When can we regard a collection of people as a community? Do they view themselves as a community?'

This chapter has outlined what you need to know about the background and thinking of the person-centred approach when working to facilitate change in communities. As you continue this journey, keep your notebook at hand so that you can keep developing your own awareness of how you think about people and change.

CHAPTER 14 How we view people and communities

14.1 Introduction

The way in which the person-centred approach views people is fundamental to the person-centred process of facilitation. Proposition 8 is the core proposition of the approach, although other propositions also give important perspectives and information.

14.2 How the person-centred approach views people

Proposition 8 should be the foundation of all our person-centred actions and development efforts in communities.

14.2.1 Proposition 8: The self

Proposition 8 explains that the focus is on the person. More specifically, the focus is on the self of the person. When working with a community, we refer to the selves of the individuals in the community, but also the self of the community. In other words, we refer to the identity or identities of the community. The selves or identities of the individuals are unique, and so the selves or identities of the community will also be unique. The selves of the community are created or constructed around certain values, concerns or shared realities that become the selves or identities of the group. This can be expressed in statements like: 'We are a proud community', or: 'We are loyal', or: 'An injury to one is an injury to all'. The selves of the community guide its actions.

The way people experience themselves and their identities may change depending on their interaction with significant others (Proposition 9) and their wider context. The community is not necessarily 'aware' of its identities and the people might not express them explicitly. However, they will express them through their actions, stories, traditions, slogans, cultural practices, rituals, preferences and so on. By listening well, the facilitator can develop an idea about the identities of the community. For example, a group of bikers can refer to themselves as Hell's Angels. From the outside, only the rough aspect of the bikers is visible in the way they dress and act, but the 'angel' aspect of the group identity is expressed when the bikers organise charity rides and collect toys for orphans. The actions, stories, rituals and preferences of the people may change as their perceptions and experiences about themselves change (Proposition 1).

It is the selves of the community that will determine or construct the meanings that are attached to experiences and perceptions. A person might experience something, but the experience does not mean anything until the person attaches meaning to it. For example, what does it mean to be part of the fan base of a particular soccer, rugby or cricket team? What does it mean to you to be an Ajax, Mamelodi Sundowns, Orlando Pirates, Blue Bulls or Cheetahs supporter? Why would you support one of these teams? Does it fit the perception you have of yourself? Can you identify yourself with the values and actions of the particular team, and what the team and its supporters represent? Along with attaching meaning to experiences, we also name them with words such as 'bad', 'good', 'happy', 'terrible', 'wonderful' or 'exciting'.

Tolan (2003: 3) views the self-structure as everything that a person holds about him- or herself and about the world. The selves of the individual developed through experience and interactions with significant others (Proposition 9). Other aspects of the selves are based on prior beliefs, for example, cultural practices, traditions and belief systems. The unique selves of the community will determine how facilitation projects or development efforts will unfold.

Example 14.1

A social worker worked in a remote rural community in the Northern Cape. The community was labelled as a poor community and was given poverty-alleviation money to drill a borehole and start a communal vegetable garden. When the facilitator arrived at the community, she saw that the borehole had been drilled and the ground had been levelled by the contractors who had drilled the borehole, but nothing further had been done. When she started asking members of the community why nothing had been done to start the vegetable garden, they explained that each person or family preferred to have their own little garden. Then they could trade vegetables with each other. It was part of how they had functioned for years. A communal garden required a totally different socio-economic and relational system in the community, one that did not fit with how they did things. They were proud of all having their own gardens and trading with each other.

Proposition 8 is the foundation of all our person-centred actions and development efforts in communities. The proposition on the self is also the basis for the belief in self-determination, individualising people and communities, and respecting people for their unique experiences and perceptions, knowledge, skills, values and expertise. This explains why people in the community are the focus of our attention and why this approach is called the person-centred approach. We do not decide, plan or act without the people. We do not work in communities, but with communities.

This attitude is reflected in the slogan of the South African disabled community: 'Nothing about us, without us'.

14.3 The self of the community and significant others

Proposition 9, which we referred to above, adds to Proposition 8 by explaining that the selves of the individuals in the community do not develop in isolation. All people live in a context in which the people have continuous experiences. The identities of the people and the community are formed through interaction with significant others and the context or environment in which they live. The values, ideas, experiences, traditions and values of communities of people have been shaped through the ages and have been assimilated into the selves of the community. If it is a newly formed community, the people as part of the group or community come with their values and traditions, and they become significant others for each other, forming a unique system. The wealth of experiences and perceptions becomes part of the group or community. Communities are also in constant interaction with other communities and new communities are formed. The communities' perceptions of themselves may change and evolve in interaction with each other and in interaction with people from other communities. Perceptions of a community may be created through the media or when the community compares itself with other communities. Communities may be labelled as 'poor', 'backward', 'deprived', 'disadvantaged', 'underdeveloped', 'rich' or 'snobbish', for example, or they can be viewed as 'survivors', 'resourceful', 'skilled' and 'knowledgeable about certain things'. The way in which they are framed will influence the perceptions about them.

In a geographical community, we seldom work with large groups of people, but with smaller groups who identify with each other because they share values or aspire to the aim of the group. Groups or communities form around aspects that the members can identify with.

Activity 14.1

1 Make a list of the groups or communities with which you would not identify yourself. Why not?
2 Make a list of the groups and communities with which you would be prepared to identify yourself. Why would you be prepared to become part of them?

Proposition 9 implies an important aspect. When in interaction with a community, the facilitator becomes a significant other for that community. As a significant other, the facilitator continually reflects on his or her actions. The facilitator, as a significant other, determines if he or she is facilitating processes of freedom, inclusion, respect and critical reflection, or if he or she is part of processes that oppress, exclude or judge people.

Another way of looking at these propositions is that we view all people with whom we are in interaction as significant others who shape each other's ideas, and together create new, richer ideas and stories. This is the strength in working in a participatory way in communities.

Proposition 14 and Proposition 16 also add another dimension to the discussion on the selves of the community. These propositions explain that the community as a whole or the individuals in the community will protect themselves from whatever appears to threaten their self-concepts, values and existence. If outsiders introduce or impose projects on the community that do not fit with the selves of the community, for example, community members will experience tension and stress. They will resist or defend themselves, perhaps by not attending the meetings any more, not working in the new communal garden or even chasing away the facilitator. Outsiders might describe the community as unmotivated, resistant or apathetic, without realising that the community is protecting itself from imposed actions that may threaten the selves of the community.

Activity 14.2

1. Think of situations in which you felt threatened, or resisted instructions or actions. Write down some examples.
2. Why do you think you felt threatened or resisted these situations? What did you experience as threatening or disrespectful?
3. How did you show your resistance?

14.4 The self and knowledge

How do we know what we know? A further application of the selves is to know what knowledge fits or makes sense to the selves of the community. This is especially important for the facilitator. He or she must ask questions like: 'Why do people think the way they do?', and: 'Why do some theories make sense to people while other theories do not make sense?'

Proposition 1 indicates that every person exists in a continuous world of experience of which that person is the centre. What is implied is that the perceptions and experiences that fit with the selves at that moment in time become the person's knowledge base. Of course, this knowledge base may change and be replaced by even more meaningful information as the person's experiences and perceptions change. What a person knows is formed by what he or she has perceived and experienced as meaningful. It becomes part of that person's unique frame of reference (Proposition 2 and Proposition 7). As experiences and perceptions change, so do behaviour and emotions. This may change the perception of the self (Proposition 3). You have probably heard people say something like: 'That really opened my eyes', or: 'After I was diagnosed with cancer, I looked at life through different eyes.' Another example of this is that people (especially Americans) said they no longer saw America as a safe place after 9/11. Changes in perceptions and experiences also occur as people are continuously exposed to the development of new technology, and changes in the environment and the economy.

Example 14.2

A community worker based in a mining company observed that most of the miners come from rural areas and neighbouring countries. Their families still live in these areas. Now the migrant workers live at the mine township. Most of them co-habit with women (also from rural areas) whom they support financially. This is how these women make a living and earn money for their own families.

During the economic recession of 2009, the mining company experienced financial difficulties and retrenched thousands of mineworkers. Think of the impact this action had on the mineworkers, the women and children in the township, and the extended families they support back home in the rural areas.

One day, a miner is the breadwinner and hero for his family back home and the woman with whom he lives in the township. The next day, he is a failure who is no longer able to look after everybody for whom he is responsible.

Along with the changes that takes place come new symbolised and unsymbolised experiences, perceptions, challenges, problems, needs, resources and relationships within the community. All of these aspects are interconnected, as described in Proposition 3 (wholeness).

The Pedi idiom *'Mollo ofisa baori'* means 'Only the person exposed to the fire can tell how hot it is'. Only the members of the community can say how they perceive the situation and what they are experiencing. This implies the need for a continuous dialogue with the people in the community that will reveal their unique changing experiences, perceptions, emotions, needs and meanings.

When working with communities, we continue to listen to the changing experiences and perceptions of the people. We also take into consideration that different individuals and groups in the community can have different perceptions and experiences (Proposition 2 and Proposition 7). The whole community will not have the same experiences in the same situations. If we only talk to the community leaders, or only to a part of the community such as the men, women or children, or the chairperson of a group, we will not elicit all of the community's perceptions. Each of these groups and sometimes each of these individuals may experience the situation differently.

Example 14.3

A couple moved from a rural town to a city. The husband complained constantly about the traffic he had to face every morning on his way to work. The wife was not happy in the rural town. Every morning on her way to work, she would say: 'Wow, it's wonderful to be in the traffic again.'

Example 14.4

The men and woman in a rural community had different perspectives about their water supply. The women focused on the clean water supply for household use, while the men gave priority to running water with which to water their crops.

14.5 The self and values

In the same way that a person's value system is part of the self of the person, the values of a community are part of the selves of that community. Some communities may be constructed around certain value systems, for example, a community of animal lovers. The individual's value systems regarding other matters might be different, but their love and respect for animals is the glue that holds them together as a community. Some geographical communities may have values that have developed over years and generations. With technological, political and environmental changes, values may also change. Changing values may bring changes to the decisions and development efforts on which people may embark. The value system that influences the decisions they make is not always known to the people. In other words, it is unsymbolised.

The values that people have are not necessarily 'grown from within' or congruent with the selves of the community or individuals in the community. Proposition 10 indicates that people sometimes adopt values from oppressors and dominant cultures. These adopted values may create stress, as they are not consistent with the selves of the community. For example, if people adopt the value system of another group, community or culture, the adopted value system may be in conflict with their own value system or their selves, but they believe that it may be safe or for the best to adopt this new value system. It is important that the process of symbolisation of the values congruent to their selves takes place before actions are planned, as it will direct these actions.

Many examples of liberation movements against colonialisation exist in the world today. (Examples include the liberation movement against apartheid in South Africa, the liberation movement of Che Guevara and various liberation movements in Africa.) These liberation movements fought for freedom, but they were also movements against adopted value systems. Freire's thinking is of great significance here. He explained that often oppressed people will take on the value system of the oppressor, even though it is incongruent to their own value system, because they believe the adopted value system is superior to their own. Freire referred to this as 'cultural invasion'. He referred to the process of symbolisation as 'conscientisation'. He said that this process of becoming aware of their own value system is important for the liberation and development of oppressed people. It is essential that they discover and appreciate their own value systems, which reflect the perceived selves of the people and the community.

Activity 14.3

So far, we have used expressions such as 'symbolisation', 'becoming aware' and 'naming the experience'. Write down words and idioms in your own language that describe this process of symbolisation or becoming aware. For example, in English, people say: 'It dawned on me', or: 'I have seen the light'. In Afrikaans, people say: 'Ek het die lig gesien', or: 'Die son het by my opgekom'.

14.6 When do people experience problems?

The self-structure is also important to explain how problems and distress are viewed. According to Proposition 13 and Proposition 14, people experience stress or problems when they are not aware of or cannot name (symbolise) their experiences and the experiences are inconsistent with the perception of their selves.

For example, let's look at communities or people who are poor. Is it poverty as such that distresses them? Yes, it can be, as they battle to make ends meet and wonder where their next meal will come from. What is it about poverty that creates stress? It is not only the fact that they wonder where they are going to get food for their children, how they will pay school fees and where they will find the money to pay the rent, but also feelings such as: 'I am not a good mother/father', or: 'I cannot provide for my children', or: 'I am worthless if I cannot find a job'. It is also the meaning of poverty and being unemployed that creates the stress. To be unemployed, not being able to provide, might conflict with the idea of the self as a responsible and competent person who is able to look after his or her family. Research done by Schenck et al. (2007) with day labourers found that some labourers would rather stand on the pavement in all weathers, even though they know that the chance of getting a job is very limited, than tell their families they are not trying to find a job. They would rather sleep in the bush than go home without money or food for their families. They cannot enter the house empty-handed.

Example 14.5

There was concern about the men in a community of farm workers on commercial farms. In spite of the fact that the men described themselves as good and caring people, they drank a lot, which resulted in violence against their wives and children. The men's view of themselves was incongruent with their behaviour. In Du Plessis's (2002) discussions with the men, they revealed (symbolised) perceptions of being disempowered and isolated without hope or vision. They existed from day-to-day, and drinking made them feel better.

Certain events are denied or not owned within particular communities as the events cannot be identified with the community's self, or the members of the community may have a different perception of their behaviour. The men might believe that they care about each other and their families, and are not violent, for example, but then the women complain about abuse on weekends when the men drink a lot.

Some communities claim to live according to the principles of *Ubuntu*, but do not do so in practice. The principles of *Ubuntu* imply that community members care for each other. However, when children are left orphaned, family members may take everything, claiming it as their right and leaving the orphaned children destitute.

Another community might regard itself as a religious community, but have exceptionally high levels of crime. These contradictory factors in communities indicate contradictory or conflicting unsymbolised perceptions, values and actions.

The following themes emerged from this chapter:

- The experience and perception of the selves of the people and the community are the core focus of the person-centred approach. They are critical when working with communities because the selves of the community determine the values, actions, processes and directions that projects will embrace.
- The process during which members of the community become aware of their experiences and themselves is extremely important. These processes will be discussed in the chapters that follow.

CHAPTER

15 The person-centred view of change

15.1 Introduction

The first two chapters of this section outlined the way in which the person-centred approach understands human behaviour. We will now consider how this approach sees the process of change in people.

According to Rogers (Kirschenbaum and Henderson 1989: 304), facilitating change processes in communities involves facilitating the creation of a community or group of learners where all members have the opportunity to participate in a safe context. (See also David Korten's (1983) learning-process approach.) Freire indicated that if we are able to transform a group of people in a community into a community of learners, then 'the excitement will be beyond belief'. Attwood (2007), whose work was based on the theory of Freire, also referred to the formation of learning circles where people collectively and critically reflect and inquire about and act on the issues that matter to them. A learning circle brings together a group of people in a process of collective inquiry to explore issues and questions that are of mutual interest to the group. The group itself decides where to focus its collective attention. It is guided by a facilitator who helps to deepen its collective learning.

Group work is usually used when we are working to facilitate change in communities because it is impossible for a facilitator to work with each member of a community individually when there are hundreds or thousand of people in the community. The only way to accomplish the change process is through groups of people.

These groups create a safe context for change (Proposition 17). Groups allow people to discover their own voices and for these voices to be heard. When people discover their own voices, they become aware that they have their own opinions and knowledge, and can take responsibility for their own social and individual growth, development and change. Their growth is based and grounded on their own values and indigenous knowledge. The locus of control and power resides with or moves towards the people to own. The professional becomes a facilitator of reflecting, learning, growth and development – the change process. Skills and ways of working that are creative, innovative and indigenous (relevant to the community) are used to achieve this change.

According to Tolan (2003:10), person-centred change is a slow process. It does not usually consist of a single significant moment of discovery or enlightment, but a series of small adjustments. These minor ripples spread gradually to affect the people's way of being, including the way in which they think, perceive and act. In community-practice terms, we refer to this as a continuous action-reflection-planning process. This is illustrated in the figure below.

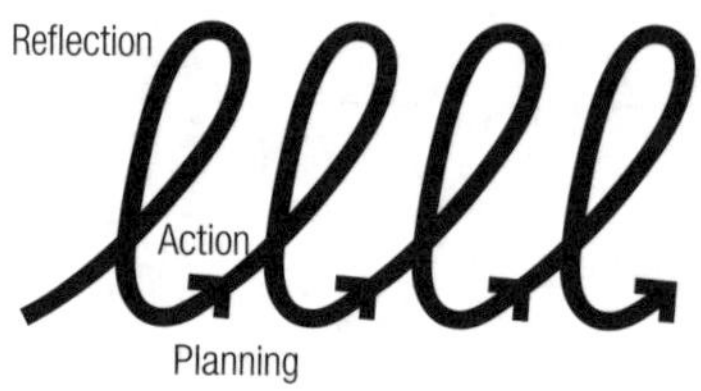

The change process unfolds in three stages that will be discussed in this chapter and the chapters that follow. The phases of the change process are a continuous process. They are described separately here to facilitate explanation, but in practice they are not 'discrete events' (Kirschenbaum and Henderson 1989: 63). Rogers states that the stages or processes mingle and shade into each other. They occur only approximately in the order described here. The propositions of the person-centred approach formulated by Rogers will be indicated as they fit with the different stages of the change process.

15.2 Humanising the context of change (Phase 1)

A person-centred process starts with humanising the context by placing the people, their perceptions and their experiences of their world at the centre of the process.

Facilitating change processes in communities may sound like a huge, unmanageable challenge. However, we start by thinking of communities as people, individuals, groups and households (in whatever form) in a specific environment or context. We remember that people are in continuous interaction with other people (Proposition 9). Communities consist of people. We will communicate with these people. We will talk to these people, build relationships with them and facilitate change processes with them.

The starting point when working with communities is to connect with the people in the community in a manner that does not threaten the self-structures of the people (Proposition 14, Proposition 16 and Proposition 17). To facilitate change within communities, we need to create a warm and safe space in which people feel respected. In this safe space, they can learn, grow, develop, change, risk, embrace their mistakes and learn from these mistakes.

> *Whenever we have warm trusting relationships, all kinds of surprising possibilities begin to open up to us, enabling and unlocking many positive things in ourselves and in others. We find that we can speak more honestly and freely, we can be more ourselves, more creative, more productive, even more generous. We are less afraid of making mistakes and more able to collectively learn from them.*
>
> [*Barefoot Guide* 2009: 48]

The creation of the conditions for change in which the self-structures of the people are not threatened (Proposition14) is important. According to Tolan (2003), the person-centred approach tells us that any attempt on the part of the facilitator to change the self-structure actively through reasoning or persuasion, whether subtly or overtly, will be threatening (Proposition 14) to the self-structure and may cause anxiety and resistance. However well intentioned, such attempts add to the people's sense of not being good enough, and not being able to draw on their own resources and abilities.

15.3 Creating a safe space

The process of creating a context that is conducive for change starts when we construct the relationship with the community as a relationship where the facilitator does not solve problems or have the answers. Rather, according to Rogers, the facilitation process creates opportunities for the members of the community to work out their own solutions (in Kirschenbaum and Henderson 1989: 66). Rogers (in Kirschenbaum and Henderson 1989: 68) continues by saying that the nature of the facilitation process will enable the members of the community to experience that the process belongs to them. This defining part of the process can be seen as a form of contracting with the community verbally and through actions. We cannot say to the community that we will create a space and opportunities where the community members can voice their concerns and collectively create solutions, but then determine the process ourselves.

The *Barefoot Guide* (2009: 49) describes this relationship as a cocoon or womb of warmth in which new beginnings may be gestated, nurtured and given birth to. The facilitator has the job of creating a relationship based on warmth, integrity and trust. This warm relationship or cocoon should be sustained throughout the facilitation process. The facilitator constantly reflects on the relationship to determine if the ingredients for the relationship still exist (Proposition 17).

The requirements for creating this safe space and non-threatening relationship (Proposition 17) for change are discussed below.

15.3.1 Respect

Respect is the central condition for establishing a safe space and a non-threatening relationship. The person-centred facilitator creates a respectful, warm, safe space for the group or community with which he or she connects. This can be done by using respectful body language and a respectful tone of voice to convey a non-judgmental attitude. It includes how the facilitator dresses and sits, his or her facial expressions and the attention given to people during meetings. It means that punctuality and honouring appointments are important. In addition, respect means that the facilitator regards the people as worthy human beings. He or she believes in their potential and abilities, and focuses on their strengths instead of on their weaknesses. The facilitator respects, believes and trusts them, and always creates opportunities for their voices to be heard. The facilitator's respect for people permeates every facet of his or her interaction with them.

Activity 15.1

1 Reflect critically about how you perceive a variety of people, for example, poor people, rich people, migrants, refugees, alcoholics, drug addicts and druglords. Think for a while, and then write down answers to the questions that follow.
   - Which people do you admire?
   - Which people do you loathe?
   - What would happen if you needed to work with these people?

2 Often we stereotype these people based on our perceptions and experiences of them. Make an effort to get to know a person about whom you have a stereotypical perception. Compare your new perception of the person with the perception you had before.

3 Would you be behaving in a respectful manner if you went to work in a poor community wearing expensive clothing and jewellery?

4 Would you be behaving in a respectful manner if you ate takeaway food in front of a group of poor people?

5 What would be the impact of this disrespectful behaviour on your relationship with the community?

6 How does your attitude towards people (for example, admiration or a low opinion) influence the way you act towards those people?

7 Make notes in your notebook of respectful and disrespectful behaviour of people whom you observe, for example, in the street, on the taxi, in the shop, in your household, in the class, your lecturers or your colleagues.

8 Reflect on your own behaviour and write down when you have acted respectfully or disrespectfully towards people. (We all do so at times.)

9 Identify patterns in your behaviour that indicate when or towards whom you tend to behave in a respectful or disrespectful manner. For example, you might notice that you tend to act respectfully towards the elderly as respect for them is embedded in your culture.

15.3.2 Acceptance and trust

Acceptance, trust and consistency are connected. Both Rogers and Freire consider trust to be very important. Freire emphasised that trust is an essential element of the relationship with people. He regarded trust as a prerequisite for growth and change in people.

We cannot accept people if we do not trust or value them. We see them as being trustworthy and capable of handling their own affairs. It is impossible to be a facilitator of learning and change without having a profound trust in people and their potential. Trust means accepting people without judgement of their ideas, values, behaviour, traditions, cultural practices and the meanings they attach to things. You may of course differ from them, but you may not judge their ideas and perceptions.

Non-judgement does not imply accepting all behaviour with an attitude of 'anything goes'. Rather, it means separating the behaviour from the person and still accepting that person. The person-centred facilitator never judges people, although he or she may not agree with or condone their actions, which might include behaviour such as drinking or committing a crime. You may be offended by a person's actions, or have a different view-point or perception from the person, but you still accept and trust that he or she has the ability to create some form of change. The facilitator's aim is to understand the person's experiences and perceptions, and not to judge that person. Acceptance of him- or herself helps the facilitator to accept others (Proposition 18 and Proposition 19).

According to Rogers (in Kirschenbaum and Henderson 1989: 309), acceptance of a person implies accepting that the person is fundamentally trustworthy with regard to his or her own affairs. When we trust and accept people and do not judge them, it encourages free expression of experiences and perceptions. People feel safe to explore, make mistakes and risk. In this safe context, we can explore and reflect on their thoughts and actions, and the effects of these actions, without judging them. The group process can be used to facilitate critical thinking about certain behaviours The aim of this thinking should not be to determine right or wrong, but to understand these behaviours. Even if the group decides to take a certain direction in the development process, the group will reflect so as to understand what the results, effect or outcome of each action will be and how to proceed next.

Social workers often feel that the people with whom they work have a certain perception of social workers. Thus, when these people meet a social worker, they say the things they think he or she wants to hear. They will only trust the social worker and share their real perceptions and experiences when they feel that the social worker accepts and trusts them, and attempts to understand them.

We have emphasised that trust means trusting people with their own affairs. We need to trust the direction people take, the decisions they make and the processes they follow. If trust and acceptance are facilitated within the group and amongst the people in the community, they will be able to listen to each other without judgment. They will become aware of the opportunities offered by their differences.

When the facilitator behaves consistently, accepting and trusting the members of the group at all times, they develop a feeling of trust in the facilitator.

Activity 15.2

1 Think about and discuss the implications of this condition. Write down what should be present in a relationship in order for you to be able to trust people.
2 Does acceptance mean that we have to accept bad, oppressive or even criminal behaviour? How can we accept a person without accepting his or her behaviour?

The facilitator creates trust by handling information confidentially, being on time for appointments and being there when he or she has promised to do so. People should be able to rely on the facilitator and experience his or her respect.

Another dimension of trust is the facilitator's belief in people. According to Chambers (1998), as soon as we engage with people and discover their potential, skills and knowledge, trust and admiration develop. The community's skills, knowledge and expertise might be different from the skills, knowledge and expertise of the facilitator, but this will make the encounter an enriching and meaningful experience. If the facilitator opens him- or herself to learn from the community (new experiences – Proposition 18 and Proposition 19), then the facilitator will develop trust in the people's abilities. The facilitator's belief in the people will create mutual trust.

Tolan (2003) also emphasised the need for the facilitator to trust in the person and the process. Trusting the process implies that the facilitator does not direct the process, but facilitates and trusts the process to go its own direction and have a unique outcome. This should not be confused with the facilitator adopting a 'hands-off' or passive attitude. It still means that the facilitator is an active listener, making empathic reflections, facilitating critical reflection, networking or facilitating networking and capacity building, but the direction and the process should be owned by the community and entrusted with the community. If this relationship of mutual trust starts to form, then the facilitator will have the credibility to start walking the journey with the community.

Activity 15.3

In your own words, write down what it means if we say we need to trust the process. What is it about the process that we need to trust?

15.3.3 Congruence or realness

Rogers saw the realness of the facilitator as the most basic characteristic of the facilitator.

> *When the facilitator is a real person, being what he or she is, entering into the relationship without presenting a front or a façade, he or she is much more likely to be effective.*
>
> [Kirschenbaum and Henderson 1989: 306]

This implies that the facilitator is aware of and can 'name' his or her own experiences (the experiences have been symbolised). It suggests that the facilitator can act congruently to the experiences and is able to communicate them if appropriate. This all sounds simple, but it requires a good deal of maturity, self-knowledge and self-reflection on the part of the facilitator. The facilitator is aware of his or her feelings and acknowledges them as such. The facilitator has no need to impose these feelings on the people with whom he or she is interacting. The facilitator is a person to the people, not a faceless embodiment of his or her requirements (Rogers in Kirschenbaum and Henderson 1989: 306). This characteristic requires that the facilitator listen to what is going on in him- or herself. The congruent facilitator will be able to express ('name') his or her feelings of happiness, discomfort or excitement. By naming and owning his or her feelings (see the discussion of immediacy on pages 97–100), the facilitator will avoid blaming or shaming other people. This requires a continuous process of self-reflection. The facilitator can ask him- or herself questions like: 'How am I feeling now?', or: 'What am I experiencing now?', or: 'Is my behaviour real or congruent?', or: 'Why do I feel the way I do?'

Rogers expresses his caution about facilitators being 'honest', as some people may use this as a licence to pass judgement on others.

> *Actually the achievement of realness is quite difficult ... Firstly one must be close to one's feelings, capable of being aware of them. Then one must be willing to take the risk of sharing them as they are, not disguising them as judgements ...*
>
> [Kirschenbaum and Henderson 1989: 119]

Acting in a congruent manner means that the facilitator speaks in direct 'I see/feel/experience ...' statements. The 'I' message also relates to the people involved in the facilitation process. When people move towards speaking for themselves and take ownership for their own thoughts and comments, it is an indication of the growth and change in the community. This value actually refers to Proposition 18, which emphasises that if we accept ourselves, then we will accept others. The facilitator needs to be where the process in the community should end – accepting him- or herself and others (Proposition 18).

> *It meant that if I am to facilitate the growth of others in relation to me, then I must grow, and while this is often painful, it is also enriching.*
>
> [Rogers in Kirschenbaum and Henderson 1989: 120]

Activity 15.4

1. Discuss the issues raised in the previous section. As facilitators, we need to ask ourselves the following reflective questions:
   - Do I know and own my experiences or feelings?
   - Can I give them names? (Now 'name' them.)
2. At the end of each day, 'name' your experiences or feelings for the day. Write them down in your notebook.
3. Next to each 'named' feeling, indicate if you acted congruently or incongruently to that experience. For example, if you are cross with a person, how did you act towards that person? Were you congruent or incongruent? Did you express your anger? If you did, how did you express your anger? Did you use blame or were you able to use the 'I' principle?
4. Give an example of a person you know who you think always acts congruently.
5. In your opinion, what makes this person congruent or real?
6. What is the difference between being honest to the point of rudeness and being real or congruent?

15.3.4 Individualisation or appreciative individualisation

Individualisation means respecting, recognising, appreciating and encouraging the uniqueness of the individuals in a community and the uniqueness of communities or groups of people (Proposition 1, Proposition 2 and Proposition 7). As a consequence of individualisation, people in the community develop an appreciation of who they are. They develop an appreciation of their assets, their knowledge, their skills, their unique experiences, and their attempts to survive and cope. Theoretical approaches like appreciative inquiry, asset-based perspectives and strength-based perspectives also value the uniqueness of individuals and communities.

The facilitator avoids using generalisations to describe people or communities. Generalisations such as 'black communities', 'white communities', 'sub-economic communities', 'poor communities', 'rich people', 'rural communities' or 'a community of squatters' proclaims communities as nouns. It is a form of labelling, and it ignores the uniqueness of people and their communities.

An article by Lee entitled 'If you build it, they may not come' (2009: 251) gives the example of a service or programme that was developed for a community of foster and adoptive parents. The parents did not respond to the programme. One parent explained the lack of response by saying: 'The agency doesn't listen to us ... I go to the store for bread and you give me a ball. We told them what we need: respite care, respite care, respite care!' (Respite care is assistance or relief with children.) The pressing issue was that the facilitators did not anticipate the load and responsibilities the adoption or foster care would demand from them. The facilitators tried to implement the same programme in different communities of foster-care parents, not taking into account that each community of foster parents is unique, so each community has unique needs. The Northern Sotho expression *'Naka tsa go rweswa ga dikgomarele hlogo'*, which means 'You cannot stick the horns of one cow on another. The horns have to grow from within', illustrates individualisation.

You can become more aware of the uniqueness of people by exploring how they survived, how they have managed or how they stayed strong in spite of poverty/HIV/Aids/drugs. Listening to the people's answers to your questions will help you to see their uniqueness.

15.3.5 Openness , transparency and participation (inclusivity)

Openness and transparency are important because they help to prevent one person or group from exerting unfair power over others. They also help to prevent oppression and corruption. On the other hand, hidden agendas, exclusion and sub-groups are factors that create opportunities for these things to occur.

Inclusivity means ensuring that all relevant parties and people are involved and participate in the process. Yaron et al. (1992: 21) mention that during their involvement in rural communities in Namibia, they found that existing social structures are often not ideal for stimulating community-based development. The reason for this is that women are generally under-represented, often to the point where they are totally absent from proceedings. However, women are involved in most village activities, including raising children, looking after the household, ploughing and harvesting, and attending to festival and funeral matters. Nearly all development efforts in the community affect women and are affected by women, yet they are not included in these development efforts or consulted about them. If you exclude groups, they are oppressed because they do not have a voice. As a result, they may resist the development efforts.

All members of the community must be given equal access to the process. The process allows all the voices and frames of references, perceptions and experiences to be heard. The result will be that interested members will create a community. They will contribute to the process and they will use it as a learning opportunity (Proposition 2 and Proposition 7).

The fundamental attitudes that support all of these concepts are respect for all people and the belief that richer experiences can develop from the differences between people. It is essential not to see differences as threatening. This is, of course, easier said than done. When we work in and with communities, there are always difficult group dynamics and political processes to consider. There are also often disruptive or difficult people, and it may be tempting to exclude them from the process in order to make it easier. The person-centred facilitator will avoid falling into these traps by keeping the principles in mind at all times.

Activity 15.5

How are transparency and openness applied when a community asks you to mediate between sub-groups in the community who have a dispute?

According to Soal and Reeler (2009), inclusion involves embracing all relevant people. On a practical level, we can check that we have remembered the principle of inclusivity by asking: 'Are all those people with whom our work is concerned included in its processes?' Soal and Reeler again refer to the slogan of the disability movement that illustrates the importance of inclusion and participation: 'Nothing about us, without us'.

Inclusion implies respecting all people, and embracing differences and diversity. Practising inclusion creates belonging, a sense of community and a sense of shared purpose.

15.3.6 Self-determination and freedom

According to Rogers, self-determination (Proposition 4) refers to the tendency of people to maintain themselves even when the pathway to their goal is blocked.

> *... it moves in the direction of greater independence of self-responsibility ... in the direction of increasing self-government, self-regulation and autonomy, and away from the control of external forces ...*
>
> [Rogers 1987: 488]

The Sepedi idiom *'Kodumela moepa rutsa ga go lehuma le le tswago kgauswi'* means 'People naturally strive and dig for what they want, no matter how difficult it may be'. Think how much emphasis is put on the concept 'self'. We speak of self-government, self-determination and self-regulation. Ultimately, the person-centred approach is facilitating the self-actualisation process and allowing the people of the community to develop 'self-responsibility'.

Activity 15.6

1 Think about situations you have experienced where it was difficult to hand over control or responsibility to another person. In your home or work context, observe where people should actually facilitate independence or self-determination, but experience difficulty. A household-based example could be that of the mother who will not allow her child to cook because of the mess the child is going to make. Instead of facilitating the process of the child cooking and cleaning up, she does the cooking herself. A community-based example could be a facilitator who keeps control by calling meetings instead of requesting the people to organise meetings themselves. By doing this, the facilitator is denying the people opportunities for learning and growth.

2 Do you think that self-determination mean passivity on the part of the facilitator? What is the 'active' role of the facilitator?

Self-determination means more just than the choices that people make. Wood (1995: 30) emphasises that self-determination must not be confused with the myth that individuals control their own destiny. People are always part of a system. They cannot always control what is happening around them, and they have to make decisions based on the information, perceptions and experiences they have. The implication for practice for the facilitator is that the facilitation of the process of self-determination means:

> ‘ *... creating freedom, creating opportunities for critical reflection, to decide, to voice, to discover, to share, to learn and ... its accompanying responsibilities.* ’
>
> [Soal and Reeler 2009: 2]

This results in the empowerment of people. People have the freedom of informed choices and responsibilities, and they have control of their own affairs.

Self-determination is built on the respect we have for the autonomous power of the people to heal. As facilitators, we create a context for this healing or development process. According to Tolan (2003), the implication is that we do not know what the outcome of the process will be. As discussed earlier, the facilitator needs to trust the process.

Freire also believed strongly in the autonomous power of self-determination. In other words, he believed that people can be trusted to take responsibility for their own decisions and actions. Freire sees the responsibility of the facilitator in this process as being to facilitate a process of critical reflection that will allow people to think critically about decisions, actions and responsibilities. In practice, it means that before people decide on actions, the facilitator will facilitate the critical reflection process. The facilitator will have gathered information, and thought about all the consequences of possible decisions and actions.

Self-determination is the aim of the facilitation process. By now, you have noted the emphasis put on the concept 'responsibility'. As facilitators, we take responsibility for our own thinking and actions in the community. In the same way, the members of the community will ultimately be able to take responsibility for their reflections, decisions and actions. In other words, the locus of control remains with the community.

15.3.7 Empathic understanding

Empathic understanding means that the facilitator attempts to understand the people from their frames of reference by listening to their experiences and perceptions, and then conveying his or her understanding of their experiences to the people. This means that the facilitator tries to stand in the people's shoes, viewing the world as they see it with empathy. The people experience that they have been understood.

Rogers (1989: 428) said that the discovery and acceptance of the fact that people have different realities (Proposition 2 and Proposition 7) will result in us living in a totally new and richer universe. These propositions are similar to constructivist and postmodern thought in their view that realities are subjective and are constructed based on people's unique experiences.

With empathic understanding, we acknowledge, respect and accept other people's different experiences and perceptions, and attempt to show understanding for these experiences.

Empathy will be discussed further during the discussion of the process.

15.3.8 Confidentiality

Confidentiality in the community is different from confidentiality when working with individuals, couples, families and even therapy groups. Knowledge and information within the groups in the community is in the open and in the public domain. So what does confidentiality then mean?

Two important points to remember when dealing with confidentiality in community groups are discussed below.

Confidentiality versus openness, inclusivity and transparency

Confidential information at the community level must be dealt with in an open, inclusive and transparent manner. As soon as the facilitator gets hooked or trapped into being told confidential information about community members, he or she may be trapped in his or her movements and involvement by not being able to be open and transparent. This immediately destroys the value or principle of openness, inclusivity and participation.

Let us consider an example that sometimes happens to therapists working with couples. A husband may come to the facilitator and share information about his wife. He will then ask the facilitator not to let his wife know that the facilitator is aware of this information. The facilitator is immobilised by this action. If the husband reveals that he told the facilitator and the facilitator had not shared the information with the wife, it may also create the impression that the facilitator and the husband are siding against the wife. Information no longer moves freely.

This can also happen in communities. The facilitator must make it clear from the beginning that he or she cannot deal with information that is not accessible to other members of the community or group (inclusivity), because this might trap the facilitator into siding with some sub-groups. If concerned members of a group come to see the facilitator about something (for example, they might be concerned that the chairperson may abuse money), the group can, with the help of the facilitator, negotiate how to deal with the issue. The group understands that it is unfair to expect the facilitator to act on a matter that he or she is not supposed to know anything about. The facilitator can rather plan with the group how to address the issue within the group. This will keep the flow of information open and transparent. The movement of the facilitator should always be free and the facilitator should always be accessible to all the people involved.

Confidentiality and donor feedback

The second issue relates to feedback that must be given to donors or outsiders with vested interests in the community. Feedback can only be given to these people with the approval of the community. Feedback reports need to be written in collaboration with the community. The facilitator can either write the report with the people, or write the report with their input and approval if the people are illiterate.

Du Plessis (2000) illustrates how to handle this aspect of confidentiality in her involvement with a rural community. She respected the community by treating every piece of information that needed to be given to people outside the community with respect for confidentiality. She never shared any information without the permission and input of the people in the community, action group or committee. She also asked the community what information should be shared and how this should be done.

People from outside communities, like donors, volunteers and politicians, often want to show off development projects to visitors. In this situation, it is essential to obtain the community's permission before bringing outsiders into the community. Agreement must be reached on how, when and where people will be allowed into the community. The facilitator also discusses what information will be shared and how this sharing will take place.

Example 15.1

When asked if a group of social-work students could visit the community to learn from them, Du Plessis replied by saying that she would consult the community. The community agreed to allow the visit, provided the visitors gave input and feedback on their observations. On the last day of the visit, the students had a formal meeting with the community during which they shared their observations and expressed their appreciation. Du Plessis's actions were based on deep respect for the people of the community.

Here are some questions the facilitator can ask him- or herself to establish whether he or she is 'living' the values discussed here when working in communities.

Do the processes I facilitate:

- Enhance or maximise freedom and participation?
- Embrace and appreciate diversity?
- Practise inclusion in all instances?
- Show respect?
- Embrace learning and mistakes?
- Respect confidentiality?
- Involve ethical actions and behaviour?

The facilitator must show his or her concern and accountability by reflecting continually on his or her own thinking, values and actions.

15.4 The qualities that make a good facilitator

The personality of the facilitator working with communities is extremely important as the facilitator is part of the process and a significant other to the group (Proposition 9). The *Barefoot Guide* (2009: 30) also emphasises that the facilitator will not be able to understand others until the facilitator understands him- or herself. The ideal qualities and abilities that enable the facilitator to establish a facilitating relationship with clients are discussed below.

- The facilitator has an in-depth knowledge of him- or herself (Proposition 8) and the agency that he or she represents. The facilitator has an awareness of his or her power, and an awareness of which of his or her own needs are being met through the relationship (Proposition 9). It might be important for the facilitator to take the journey of symbolising or becoming aware of the issues raised before starting the process with the community.
- The facilitator has an awareness of how he or she is perceived and experienced by the participants and what the facilitator represents to them (for example, hope, congruency or trust – Proposition 9, Proposition 2 and Proposition 7).
- The facilitator has the ability to articulate clearly and honestly who he or she is, and his or her purpose and intentions (congruency – Proposition 8).
- The facilitator has a warm, non-judgemental, accepting personality. He or she relates well to the individuals and group (Proposition 17).
- The facilitator has an awareness of how change processes take place in groups, and the ability to respond appropriately (Proposition 17, Proposition 15, Proposition 18 and Proposition 19).
- The facilitator has the ability to listen consciously, deeply and actively in order to appreciate the purpose and intentions of others (empathy – Proposition 17 and all the other propositions).
- The facilitator has the ability to build trust by being worthy of trust in all that he or she does and undertakes to do. This makes the facilitator significant for the person or group. Freire (1972: 41) regards trust as the most critical aspect in the relationship:

'They (facilitators) talk about people but they do not trust them; and trusting people is the indispensable precondition ... A real humanist can be identified by his trust in people.' (Proposition 9 and Proposition 17).

- The facilitator is knowledgeable and enthusiastic about what he or she is doing because he or she believes that people can change under the right conditions (Proposition 17).
- The facilitator is able to generate ideas and new meanings with the participants, and to use their skills (Proposition 9).
- The facilitator has the ability to negotiate agreements (contracts) that honestly reflect the interests of all parties and encourage co-ownership (trust) (Proposition 3).
- The facilitator has the ability to allow and encourage his or her relationships to change over time. He or she is flexible in responding to the changing realities and experiences of participants (Proposition 1).

Rogers (in Kirschenbaum and Henderson 1989: 306) said that when the facilitator enters into a relationship with the client, the facilitator is much more likely to be effective if he or she is being a real person, being what he or she really is, and not presenting a front or façade. The facilitator must be him- or herself, not deny him- or herself. This sets the foundation for reflective practice.

What do we mean by reflective practice? Reflective practice means that we look back on what happened and what we did in the process. We reflect during the process and on the process. This includes considering our own thoughts and actions as part of the process. The facilitator is part of the reflective process. The facilitator could ask him- or herself questions like: 'What did I do in the process?', or: 'What happened between me and the community?', or: 'Where did I do what or where didn't I do what?', or: 'How could I have done it differently or better?' The facilitator can ask the community members similar questions to enable them to reflect on the process. The community members could respond to questions like: 'What could we have done differently or better?', or: 'What did we do?', or: 'What didn't we do?'

These reflective processes also create trust. They are not intend to assign blame, but to look at what was good, what worked and what could have been done better. They allow us to plan and act further.

As we have already discussed, people can only change in a context that is conducive to change. This implies a context in which the self-structure experiences no threat to the self (Proposition 17). Proposition 14 indicates that the facilitator can create unsymbolised psychological tension if he or she introduces or imposes change that is in conflict or incongruent with a community's self-perceptions and values. No learning or change will take place in such a context because the community does not have control over the changes.

Example 15.2

Parkash and Esteva (1998: 52) gave the example of teachers who came to teach at a school in Gautemala. The teachers wanted the children to wear school uniforms >>

so that they would all look the same. Previously, the children had worn colourful dresses and their parents had taken pride in weaving the colourful material from which the dresses were made. What angered the parents even more was that the teachers expected the parents to buy the uniforms. This was against their custom. They usually wove cloth and made their own clothes and other goods, and then traded with each other. The parents demanded that the teachers leave the community immediately and refused to allow their children to wear clothes made of material that was all the same colour.

The anger of the parents was symbolised or expressed. However, the feelings of humiliation, lack of control over their children's education, not being respected and that their values were not appreciated were not symbolised (because the parents were not yet aware of these feelings), and created tension and resistance. The *Barefoot Guide* (2009: 51) speaks of power imbalances in relationships. More often than not, development is hampered when an unequal balance of power in a relationship prevents cooperation. These unbalanced relationships oppress, stress and limit the potential of people.

> *Therefore if we want to see shifts or transformation of power, we have to help transform relationships.*
>
> [*Barefoot Guide* 2009: 51]

Attwood (2003: 6) gives an example of how she assisted a community in Malealea, Lesotho, to transform the unequal power relationships in the community without threatening existing structures. Men in Lesotho are legally and culturally the heads of the household. When groups were established in the community, certain rules were put in place. One of these rules stated that the groups would function according to the principle of equal participation for men and women. The group debated cultural attitudes and practices, and discussed what changes needed to be made.

It is essential to create a warm, respectful relationship in which change can take place throughout the facilitation process.

CHAPTER 16

Facilitating symbolised experiences of the community (Phase 2)

16.1 Introduction

In the first three chapters of this section, we considered the first phase of the facilitation process. We indicated the importance of creating a context that is conducive for change and development when connecting and engaging with a community. We looked at how the person-centred approach puts the person, people or community, along with their experiences, perceptions, feelings and realities, at the centre of the facilitation process.

In the second phase, which we will discuss in this chapter, the facilitator explores, listens to and deals with the symbolised or conscious experiences of the people in the community. (By symbolised or conscious experiences, we are referring to the things that the people talk about, that they name and of which they are aware.) The facilitator also discovers and explores the unsymbolised experiences.

16.2 The stages of the facilitation process when working with a community

Most projects described in traditional literature on the community development process follow stages during which the community is explored, its needs are determined, and then projects are planned, implemented and evaluated. *People-centred Community Practice* (Schenck, Louw and Nel: 2009) identifies these five stages:

- Connection with and discovery of the community
- Creation of a vision or dream
- Design of a plan
- Delivery and implementation of the plan
- Reflection, disconnection and termination.

The facilitator begins exploring and listening to the symbolised and unsymbolised experiences of the people in the community during the first phase of the development process, the stage of connecting with and discovering the community. (Remember that we are using the term 'phase' to describe the broad person-centred processes and the term 'stage' to describe the facilitation of a development process in a community.) During the first stage of engagement with the community, the facilitator may create conditions in which some unsymbolised experiences can be symbolised. Throughout the process of change, there will be symbolised experiences that the facilitator will deal with empathically.

To understand this process, think of a sandwich. The bread and butter represent the basic empathy used to express understanding for the symbolised experiences. The ham, jam, cheese, peanut butter or other filling represents the advanced skills that must be used to facilitate the unsymbolised experiences. The slices of bread that make up the sandwich remind us that the advanced skills are preceded and followed by basic skills in an attempt to show understanding.

When we explore the symbolised experiences of the people in the community, we engage with them to discover 'what is' in the community. In other words, we seek to understand their reality and their experience of the community.

16.2.1 Proposition 2 and Proposition 7: Exploring and listening to symbolised experiences

To connect with the people in the community and discover 'what is' in the community means to explore the people's frames of reference. Proposition 2 and Proposition 7 tell us that every community, every group and every person in the community have their own frames of reference, and their own experiences and perceptions. It is important to work from the frames of reference of the people and to take cognisance of the fact that people's realities and experiences change (Proposition 1) and differ.

When the facilitator engages with the people in the community, his or her main aim is to get to know and understand the people, their context and how they perceive it. The facilitator listens and learns about their experiences and perceptions, and attempts to express his or her understanding of the people's experiences, perceptions and frames of references. In other words, the facilitator responds with empathy. The facilitator explores what the people find painful and what makes them sad, what worries them, what makes them happy, what knowledge, skills, assets and strengths they have, how they view their world and what they talk about.

The importance of Proposition 2 and Proposition 7 is that they guide us to understand that whatever people experience and perceive is their reality. Their reality will be different from the reality and frames of reference of the facilitator. The facilitator listens to and respects this reality, and does not judge it. The people may live in a different world with different realities from those of the facilitator. The facilitator has to reflect on the cultural, religious and theoretical filters that may stop him or her from listening to and understanding the community. We will take a closer look at some of these filters next.

Filters determine what we hear and see.

Activity 16.1

Is there anything about your own values that may prevent you from listening to a community, or may allow what a community says to threaten your own value system and self?

16.2.2 Situations that may influence the facilitator

The mission of the facilitator may filter or affect his or her ability to listen to the frames of reference of the people. By mission, we mean what the facilitator wants to hear, the mission of the organisation or donor that he or she represents. If a facilitator works for an agency whose mission is the prevention of alcohol-and-drug abuse, he or she will look for issues related to alcohol and drugs, and ask questions concerned with alcohol and drugs. Other, more urgent issues may not be heard by the facilitator.

Robert Chambers (1983: 13–25), an important thinker in the development field, identified six situations or biases that may filter what the facilitator hears and sees in the community.

Spatial bias

According to Chambers, when a facilitator visits a community, he or she usually does so by car, using tarred roads or roads that are accessible by car. It is seldom that the facilitator gets out of his or her car and walks to remote, unseen places. The result is that certain communities, or certain parts of communities, are excluded. Important voices are not heard. The facilitator needs to walk around the community so as to see it from different perspectives. This will also allow the facilitator to see the community from the perspective of those people who are usually excluded. Chambers also noted that facilitators prefer to visit communities that are close to cities. They seldom go to very remote areas.

Example 16.1

Social workers in a very remote mountainous community on the border of Swaziland said that they never visited the people living in the mountains around the community. Their cars could not cope with the poor access roads. As women, they did not feel that it would be safe for them to walk to these areas.

Project bias

Often people or donors who have contributed to a project wish to visit the community. The projects that are usually shown to visitors are the well-groomed, good-looking projects. The less-groomed and less-successful projects are not displayed, as they reflect badly on the agency or community. When entering a community, the facilitator engages with the community in such a way that he or she has access to all aspects of the community. The facilitator needs to be careful that his or her attention is not directed away from the poorer people in the community.

Example 16.2

A newspaper article reported on a visit by the Minister of Health to a hospital with a bad reputation. Many patients had complained that the hospital was always in a dreadful state. It was filthy, the nurses were lazy and patients were not attended to. When the Minister of Health arrived, everything looked wonderful. The hospital was clean, the garden was well tended and the nurses were running around looking after their patients. This biased the Minister of Health's perception of the state of hospitals.

Person bias

The practitioner will often talk to the rich people or important people in a community, such as the leaders, the schoolmaster or the chief. The practitioner tends not to speak to the poor people or the less verbal people in a community. The practitioner may also talk to the males in the community, and not the females and the children.

Example 16.3

In Chapter 15, we mentioned a community in Namibia where the women are engaged in almost all the village activities, but have no say or representation (Yaron et al. 1992: 21). Only the men, who are the decision makers, may attend meetings. Thus, the voices of the women may not be heard unless an effort is made to listen to them.

All levels and groups of people in communities need to speak and be heard. The boss of an agency cannot speak for his or her employees. The principal of a school cannot speak for the teachers and children of the school. Every person must have the opportunity to speak and to present his or her frame of reference.

Another aspect of this bias is the tendency for the facilitator to talk to the people who are using facilities. The facilitator will go to the clinic and talk to the people attending the clinic, for example, but what about those people who are too sick to go to the clinic? What about those people who live too far from the clinic? What about the children who do not attend school because they are too poor, live too far from the school or are too ill to attend school? These helpful questions will remind the facilitator to be sure to hear all of the different voices of a community.

Active, present, living bias

When we visit an area, we may see fit, happy, active children running up to the car. We do not see the children who are weak, apathetic and ill. Sick people lie out of sight in their beds. Old people are also often out of sight. Chambers refers to a socio-anthropologist who camped outside a village in Uganda for some time before he realised that old people were starving in the village. He would not have known about the old people if he had not spent time in the village or lived near the village.

Example 16.4

Gillian Attwood, an educationist who is involved in a community in Lesotho, wrote that a school sponsorship programme had been established at local schools. Tourists could donate money and sponsor children. They soon changed the policy because only the children attending school received sponsorships. The children who did not attend school because they were ill or could not afford school fees and school uniform were not 'seen', and so they did not receive sponsorships. Some children also walked for hours to get to schools where tourists gave sponsorships, leaving their own schools empty (Attwood 2007).

Professional bias

Chambers identified that the professional training, the values and the level of interest of the practitioner may present problems. The practitioner in a rural area can become narrow minded. There is never enough time to do everything, and the practitioner will probably have decided in advance what information to look for. As a result, the practitioner will not ask open-ended questions that encourage exploration. Just as the soil scientist only asks about soil and the hydrologist only asks about water, the social worker only asks questions about social problems. It is important for the facilitator to reflect critically on the biases that may be applicable to his or her involvement in a community.

Politeness bias

Here we will consider the facilitator who refrains from questioning members of the community too frankly for fear of being rude.

In terms of the person-centred approach, we do not ask frank questions, but rather facilitate a process of critical reflection. So the facilitator facilitates the process that allows the group or people to look at their own situation critically.

Proposition 2 and Proposition 7 help us to appreciate the differences and complexities of people. They guide us to reflect critically on ourselves and what we do, and to learn from each other. Rogers put it like this:

> *If I accept that we live in different realities; if we can see different realities as the most promising resources for learning ... We can live together in order to learn from one another without fear ...*
>
> [Rogers 1989: 428]

When we are working in communities, we have a vast richness of differences to learn from.

Later in this section, we will focus on the importance of good listening. Good listening allows us to listen to people's experiences and frames of reference. For now, we can summarise by saying that when the facilitator engages with people in the community, he or she explores people's experiences and perceptions, and accepts them as unique and different. The facilitator also accepts without judgement that this is the reality of those people. The facilitator listens actively to their perceptions and experiences, and responds with empathic understanding. The facilitator acknowledges all perceptions and experiences, and includes them in creating or constructing new perceptions and experiences.

16.2.3 **Proposition 3: Wholeness**

When engaging with the community, listening to and learning about the community's symbolised perceptions and experiences, the facilitator views each person in the community and the community itself holistically. Here follows an explanation of this concept.

- The community (including the community members' values, attitudes, behaviour, emotions, ideas, desires, aspirations, meanings, perceptions and experiences) is regarded as a whole. These dimensions all interlink with each other. As a result, change in some or even one of these dimensions will also bring change in other dimensions. If the community members' perception of a situation changes, their actions might also change. When the facilitator engages with a community, he or she explores all aspects of that community. The facilitator listens to the community members' values, perceptions, experiences, aspirations, dreams and so on. The facilitator also listens to the meanings they attach to things and experiences. The facilitator observes their behaviour, and takes into account the perceptions and experiences that motivated their actions or behaviour. Think of the community members who chased away the teachers in Example 15.2. Their behaviour was motivated by the feeling that the teachers did not respect what they were proud of.

- The community as a whole also consists of individuals and groups of people that form part of a larger environment or context. Change in one section of the community may affect the rest of the community. For example, if the women of a community become more empowered, this might threaten the men. It could also bring relief to the men, because they would no longer be the sole providers for their families. It might also allow men to move into women's roles, such as cooking and looking after children. Development efforts might also have a great impact on the physical environment. A bread-baking project using wood from the veld or a brick-making project using sand from a river could pose a threat to the environment. Good planning is required to find solutions to problems that do not simply create further problems.

Manfred Max-Neef, a Chilean economist and environmentalist, illustrates another dimension of holism or holistic thinking regarding development and change in communities. Max-Neef identified nine fundamental human needs that all people and communities experience. (We have added transcendance or spirituality to his original list, making ten fundamental human rights.) These fundamental human needs are all part of the whole human being. Max-Neef further indicated that poverty is usually measured in financial terms, but he maintains that it is possible to experience many different kinds of poverty. If any one of the segments or fundamental human needs is not met, the person or people concerned may experience poverty in that dimension.

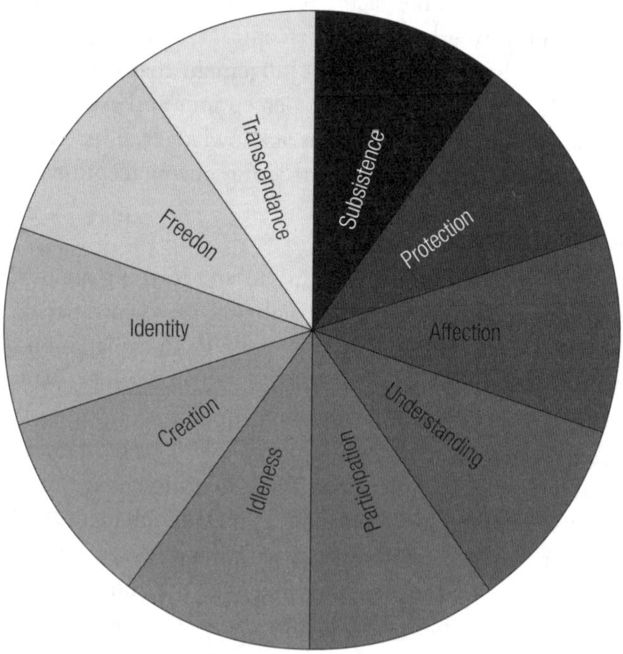

Max-Neef's holistic wheel of fundamental human needs

Each segment in this wheel can be seen as a need or an asset in the community. A short explanation of these fundamental human needs is given on the next two pages.

- Subsistence is the most fundamental form of need. This need exists where there is inadequate income (from work and employment), where there is not enough food, water or fuel, where a family or individuals do not have access to decent and affordable housing, where there is a degrading natural environment or where there is a lack of transport (Shiffman 1995: 2).
- The need for protection exists as a result of inadequate and unreliable protection systems against crime, unfair labour practices, inadequate health care, inadequate social security, or unjust limitations of freedom of movement, speech and association. Shiffman explains that lack of protection exists:

> *[w]hen poor sanitation and public health standards deteriorate to the point where disease is rampant, where access to health and medical services is limited, when violence and crime combine to imprison people in their own homes – that is if they have a home – or in any way limit their freedom.*
>
> [Shiffman 1995: 2]

- The need for affection exists as a result of lack of relationships. It also exists where people experience oppression, exploitation, authoritarian relationships or where they live in fear of retribution. Shiffman (1995: 2) also explains that people are poor when they are oppressed or fear retribution, when authoritarian governments ascend to power, or when people are exploited by a public or private sector that cannot be held accountable for its actions.
- The need for understanding exists as a result of poor education, lack of access to good education, or lack of recognition of innate knowledge, skills, wisdom and resources. Poverty of understanding owing to lack of education contributes to poverty of subsistence since people are not able to obtain employment (Shiffman 1995: 2).
- The need for participation exists as a result of social, economic (lack of work) or political exclusion or isolation, marginalisation or discrimination. The poverty of participation manifests as exclusion and isolation (Shiffman 1995: 3). Poverty of understanding can contribute to poverty of participation, and social and economic exclusion.
- The need for idleness, recreation or enjoyment ensues from the necessity to work constantly to survive, leaving people with little free time or relaxation that can result in peace of mind. Such poverty includes dismal and ongoing drudgery, hunger and struggle that offer no time for recreational rest or activity.
- The need for creation exists as a result of the lack of opportunity or choice to work, produce, design or invent. It is exacerbated when people help others without their participation.

> *Because man is a creator he does not want others to do things for him.*
>
> [Rahman 1993: 113]

- The need for identity exists as a result of the imposition of alien values, loss of language and customs, lack of social rhythms, forced migrations and exile, or lack of tolerance for diversity. All of this gives people a sense of not belonging. (It is interesting to see how the need for a sense of identity was demonstrated at an organised hiring site where Mexican day labourers gathered in Los Angeles. The men displayed their Mexican identity in different ways. For example, a small Catholic shrine was erected at the entrance to the site, Mexican arts and crafts were displayed and a Mexican woman sold tortillas to the men.)

- The need for freedom exists as a result of lack of security or protection, or lack of income, rights, self-determination or legal protection, for example, equal rights. The poverty of freedom exists when people do not experience equal rights, including the right of access to services.
- The need for transcendence or spirituality exists if the fact that people are spiritual beings is not recognised, their spirituality is not recognised or it is ridiculed, or they are prevented from expressing and maintaining their forms of ritual and religious affiliations. (Although Max-Neef sees spirituality as part of the identity, we believe it is a fundamental human need. We have made it a separate need because it is so important to many people, but it could also be seen as an aspect of understanding. The need for spirituality includes the need to believe in a god, spirit or ideology that guides our actions and thinking processes.)

According to Max-Neef, development and change efforts must facilitate as many of these areas as possible in order to be effective and sustainable. Affecting one area of the fundamental human needs may also have an impact on the other fundamental human needs.

This wheel of fundamental human needs is a helpful tool with which to explore all the aspects of a community's existence. When engaging with the people in the community, we discover many things about them. All of these things are linked to the fundamental human needs. The fundamental human need that relates to each thing we learn about the community is identified in brackets in the list below:

- How they survive physically (subsistence)
- Their safety or lack of safety (protection)
- Their relationships (affection)
- Their literacy levels and access to schooling and education, which assist the community members in understanding and reading the world (understanding)
- Their ability and opportunities to participate on different levels (participation)
- The opportunities that the people have to relax and rest (idleness)
- Their access to work and skills (creation)
- Their ability to live and display who they are (identity)
- Their ability to express themselves freely and make decisions (freedom)
- Their opportunity and freedom to practise their chosen form of spirituality (transcendance).

The wheel of fundamental human needs allows us to identify the needs or poverties that people in a community may experience. It also allows us to identify the assets and strengths they may have in all these dimensions. If a project focuses on fulfilling the fundamental human need for understanding by upgrading schools and education in a community, for example, but people cannot participate in decision-making or there are no democratic processes, a situation that results in uneasiness and discomfort may be created.

The wheel of fundamental human needs can also be used to explore people's unsymbolised perceptions and experiences, as people do not express themselves holistically. They usually focus on one or a few dimensions. Proposition 3 implies that we cannot look at the community as an entity consisting of isolated and unrelated components. Rogers stated:

> *The outstanding fact that may be taken into theoretical account is that the organism (community) is at all times a total organised system, in which alteration of any part may produce changes in any other part.*
>
> [Rogers 1987: 487]

Example 16.5

A local community had started to complain about day labourers (men waiting at the side of the road, hoping to be picked up for a day's work) in a South African suburb. The community felt that these men masked crime and were affecting the value of their properties, and demanded that the police remove the men. The police removed the men, but they were back at the side of the road the following day. Then social workers started to talk to the men. The men revealed that they mostly came from rural areas and other countries where poverty levels are high. They were unable to make enough money at home to look after their families. They came to this particular community because a nearby shop sold building materials and there was a lot of construction in the area, so they were occasionally able to get work. The building contractors paid fairly well and the local residents paid higher wages than other, less-affluent communities. At the same time, local churches that were concerned about the men had started providing them with food and most of the employers provided food to the men they employed. The day labourers had also befriended domestic workers in the area and so had access to certain basic facilities. The day labourers made friends with other day labourers and they all supported each other. If one man did not succeed in getting a job, then the others would support him by sharing their food and sometimes even their earnings for the day. It later emerged that the police even benefited from the day labourers by using them as informants about criminal and drug-smuggling activities in the neighbourhood.

Seen holistically, the community provided the ideal context in which the day labourers could survive. The community unknowingly created a context that fulfilled the men's needs.

Note that it would be short-sighted to see the labourers simply as people with a need for work (creation) without taking their other needs into account. They also have a need for subsistence (food and shelter) and understanding (skills and training), for example. Neglecting these needs would make any development attempts unsustainable. We also need to acknowledge their strengths and assets, such as their creativity in networking and accessing resources.

16.2.4 Proposition 5: Needs and behaviour

Proposition 5 reminds us that people's behaviour is always purposeful. The Northern Sotho saying '*Ngwana a sa llong a swela tharing*' means 'A child does not cry for nothing'. He cries because he is hungry, needs attention or is experiencing some form of discomfort. He cries to get attention from the caregiver for his needs. His behaviour is not seen as mad or bad, but as purposeful. Another Northern Sotho idiom that relates to this proposition is '*Manna o dira ka boomo*', meaning 'Man acts with intent'. This proposition takes a positive stance towards people's behaviour. It views behaviour as an attempt to achieve self-determination or self-actualisation.

Example 16.6

A mining company built a brick apartment building to house miners who had previously lived in shacks. However, it was not long before the miners moved out of the well-built apartment building and back into their shacks. From the outside, this seems odd and difficult to understand. The miners preferred to live in shacks made of corrugated iron instead of well-built brick apartments because this fulfilled their need to create a more rural atmosphere that fitted with the rural lifestyle they were used to. They also had more freedom and independence, as they did not have to abide by the rules and regulations of the mine's housing policies. They put their own system in place, fulfilling their needs for freedom, participation and identity.

When engaging with individuals and groups in the community, the facilitator sees the behaviour of the community as being purposeful and having intent. The facilitator explores the meaning and intention of this behaviour with members of the community in order to understand how they view it. The intention of the behaviour will emerge through the stories of the members of the community. This may set the stage for the next level, at which the facilitator deals with the unsymbolised experiences. The process of symbolising the unsymbolised experiences begins with the emergence of the intention of the community members' behaviour. Unsymbolised experiences may become symbolised as the people become aware of their actions.

The Guatemalan parents who chased the teachers away in Example 15.2 did not intend to harm the teachers. They simply needed to protect their own pride, values, culture and ways of caring for their children.

As facilitators, we reflect on our own behaviour and intent when working with people. We reflect on questions such as: 'Why do I want to help people?', and: 'What do I expect of people?' We ask ourselves: 'What do I want to achieve?', and: 'How do I want to benefit from my involvement with these people?' You may find that you are seeking to fulfil a need for praise, acknowledgement or to feel worthy. Understanding our intention and motivation helps us to be better facilitators. For example, a facilitator could either try to convince clients to take certain actions, or the facilitator could create a warm, safe space in which clients can develop. A facilitator could try to prove his or her own expertise to clients, or the facilitator could facilitate the process in such a way that clients discover for themselves how to change and develop. Awareness (symbolisation) of our own behaviour is crucial for us to be able to act congruently toward the people in the community.

16.2.5 Proposition 6: Emotions

This proposition is one of the most important propositions for the facilitator to remember when working with people in communities. According to Rogers, all behaviour is accompanied by emotions. When we experience an event, we also experience emotions about the event. We might experience emotions such as happiness, gladness, excitement, sadness, pleasure, discomfort and anger, for example. Emotions also differ in intensity. The level and intensity of the emotion will determine the actions of the people. In other words, the intensity of a person's emotions will determine how forcefully that person will act.

Paolo Freire confirmed this proposition and referred to the concept 'generative themes' in the community. By this, he meant that we should explore the experiences about which the community feels strongly. Freire refers to the direct link between emotion and motivation to act.

> *People in communities will only act upon something if they have strong emotions about it.*
>
> [Freire in Hope and Timmel 1995: 53]

People may sometimes mention something they have a need for, such as better roads or better schools, but if they do not express the issue with intense emotion, they may not be really motivated to do something about it or make an effort to change it.

Example 16.7

A social worker working with farm workers with the aim of informing them about HIV/Aids spent a lot of time with the workers listening to their stories, wishes, hopes and dreams. An aspect of their lives that they felt really strongly about was domestic violence, and the fighting and beatings that occurred among members of the community, especially when they had abused alcohol on the weekend. The women had had enough of this. HIV/Aids was not yet real for them. It did not make sense, as the women in this community were not in a position to refuse their husbands sex or ask them to use condoms. According to the women, the husbands had the power to beat them or chase them away if they refused sex, especially if the men were drunk. The women's experiences of being abused, voiceless and humiliated were stronger than their fear of HIV/Aids.

The issue about which a community feels strongly at a particular moment will most probably be the issue that community members would like to deal with immediately. This will already bring community members some understanding of themselves and their actions.

16.2.6 Proposition 10: Values of the community

People make decision based on their values. When engaging with people in communities, it is important to explore their values. In certain geographical communities, value systems have developed over many years. In newly formed communities, value systems are often what brought the people together. Values can be symbolised or unsymbolised. Symbolised values can be seen and heard. The people will display these values or talk about the values. Other values can be implicit and unsymbolised (the people are not aware of them). We will look at how these unsymbolised experiences can be explored and become symbolised in Chapter 17.

Here is an example in which the value system of a community was not respected.

Example 16.8

In a rural area in South Africa, houses were built for a community that had complained of a shortage of housing. The contract was given to an outside contractor who built formal, square houses with four rooms. The houses were allocated to families in the community, but nobody moved into them. When asked why the houses remained unoccupied, the members of the community explained that they usually build mud houses in circles. They build four mud houses linked together so that the extended family can live together and each wife can have her own hut if the husband has more than one wife. They could not identify with the square houses and they were too small for extended families to live together.

In the next example, the value system of the community was respected.

Example 16.9

In another rural area in South Africa, a company that was concerned by the high number of child-headed households wanted to build a children's home in the area. The local social worker discussed the issue with the community. The community stressed that the children's home must look like the other houses in the community so that the children living there would not be stigmatised or seen to be different from the community. The community was situated in an area that had previously been a homeland. The four-roomed matchbox houses like the one in the photo on page 205 had all been built during the apartheid era. The company built a children's home like this house so that it would fit in with the rest of the community.

[Photo: Rinie Schenck]

The children's home blended in with the rest of the community.

16.3 Important skills during this stage

The facilitator's most important skills during this stage are his or her communication skills. These skills include attending, listening and basic empathy, also referred to as 'testing understanding' (Rogers in Kirschenbaum and Henderson 1989: 128). To test understanding first requires good listening.

Good listening can take place in two ways:

- Unstructured listening
- Structured listening.

These ways of listening are discussed below.

16.3.1 Unstructured listening, attending and observing (listening with your eyes)

This kind of listening can take place in a variety of contexts, including in the street, at shebeens, in pubs, at meetings of various kinds and in people's homes. Unstructured listening involves listening to conversations that take place in contexts where people feel relaxed and able to talk about things that they are concerned about (Hope and Timmel 1995: 24). This means that the facilitator must spend as much time as possible in the community.

> ***Example 16.10***
>
> Louw (2002: 45) refers to an example where a community member made this comment about a facilitator who came to the community and started listening to them: 'Some time ago, a young woman showed up at the gathering place (the pay point for the aged) where we waited in long queues for our pensions. She listened to our complaints (what else is there to talk about?). Here was someone who made it her job to listen to old people's stories. We also started to listen more carefully to each other's stories.'

16.3.2 Structured listening

We create listening opportunities through different forms of group discussions. These include focus group discussions, nominal group discussions and learning circles (groups where activities are facilitated that help people to share their stories and experiences more freely). A variety of creative techniques exist to facilitate the community in sharing their perceptions and experiences (stories) of themselves and community life. Participatory learning techniques include:

- Mapping the community
- Writing plays, stories and poems reflecting what is happening in the community
- Creating drawings, murals, diagrams and songs that reflect what is happening in the community.

Example 16.11

A group of physically disabled people in a community wrote a play dramatising the problems that disabled people experienced with taxi drivers. Sometimes the drivers would not stop for long enough for them to get onto the taxi, for example. Some drivers exploited disabled people by asking them to pay double for their wheelchairs.

The play reflected the intensity of their feelings of powerlessness. This created stronger connections between the members of the group of disabled people and they decided to take action on the matter.

Example 16.12

A young man who had never dealt with his war experiences wrote the following poem about the experiences that still haunt him:

The echoes of war
forever pursuing me
in my dreams
when I am awake
I can hear the guns
Ever-present death
The thunder
Gnaws my soul
For how long?

[Batley 2007: 64]

Listening holistically means listening to all the dimensions of the community's needs (the fundamental human needs as identified by Max-Neef). It also means listening holistically in the sense of listening to the head (perceptions and experiences), the heart (feelings and emotions) and the feet (the actions and intentions of action) of the people.

The *Barefoot Guide* (2009: 30) explains the three aspects of listening as follows:

- Listening to the head implies listening to people's perceptions, thoughts, facts, ideas, beliefs and so on. The facilitator must listen non-judgementally to people's thoughts, perceptions and beliefs, showing interest in what and how they think, and in how they perceive the world.
- Listening to the heart means paying attention to the emotional level to establish how people feel about things. The facilitator can do this by paying attention to a person's tone of voice, facial expression, eyes and gestures. The facilitator will see and hear the intensity of the person's emotions.
- Listening to the feet of people means listening to their actions and what they want to achieve with these actions. The *Barefoot Guide* (2009: 30) refers to the will. The facilitator must decide what the intentions of people are, what motivates them and what they are trying to achieve. For example, if nobody in a community attends a meeting, the people are communicating something. In the same way, if the whole community attends a meeting, the action expresses an intention.

The *Barefoot Guide* (2009) indicates that we need to listen holistically (Proposition 3) to people's:

- Emotions and values (heart) – Proposition 6 and Proposition 10
- Behaviour and intentions (actions) – Proposition 5
- Experiences and reasoning (mind and reasoning) – Proposition 2 and Proposition 7.

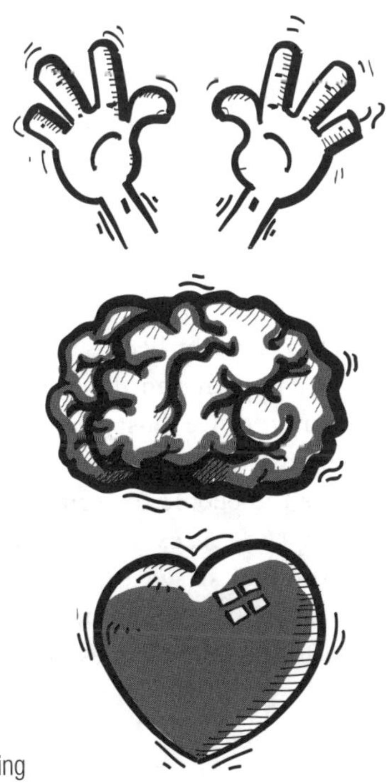

We need to listen to people's emotions, behaviour and reasoning

16.3.3 Empathy

Empathy means that the facilitator listens well and tests that he or she has understood what people have said. It is a skill or attitude that becomes part of the facilitator's being or self-structure, and is shown to all people in the community with whom the facilitator is in interaction. The facilitator adopts the position that he or she does not already know what people have to say. Instead of the facilitator imposing him- or herself and his or her ideas on people, the facilitator attempts to listen to what people say. The facilitator shows a willingness to learn from people. He or she also attempts to show understanding of their perceptions, experiences, emotions and actions. This is done by responding in a way that tests or checks the facilitator's understanding of what people have shared with him or her. Phrases such as: 'What I hear you say is ...', 'I can see this is very difficult for you, am I right?', 'That must have been hard ...', 'This must have been an exciting day ...', ' ... you feel so excited ...', 'Tell me if I heard you correctly ...', 'I can hear your insecurity', and: 'What I hear is unfairness ...?' invite the person to confirm or correct what the facilitator thinks he or she has heard and understood.

When the facilitator allows members of the community to correct him or her, shows a willingness to learn from people and listens to them, this demonstrates the facilitator's empathic way of being within the community. Good listening and empathy may already empower the people.

It may also happen that the facilitator hears mixed feelings and contradictory experiences at the same time. Both can be reflected back to the people.

Example 16.13

The principal of a school was suspended owing to mismanagement of money. The teachers reacted with anger, sadness and relief. They felt anger about the actions of the principal, sadness that they had lost a person with whom they had had a relationship and relief that the problem had at last been addressed.

Rogers (in Kirschenbaum and Henderson 1989: 128) moved away from the term 'reflection of feelings' when referring to empathy because this term encouraged people to use empathy in a mechanistic way. He preferred the term 'testing understanding'. So when we listen to people in a community, we must continually show them that we are trying to understand what they are telling us. This can be done by feeding back what we have heard in a way that allows the people to correct us if we do not understand it the way they do. We must attempt to see, experience and understand the world as they do. When we test our understanding of what people are telling us, they can hear we are actively involved and listening. It is important to listen without judgement, showing respect and appreciation for people's frames of reference and feelings about what is happening.

Example 16.14

An elderly lady in a community made the following comment about an empathic social-work student: 'She admired the plans that we made to stretch our budgets and how we survive. Somehow we realised that we had some dignity ... We started to enjoy the company that emerged out of her visits to Matjila (the village). She shared with us what she became aware of while talking and listening to us. We experienced that she cared about our nearly desperate situation. She also shared her admiration for our coping skills.'

As this quotation illustrates, empathy is not only about a technique, but about a way of being. The people of Matjila could feel the student's appreciation, her attitude, her listening and her attempt to understand them, and they experienced a feeling of dignity. Empathy is an effort to understand and respect the people holistically: their feelings, their ideas, their perceptions, their actions, their selves, their meaning and their values (Proposition 3 – wholeness) in all their dimensions.

16.3.4 Listening to the pain and the positives

Holistic listening means listening to people's pain and their positive feelings. Rogers (in Kirschenbaum and Henderson 1989: 71) explained that when the negative or painful feelings have been fully expressed, they might be followed by faint positive perceptions and experiences. These positive feelings (assets and strengths) can only be expressed if the painful experiences have been expressed and understood.

Helpers tend to move away from painful experiences expressed in the community. Sometimes it is difficult for the facilitator to listen to very painful stories, but they need to be heard and understood.

According to Rogers, the positives (assets and strengths) of the people and the community should be recognised and accepted, heard and understood in the same way as their negative or painful experiences and perceptions. The positives cannot underplay or negate their painful experiences and vice versa.

16.3.5 Minimal encouragers

Not all members of the community will or can speak freely and clearly. The facilitator can use some of the phrases listed below to encourage people to talk more, explain and be clear when sharing their stories. These encouragers assist the facilitator to empathise and understand better, and to feed back this understanding to the community more clearly.

- 'Tell me more about ...'
- 'I am not clear about ...'
- 'Elaborate please ...'
- 'What do your mean by ...'
- 'Help me to understand ...'
- '... and ...?'
- 'How come ...?'

In summary, we listen holistically during the process of dealing with symbolised experiences. We convey our understanding of what people are telling us and test this understanding through empathy. Basic empathy entails taking a not-knowing and not-assuming position. We listen to people's perceptions and experiences without judging them in an attempt to support and understand the people in the community.

An empathic attitude and understanding should be present throughout the facilitation process. Good listening and understanding will lead us to the next stage: facilitating the unsymbolised experiences.

CHAPTER

17 Facilitating unsymbolised experiences in the community (Phase 3)

17.1 Introduction

As discussed in Chapter 16, Phase 2 of the facilitation process starts when we explore the already-symbolised experiences of people holistically. It begins as they become aware of their frames of reference (head), emotions (heart) and intentions of their actions (feet), and as they start to understand their attempts at self-actualisation. Good listening to their pain (the things that people feel strongly about) and the positives (people's assets and capacities, hopes and dreams) can set the process of symbolising the unsymbolised experiences in motion. (Remember that good listening means that we convey our understanding of what people are telling us and test this understanding through empathy.) Facilitating the experiences that have already been symbolised may not necessarily facilitate the reconstruction of the self, but it does set the stage for symbolising the unsymbolised experiences and the reconstruction of the self. In the community context, it means we need to bring to the fore the things that people do not speak about, even though they are dominant issues in the community, and help them to make connections.

If a group makes decisions based on the already symbolised experiences, they might make decisions that are not really sustainable, as will be explained. Further and deeper exploration of the unsymbolised experiences (those experiences they are not aware of) is required. The focus of this section is to understand the process and skills used when facilitating the unsymbolised experiences with the community or with groups of people in the community. When dealing with the unsymbolised experiences in a group or a community, the group will need more trust in each other and the facilitator. This means going deeper and further 'under the water' (refer to the explanation of symbolised and unsymbolised experiences on pages 20–21 of Chapter 1) to bring the unsymbolised (unaware) experiences into the open.

The unsymbolised experiences are the experiences that are implied, but not spoken of or expressed. People may express their anger, but what they do not express is their experience of humiliation. They may express poverty, but not the experience of not having dignity. They may view their circumstances in isolation and not as part of a bigger whole or in a context (Freire).

Other authors use different terminology to express this idea that facilitators should look deeper and explore the unconscious, unsymbolised issues in a community before deciding on and planning projects in that community.

17.2 Max-Neef and need satisfiers

Max-Neef's description of needs and satisfiers might also help you to understand the difference between symbolised and unsymbolised experiences. According to Max-Neef (1991: 29), people express their needs in terms of satisfiers (a satisfier is the thing that will satisfy the fundamental human need that a person is experiencing) and not in terms of the fundamental human needs as discussed in Chapter 16. They will express having a need for a crèche, an income, skills training, support groups and so on, but according to Max-Neef, these so-called needs are actually satisfiers. In terms of Max-Neef's approach, people can only decide on the satisfier after they have identified the need as indicated in the wheel of fundamental human needs (see page 198).

People choose a particular satisfier by being aware of their context and the fundamental human need that they are experiencing. Identifying the fundamental human need allows them to identify which satisfier they wish to achieve. For example, food and shelter are satisfiers to the need for subsistence.

Max-Neef identified five satisfiers. The fundamental human need behind each satisfier is identified in brackets in the descriptions of these satisfiers below.

- Destroyers are also referred to as paradoxical satisfiers. A destroyer is supposed to satisfy one need, but it ends up destroying the community's ability to meet many other needs. For example, starting a baking project (satisfier) using wood from the land might destroy the ecology. It could destroy the environment that should have continued to sustain the community in the future (subsistence). Trees may also have spiritual significance for some communities, so using wood from trees for fuel may have an impact on the community's gathering places (need for affection).
- Pseudo satisfiers create a false sense of satisfaction. Examples include status symbols (identity) and prostitution (affection).
- Inhibiting satisfiers can prevent the fulfilment of certain other needs. For example, building walls around a house may satisfy a person's need for protection, but inhibit his or her need for freedom. A strong leader may satisfy a community's need for protection and identity, but stop people from taking responsibility and being creative (participation and freedom).

Example 17.1

A community expressed the need for strong leadership (satisfier) to take them into the future. The strong, charismatic leader that resulted inhibited the community's need for participation. The people were also prevented from creating their own identity because they were forced to adopt the identity and directions of the leader. This kept them dependent on the leader and stopped them from discovering their own abilities.

- Singular satisfiers only satisfy one need. The more needs are satisfied by the satisfier (project or actions), the more sustainable the project will be. Providing food (satisfier) may satisfy the need for subsistence, but it will not satisfy any other needs. On the other hand, creating jobs and training people may satisfy more than one need (subsistence, understanding, creation and protection).

- Sinergic satisfiers satisfy more than one need at the same time, as described in the previous point.

Max-Neef advocates that the facilitator reflect on and analyse the fundamental human needs of the community (the people's unsymbolised experiences). The facilitator can then investigate and decide on possible satisfiers that could satisfy more than one of these needs for the community (Hope and Timmel Book 1 1995: 86).

The activity that follows is an example of how to facilitate the symbolisation of unsymbolised experiences or how to become aware of the fundamental human needs in a community (Hope and Timmel Book 1 1995: 90).

Activity 17.1

1. Make sure you understand what is meant by the fundamental human needs as discussed in the previous chapter.
2. Clarify your understanding of needs and satisfiers.
3. Draw the wheel of fundamental human needs on a sheet of newsprint. Shade each section, indicating to what extent each of these needs is met in your own community. What is stopping the community from meeting this need?

This exercise facilitates the process of thinking deeper about the community, its context and the direction it should take by linking islands and bringing forward issues that have not previously been expressed. It brings out the issues that have been 'under the water'. This process is based on good listening and empathy.

Example 17.2

A rural community drew the wheel that follows in response to this exercise.

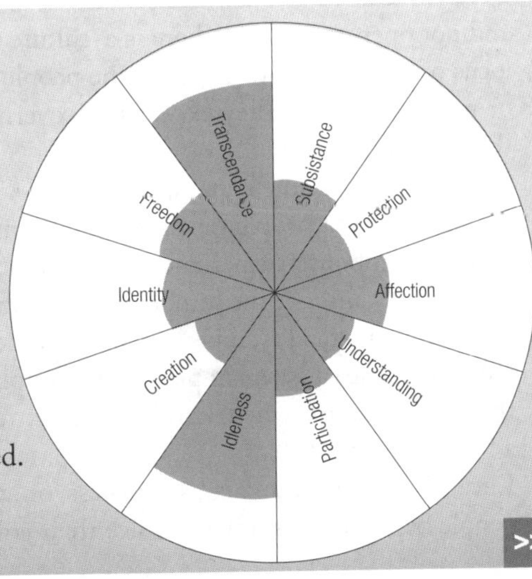

After completing the sketch of the wheel, the members of the group realised that it gave a very holistic representation of their community. They also realised that according to their sketch, only the community's spirituality dimension was fully satisfied. Critical questions arose during the discussion on how the strength of the

>>

spirituality could be used to support the other needs and why there was so much crime in the community if it was such a religious community. Note that in this example, the high level of the idleness dimension indicated too much idleness as a result of the high level of unemployment in the community.

The use of the wheel of fundamental human needs and the idea of focusing on needs instead of satisfiers led Freire to develop the concept of the critical-awareness process.

17.3 Freire's process of conscientisation

Freire refers to the process of symbolisation as the process of becoming aware, or the 'conscientisation' process. According to Freire, conscientisation is the process of critical reflection by people on their own world, perceptions and realities. This explanation helps us to understand how the symbolisation process described by Rogers takes place within communities.

The process of conscientisation should not be confused with the concept 'awareness-raising'. These are two totally different concepts. Awareness-raising is when we have an awareness day or an awareness campaign to make people aware of the consequences of something, for example, HIV/Aids or the importance of using clean water to avoid contracting cholera. Conscientisation, on the other hand, implies facilitating a process where people become aware of their context and what processes are taking place in their community.

The process of becoming aware that was illustrated in Example 17.2 is a good example. It requires a much more critical thinking-and-reflecting process by the people of the community, with good listening and empathy from the facilitator. Good listening helps the facilitator to pick up themes and implied messages.

Hope and Timmel (1995:78–79), who based their work on the ideas of Freire, identified four levels of conscientisation or awareness in the process of change in communities:

- Level 1 – Closed (broken) consciousness or awareness: Here the community is closed and not open to change. There is a 'culture of silence' (see page 215) and an external locus of control. In other words, the people believe that events are caused by outside or magical powers. They expect the government or outsiders to solve problems for the community.
- Level 2 – Awakening consciousness or awareness: There are signs of limited change, for example, the people develop an awareness of inequality and injustice. They deal with the symbolised experiences (like symptoms such as alcohol abuse, poverty, crime or satisfiers) and not the implied or unsymbolised experiences (such as hopelessness, destitution, inequality, injustices or the fundamental human needs). They will probably put single satisfiers in place, for example, a soup kitchen or handouts. (Note that there are instances where handouts are extremely important and necessary as part of a broader plan.)
- Level 3 – Reforming consciousness or awareness: Collective actions start. The people begin to question and voice their concerns. The desire for self-determination

emerges. People want to rely on their own reserves and resources. They start to take responsibility for their own situation (internal locus of control) (Proposition 18).
- Level 4 – Liberating and transforming consciousness or awareness: New relationships develop. The people question their old values and develop new values (Proposition 19).

Freire said that people are able to 'read the world' through this conscientisation process. They will base their actions on their understanding of their world and their circumstances. This understanding will assist them in taking responsibility for reconstructing their selves and their world. The locus of control resides within the people.

Freire developed the term 'culture of silence' to describe the tendency for people living in poverty and under oppression to become quiet and passive. They expect outsiders or other people to provide assistance and leadership (Level 1 awareness) and blame their situation on others. All responsibility is placed in the hands of the oppressor or the dominant group. The people do not question their existence or the processes that are happening. They adopt the values of the oppressor or dominant group, and do not appreciate their own values. They might even believe that their own values are not good enough. They do not own the issues in the community and wait for outsiders to solve them (external locus of control). The symbolisation or conscientisation process is therefore a very important process that needs to take place if real change of the self-structure is to commence. As seen in the description of the levels of awareness, it is a process. It takes time to facilitate the awareness of the people from one level to the next level.

The use of minimal encouragers and different creative techniques can facilitate this process of conscientisation or awareness. These creative techniques can include the use of community drama, murals, singing, community walks and codes (for example, pictures). Attwood (2007: 7) described how she used the construction of a seasonal gender workload calendar with a group of men and women in Lesotho. The calendar gave the men and women of the community the opportunity to discuss issues such as what it meant to be a man or a woman, cultural attitudes and cultural practices.

The process of awareness or becoming conscious is also a process of appreciation for the self of the group or the community. The members of the community will develop an appreciation for the skills, culture and knowledge of the individuals that make up the community as they become aware of these skills, culture and knowledge. The facilitator focuses on the development of this appreciation.

17.3.1 Facilitating a process of appreciative inquiry

The needs and the processes within the community (what is) are explored during the awareness or conscientisation process. The process includes the members of the community developing an appreciation of themselves, their skills, their values and their knowledge (Proposition 18 and Proposition 19). The process of appreciative inquiry explores what the people have, what they have achieved, how they have survived, how they have managed to this point, how they have dealt with issues in the past, what resources they have, what skills and capacities exist in the community and so on. Chambers (1978 and 1983) believed that the people's unique knowledge and skills should be discovered and appreciated. Their skills, knowledge and values may be different from ours and they are experts in their own right. They can do things and they know things that the facilitator might not do or know about. The dignity and worthiness of the people are enhanced as they became aware of their assets, skills and knowledge. Meyers (1999: 175) proposed that the facilitator focus on appreciative questions and encouragers, and on the discovery of what enriches the life of the community.

Here is an example of the difference in the quality of information obtained when the facilitator explores an issue using appreciative inquiry.

Example 17.3

During research on child-headed households (Gauteng DSD 2008: 43–140), the children were asked two questions:

1 What are your needs as a child-headed household? (This is a problem-focused question.)

2 What has enabled you to survive as a child-headed household? (This question uses appreciative inquiry.)

The children gave the following answers:

Answers to Question 1 (question focused on needs)	Answers to Question 2 (appreciative inquiry)
• 'No one cares for us or tells us if we are doing right or wrong' • 'Other people take advantage of us and abuse us because we stay alone' • 'We are poverty-stricken and we struggle every day to survive' • 'No one helps me' • 'I have to study by candlelight and that is difficult'	• 'With the help of the neighbours things are not so bad' • 'My little siblings respect me' • 'With the help of a friend I am able to survive hard times' • 'My younger sister is cooperative and we share the responsibilities' • 'I go to church often' • 'This teaches me to have guts' • 'Being part of a child-headed household taught me how life is and to be responsible' • 'We get donations from school and church' • 'The community helps us'

The quality of the answers is vastly different. The answers to the second question tell us how the children are supported by the community and that they are able to network.

Appreciative inquiry facilitates awareness and co-creates new perspectives with the community. The co-creation of new stories and new perspectives helps to mobilise and reactivate the community in new directions. If these new stories fit the self-structure of the community, community members' perceptions of themselves, their actions and their emotions will change. For example, the children in child-headed households will realise that they can network and that they know how to survive.

The example that follows illustrates the process of dealing with unsymbolised experiences in a community.

Example 17.4

A social worker was approached to assist a farm school situated just outside a city. The farm owner, a woman, really cared about the school and was dedicated to its functioning. She formed a trust from which the school's funds were augmented. Many township parents who were unhappy with city schools took their children to the farm school. They felt it was safer and that the children would get a better education as the teachers were more dedicated. As a result, the learners were a mixture of children from the surrounding farms and children from the nearby townships.

Some of the families were very poor and their children went to school hungry. The school originally asked a local soup kitchen to provide food to the children as they came to school hungry (need for subsistence). The feeding scheme at the school went on for three years. The teachers at the school realised that they should not be dependent on the soup kitchen. They decided that they should embark on a vegetable garden project (needs for subsistence, creation and understanding) that would provide food for their own soup kitchen and educational opportunities for the children. When the facilitator discussed the issue of a possible food garden with the principal of the school, he mentioned many obstacles that stood in the way of maintaining a vegetable garden. He said that there was no running water, there was no fertiliser, the land was not fenced off and so on. In other words, he did not support the creation of a vegetable garden.

According the principal, the parents needed education and literacy classes (satisfiers to understanding and creation) to be able to access work, and look after and feed their children. The farm owner again confirmed that the vegetable garden (satisfier) was a need and said that she would provide the fences and the fertiliser. The principal was still not happy. He felt that the garden would become his responsibility during holidays as the parents and children stayed far away from the school. He could not see how it could be viable. At this point, the facilitator was still dealing with the symbolised experiences of the farm owner and the principal.

The facilitator then decided to find out what was important to the children. The teachers asked the children to make drawings of their 'needs'. The children misinterpreted the request to draw their 'needs' for the school as their 'wants' for the school, as the meaning of the word was not discussed. The children drew things like school clothes, a swimming pool, and heaters and television sets for the classrooms.

>>

The facilitator then realised that when she asked what the children's needs were (focused on the problem) without first discussing and exploring what this implied, and questioning their understanding about it, she would only be told about their wants and need satisfiers. She then started to conduct in-depth discussions with the teachers and parents. She took with her a colleague who could understand the language of the people well. This enabled her to develop a clear understanding of what the parents and teachers were saying, to convey her understanding to the people and to avoid misunderstandings. The issues that emerged then were totally different from the original 'wants' that the children had raised. The parents had lots of appreciation for the safe environment the school created for the children. However, they started to question what was going on at the school. They asked why teachers were not always in their classrooms, why some teachers swore at the children. They mentioned problems with the bus services, the poor condition of the school toilets and so on. The teachers expressed their concern that parents were not involved in their children's work and not interested in the school activities.

At the same time, the facilitator got the children to write plays and draw pictures to illustrate the issues that concerned them about the school. The plays revealed what was good about the school, but they also illustrated that there were some problems between the staff and the children. For example, children complained that teachers were not always in their classrooms, but were attending to other matters instead of teaching. They also expressed their concern that their parents did not participate in the management of the school.

After much discussion, the parents realised that they needed to get involved in the school and accept more responsibility for the education of their children. They formed a school governing body and other structures through which they could raise their concerns. They took responsibility for what was happening at the school and with their children's education.

Over time, the group of parents, teachers and children addressed many issues to improve the quality of the school. These included guidelines for the teachers so that they knew what was expected of them. The problems with transport and buses were resolved. Parents and teachers became members of the trust fund that was started for the school by the farm owner.

Note the development of the following aspects in this example:

- The parents, teachers and children did not view or construct themselves as a community, but this process made them all into a community – the community of 'mind'.
- The process of communicating with the teachers, parents and children in a variety of ways facilitated the unsymbolised experiences in different ways and facilitated the reconstruction that took place. The school community changed from being a dependent school community to being a school community that took responsibility for its own matters (internal locus of control). The staff, children and parents now all

identify themselves with the school and do not blame each other for what is happening or not happening at the school. During the discussion, all members of the school community developed a better understanding and appreciation for each other. They now decide together on the issues that need to be tackled to improve the school.

- The process in which they became involved offered the members of the community the opportunity to develop and discover new dimensions of their selves as a community, but also as individuals. In the process, the parents became aware that they had the ability to negotiate, they experienced dignity and they realised that they were caring parents. The aim of the project was to improve the quality of schooling for the children, but it also allowed the reconstruction of the parents and teachers as a school community.

Some members of the school community might decide at a later stage to take on the original project of establishing a vegetable garden. Their motivation might be to provide food to those who need it, to provide an educational facility for the children and to build the school community by involving parents and teachers. They would build a sense of community by working together in the food garden and by preparing food for the children together (affection). The purpose would now be different. The garden would feed the children (subsistence), assist the children and improve the quality of their schooling (understanding) (Van den Berg 1997).

It is important to note the nature of the involvement of the facilitator in this example. The facilitator was not a passive onlooker. Throughout the project, she actively reflected the experiences and feelings of the community, and asked critical questions. She used encouragers, activities and creative techniques to explore the experiences and feelings of the community more deeply. ('How come …', 'For whom is this also important?', 'Who are we going to invite?', 'Can you tell me more about this …?') However, she did not direct or advise. The members of the school community had to find their own answers and direction. This process required active preparation and planning from the facilitator.

Let us look at another example.

Example 17.5

A women's club in a poor rural community became very concerned about the care given to disabled children in the community. They decided to start a care centre for these children in a two-roomed mud house. The caregivers donated some food and requested the parents of the disabled children to contribute to the centre. They call it the *'Tsoga O Iterele'* ('Wake up and do things for yourself') centre. The local social worker was so impressed by the women's motivation and enthusiasm that she helped them to apply for money from a government poverty-alleviation fund. The money allowed them to move into a better house and offer better facilities (subsistence, identity and protection for the children). The women asked the social worker to help them develop the project into a sustainable care centre. At first, the women listed many things that they felt they needed for the care centre. The facilitator

>>

actively facilitated sessions in which the women used brainstorming and techniques such as community walks. As a result of these sessions, the women realised that they would be able to run the centre on their own if they acquired certain skills. They had done very well in establishing the centre with the limited resources available to them, but to make it sustainable they had to fill the gaps in their own skills, abilities and access to resources. The focus shifted from the children to the group of women (Ntsoane 2000). In the end, they realised that the project facilitated their own development and growth as people and caregivers (it fulfilled their needs for subsistence, identity, understanding and creation).

17.3.2 Proposition 15: Reconstructing the self

Example 17.4 and Example 17.5 attempted to illustrate the facilitation process in which people's unsymbolised experiences and perceptions are symbolised. The individuals in the groups and the groups themselves based their decisions and direction of planning on what they wanted to change and how they wanted to change it, according to their newly symbolised experiences. (Bringing the unsymbolised experiences to the surface is not instant or easy. It is the result of a gentle process of exploring the unexpressed and unconscious experiences.) The decision to start with a certain project was based on good, thorough exploration and reflection. The process of symbolisation will continue during the implementation of the project. The individuals in the group and the group itself will be able to reconstruct themselves. The behaviour or actions of the people in the group are based on newly symbolised experiences. These newly symbolised experiences, which are sometimes still painful, become part of the self of the individuals and group.

This implies that the people in the community will develop new perceptions of themselves. For example, they may come to see themselves as concerned parents, competent caregivers or good teachers (identity). They will be aware of the intentions (we want to do the best for our children) for their behaviour. The people will be accountable for and aware of the emotions that accompany their behaviour (identity). They will express these emotions. They will be able to verbalise their experiences and perceptions in the here and now. They will be able to view what is happening in the community critically and in context. They will take responsibility for their decisions and actions (participation and internal locus of control). They will experience that they have made their own changes (participation – 'We did it ourselves') and their own decisions (participation and freedom). They may be involved in projects that create an income (subsistence), and where they decide for themselves, plan and execute the plan (freedom, participation and creation). They may be involved in projects that allow them to learn new skills (understanding) and care for the environment (subsistence). They may experience belonging to a [illegible] (affection), and feel that they are valued and better parents for their children [illegible]ce, affection and identity).

[illegible] 2002) gives an example of the self-actualisation and reconstruction process as [illegible]e in a group of diabetes patients in a community.

Example 17.6

The facilitator met the diabetic patients when she visited the local clinic. They came to the clinic on a weekly basis to receive their medication and attend lectures, which they perceived as boring, on how to manage their diabetes. The patients shared with the facilitator that the nurse was very rude to them. The information given to them about the food they were supposed to eat was of no use to them because they were poor, and could not afford the food and vegetables prescribed by the nurse. They felt disregarded by her as she knew that they were poor. The facilitator spent a great deal of time listening as the diabetic patients recounted their stories of being diabetic (pain), not being able to work, not being able to buy vegetables and not having access to cheaper vegetables. After many sessions, the patients decided to start a vegetable garden (satisfier). They felt that a vegetable garden would satisfy their need for healthy vegetables (subsistence), would provide an income (subsistence) and would give them the opportunity to get the physical exercise that they needed. It would also allow them to work (creation), to work together (affection) and it would give them a name (identity). They expressed their excitement about the process and the fact that nobody had prescribed what they should do, but that they had been able to determine their own process (freedom and participation). During the appreciative process, they also discovered enough skills and expertise to be able to start the garden.

The process developed faster than the facilitator could attend to. Without her knowledge, the diabetic patients negotiated the use of a local school's land (participation, identity and freedom). With the facilitator's help, they sent a proposal requesting help with ploughing the land and drilling a borehole (understanding) to the Department of Agriculture. They worked in the garden on a daily basis (creation). As a result, they felt good about themselves (identity). They opened their meetings with prayers (spirituality). They sold some of the vegetables (subsistence) and took some of the vegetables for themselves (subsistence). They ate the vegetables to help their bodies handle the diabetes (protection and subsistence). They managed their own meetings (participation) and planned their own working schedules (freedom and participation, understanding and creation). The MEC for Agriculture came to visit their project and gave them a certificate acknowledging their efforts (identity). They were self-driven and the facilitator became redundant. The project had elements of sustainability, but the people were able to reconstruct themselves from helpless, frustrated people to people who took the management of the illness in their own hands (internal locus of control). They also relabelled diabetes as a 'condition' instead of an illness or a disease (reframing). Their perception of themselves and of the illness changed, and their actions changed. The people changed from being passive recipients of medication to being active managers of their own condition. They discovered their ability to negotiate and to be acknowledged. The unintended change took place on more than one level (wholeness).

>>

This does not suggest that the people will never experience problems again. However, the next time they encounter a problem, they will approach it knowing what they have already learnt and achieved. They will probably be able to deal with new problems more easily.

17.3.3 Proposition 18: Acceptance of self and others

The individual and the group now experience their competencies, gain confidence, learn skills, express themselves and feel empowered. They will discover what they may be able to do now. The result is the process of acceptance of themselves and others as people. They will come to understand that other people may have different realities and experiences from them, but they will no longer feel threatened by these different realities and experiences.

This proposition is extremely important in this phase. If we facilitate the process in such a way that the people we are working with experience failure and are not empowered, then we are working contrary to the principles of the person-centred approach. In some instances, facilitators start projects with the best intentions, but if the members of the community who are involved in the project do not learn to value themselves and do not feel able to participate, they will not have symbolised their own unsymbolised experiences. They will not be able to accept themselves or others.

Nobody can promise that a project will be successful, but it is essential to facilitate the process in such a manner that the people concerned gain and learn about themselves, even if the project itself is not a success. When the people involved have symbolised and accepted most of their experiences, values, needs and behaviour, then they will be able to appreciate others.

This proposition is also important for the facilitator. The reflection process about our own unsymbolised experiences is important when we are working with people. The facilitator needs to accept his or her self and the selves of others in order to be able to deal with differences and different realities.

This is also a significant proposition for communities. If we can really facilitate this acceptance of self and others, then people will not be afraid of each other or hate each other. They will understand each other or attempt to understand and accept each other as people with different points of view. They will be able to listen to themselves and to deal with symbolised issues constructively.

17.3.4 Proposition 19: Developing your own value system

This proposition explains that adopted values are now replaced with internal home-grown values and actions that are indigenous to the community. The members of the community have discovered their own values. They can now value and appreciate themselves and their own values. They now take ownership of their projects and proudly show them off to others. They may, for instance, invite their sponsors, other community members or their traditional or political leaders to come and see what they have achieved. At this stage, the members of the community will be ready to continue on their own and the facilitator can leave or terminate with the people. According to Swanepoel (1992: 3–4), growth, development and empowerment have occurred through the learning process that took place in the community, causing the people to become self-sufficient, to develop self-esteem and to maintain their own values. They no longer look to other people as the experts and can build networks to access resources on their own. They value their own skills and knowledge.

The aim of change is for people to actualise themselves. They do this by working through their uncomfortable feelings, dissatisfactions and experiences with the help of the facilitator until they are able to acknowledge their experiences, reconstruct their selves, and appreciate and value themselves (symbolisation) (Tolan 2003: 7).

The symbolisation or conscientisation process is a subtle and gradual process. It is the process during which a person re-experiences and resymbolises his or her self-structure. It involves loosening the self-structure to accommodate previously denied or distorted experiences (Tolan 2003: 11). If experiences are not symbolised, they are blocked somewhere in the person's self, waiting for the moment when they can be freed. The importance of the skill of advanced empathy comes in here. We use advanced empathy when we name the experience and give it new meaning.

Example 17.7

Let us return to the rural community (Du Plessis 2002: 82) where the men drank and physically abused their wives. If the facilitator addressed the drinking problem on its own by discussing alcohol abuse and the problems of being poor, only the already-symbolised experiences would be dealt with. If, however, he or she facilitated the symbolisation or conscientisation process and allowed the men to deal with their experiences of hopelessness, disempowerment and the feeling of not having a future, then the facilitator would be helping them to symbolise their unsymbolised experiences. The men would look at what they have and what they have achieved despite their circumstances. They would realise what they have learnt and how knowledgeable they are, and plan according to their assets how to proceed and act towards self-actualisation. They would probably embark on processes that they can manage and control themselves without expecting the farmer or the government to improve their situation (internal locus of control). The entire project will be planned in a manner that encourages participation. The implementation process will be a learning-action-reflection process until the men have reconstructed their experience of themselves, and they accept and value themselves and others (Proposition19).

If we do not attend to the unsymbolised experiences, no change will take place. A person who had experienced a traumatic incident wrote the following to indicate what happens when the unsymbolised issues are not symbolised: 'Sometimes memories will just surface like sewage bubbles up through the manhole of a blocked drain bypassing some kind of valve that should keep them hidden in your deepest sub-conscious where they fester and rot and mingle ...'

Unsymbolised experiences in communities emerge in symptoms like crime, disrespect for others, anger, hopelessness, apathy, and high levels of drug and alcohol abuse.

The table that follows (adapted from Tolan 2003: 116) summarises the process of change. It explains the direction of change within people. This direction of change summarises the processes in Proposition 15, Proposition 18 and Proposition 19, and describes the end result of our development efforts with communities.

From ...	To ...
1. Rigidity (not open to experiences)	1. Fluidity (open to experiences)
2. External locus of control, blaming others ('The government should provide ...', 'This is how the world is ...')	2. Internal locus of control, taking and accepting responsibility for own thoughts and actions, aware and owning the constructs ('This is how I perceive the world ...')
3. Believing in the truth ('This is a fact ...')	3. Accepting and appreciating other constructs and realities
4. Fearing feelings	4. Accepting and 'naming' feelings, both painful and positive
5. Expressing experiences and feelings in the past	5. Able to experience and express feelings in the here and now
6. Not believing in own ability to change	6. Welcoming own capacity for change
7. Living according to other's values ('I need this car/house/dress to be accepted') (Proposition 10)	7. Living according to own values, clear about and proud of own values (Proposition 10)
8. Judgmental	8. Accept self and others; less judgemental
9. Fearful of the unknown and change	9. Unthreatened by changed circumstances
10. Wanting quick fixes	10. Working towards long-term solutions
11. Preferring rules and structures	11. Preferring flexibility
12. Set or fixed ideas about meaning	12. Searching for meaning
13. Predictable and constrained	13. Spontaneous and creative
14. Judging success or failure	14. Believing in growth through experience (embracing mistakes)
15. Preferring distance	15. Allowing closeness (affection)

17.4 Skills used to facilitate the process of symbolisation

The basic conditions for facilitation and the basic skills for facilitating communication (for example, listening and empathy) are all necessary for the process of symbolisation or conscientisation. During the earlier phases of the process, the facilitator reflected on the experiences (heart – Proposition 6), perceptions (head – Proposition 2 and Proposition 7) or actions (Proposition 5). The focus was on the basic skills, as they help the facilitator to understand people and processes in the community, and to convey this understanding to the community. As indicated earlier in this chapter, a variety of advanced skills can be used to help members of the community to bring implied or unsymbolised experiences to the surface, to make links between heart, head and actions, to reflect critically, and to connect patterns and generative themes (experiences about which the community feels strongly). Examples of creative advanced skills include the use of the wheel of fundamental human needs, mapping, creating drawings, and writing and presenting plays. The facilitator listens deeply and holistically to be able to link the heart, head and action, or hear the themes that emerge in the community, and assist members of the community to reflect on their own situations.

Think about Example 17.4. Originally, the children, parents and teachers addressed issues linked to poverty and the hunger that the children experienced. When the facilitator started using advanced skills to listen more deeply, the generative themes emerged, indicating concern about the quality of the education. The parents' concerns about their responsibility for and involvement with their children's schooling and their own development also emerged. Feeding the children became part of a bigger project to improve the schooling that they received.

17.4.1 Advanced empathy and immediacy: Conveyors of the unsymbolised experiences

These skills have already been discussed in detail in Section A of this book and will only be reflected on briefly here in terms of their use when working with communities. The skills facilitate the symbolisation of the unsymbolised experiences. The facilitator uses advanced empathy and immediacy to convey his or her understanding of these unsymbolised experiences.

When using basic empathy, the facilitator reflects their already-symbolised experiences back to the members of the community. The facilitator strives to make the people feel deeply understood (Martin 1983: 3). Advanced empathy attempts to bring to the surface the implied messages and make the connections (connecting islands) between issues, practices, behaviour and so on, so that the person can see the whole picture. In many instances, the members of the community will be able to make the connections themselves. An example of the facilitator finding the implied message or connection can be seen in Example 17.4. The facilitator listened holistically by listening to the children, the teachers, the parents and the farm owner (supplier of funds), and noted that they were all deeply concerned about the education of the children. To address only the need for food would have been to address only one aspect (single satisfier) of the children's education. All the role-players expressed the same concern in different ways.

The concept 'immediacy' implies three aspects: closeness, transparency and the here and now (the immediate present). Immediacy refers to the relationship between or amongst the people in the community, and between the community and the facilitator in the here and now (the immediate present). With this skill, the facilitator can reflect and symbolise the relationship between him- or herself and the community in the here and now.

Why is immediacy such an important skill? The aim of using immediacy is to strengthen and clarify the relationship with the people, not to destroy the relationship. However, relationships between members of the group, and between the group and the facilitator can become troubled during the facilitation process. For example, issues of trust might hinder the facilitation process. Sub-groups, political aspirations and individual aspirations could present obstacles. A leader in the community could start dominating the process, preventing the participation of the rest of the group. Suspicions of abuse of funding could develop. Political leaders might try to take over the projects to enhance their own reputations.

Immediacy is one of the most helpful skills when working in a community as it helps the facilitator to symbolise the relationship processes between the participants. The facilitator can use self-based statements ('I ... in the here and now.') to indicate that he or she speaks for and on behalf of him- or herself and nobody else. The facilitator always starts the sentence by referring to him- or herself ('I ...'). He or she owns the statement (internal locus of control).

For example, it may happen that the facilitator experiences problems with the process or the project. The facilitator can phrase his or her response by saying: 'It seems to me that not everybody is happy with where we are going with this process.' The facilitator may experience frustration with the pace of the project: 'I am a bit concerned about the pace of the project. It seems as if everybody is not moving in the same direction, and that makes people anxious. I may be wrong.'

Note that the facilitator takes responsibility for his or her concern or frustrations, and conveys the message tentatively. The members of the group may not have the same view and may wish to differ from the facilitator. This statement also empowers the members of the group as it invites them to guide or inform the facilitator.

Another example could be if the facilitator detected some mistrust within the group. He or she could address the issue by saying: 'I am not sure if I am experiencing this correctly. I am not sure that everybody trusts me and each other. What can we do in this group to develop trust amongst each other?'

Read Example 17.8, paying attention to the tentativeness with which the facilitator phrases her response. This allows for the people to differ with her as facilitator and express their points of view.

Example 17.8

A teacher in a poor semi-rural informal settlement was approached to act as facilitator for a group of local women who had started a crèche in the community. The teacher helped the women to work out daily programmes and stimulation activities for the children. She experienced some difficulties with the group of women in the early stages of the project.

In the first few weeks, the facilitator was constantly met with complaints like: 'The mealiemeal/chicken/rice/sugar is finished.' She sensed that the group members felt that the food was not well managed and was probably abused by the cook. The cook felt that she was not trusted by the group. Some of the parents even accused the cook of using the gas and food for her own family. The facilitator called a meeting and expressed her uneasiness with what was happening in the group. She was careful to use a turn of phrase that would encourage the women to express their opinions: 'I am very concerned about what is happening in the group. I may be wrong, but this is how I see what is happening here ...' She then explained her understanding.

During the community meeting, the group addressed the issue of trust in the group and decided that the best way to deal with the issue was to keep the food locked up. They decided to ration the food, changing the menu from two full meals per day to one meal at midday. They also switched to cheaper meals that were easier to prepare, and used more fresh fruit and vegetables. What was amazing about the process in the group was that they all took responsibility for the issue with the food and did not leave the problem for one person to resolve. This strengthened the relationship between the members of the group, and the relationship between the facilitator and the members of the group. It also made the processes more transparent.

Phase 3 is a complex process. It is impossible to predict how long it will take and how it will end. The focus is not on the type of project (food garden, crèche or income generation, for example) that will be facilitated, but how the person-centred process of change will evolve. Each development effort has it own unique process. We have illustrated the theoretical explanation, the direction and end result that a person-centred development effort should take as described in Proposition 15, Proposition 18 and Proposition 19.

17.5 Phase 4: Termination or the process of disconnection with the community

The termination with the community can be a difficult and complex process. The termination process will not be discussed in detail in this book as it is discussed in many books describing the development process, but it is important to reflect on some aspects of the person-centred approach.

In some communities, if the process develops well, the facilitator will gradually become redundant. The people of the community will take over the process and manage it themselves. They will celebrate their achievements and terminate with the facilitator.

However, in some instances, the facilitator may not be able to continue the process with the community for one reason or another. For example, the facilitator might leave his or her organisation, be transferred to a different area or be promoted. The principle to remember about termination is to leave in a gradual, respectful and ethical manner, and to see that structures are in place for the process and project to continue until it will be able to stand on its own feet. Handing over the community to another facilitator is a sensitive process. The new facilitator needs to build relationships with the community. He or she needs to create trust and the basic conditions for change from scratch. Relationships cannot be transferred from one person to another person. Each facilitator creates his or her own safe space for the community.

Termination does not necessarily mean the ending of a relationship, but it involves the creation of distance and space to allow the community to continue on its own. The facilitator can still show interest, share ideas if consulted or assist when required.

O' Leary (1989) said that in formulating the person-centred approach described in this book, Rogers had developed a powerful method for creating second-order change. Second-order change is change that involves a significant shift in the cognitive framework (perceptions), habitual behaviour (action) and experiences (feelings) of an entire system. (See also Max-Neef's fundamental human needs). First-order change, on the other hand, refers to a shift in one particular behaviour and does not really have an effect on the rest of the system. Working with the symbolised and unsymbolised experiences facilitates this second-order change process.

According to the person-centred approach, change does not mean solving problems for people or that people will never feel bad again. It means that people who have been through the process of facilitation during which their unsymbolised experiences were symbolised will experience their feelings in all their intensity, whether those feelings are welcome or not. The difference is that they will now acknowledge and express the feelings. Experiences will not be denied or distorted, but managed. People will take control and responsibility, and do something about a problem themselves. They will have internal locus of control ('We can do it ourselves'). They will not wait for people from the outside to deal with the problem. They will be able to manage it or become part of the process of changing the situation if they feel strongly about it. They will be free to respond to their own inner actualising tendency, and not be restricted by the views and beliefs of others. They will be controlled by their own values and not live up to the expectations of others. They will not make their self-worth dependent on others so that they experience only conditional positive regard. They will be able to accept themselves and others.

The theoretical base of the person-centred approach gives the facilitator an anchor (Tolan 2003: 16) and guides his or her actions so that facilitation takes place in an ethical and accountable manner. The facilitator knows how to think about people and communities, and what conditions must be created to start the process of change. Within this safe context, people will be able to explore their own experiences and perceptions, alter their self-structure and move towards self-actualisation.

SECTION

D

Some special considerations

We are often asked if the person-centred approach can and will work under all circumstances. While it is not possible to give a guarantee, we have found the approach to be useful in most situations. However, it is not without problems.

We would like to share some of our ideas and practical experiences with you. We would appreciate any comments, experiences, examples and criticism for and against the approach.

In the next three chapters, we will try to demonstrate how the thinking, attitudes and communication skills (both basic and advanced) discussed in the previous chapters can be implemented in specific circumstances. We will look at issues related to:

- Cross-cultural encounters between people
- Conflict situations between people
- The self of the facilitator.

CHAPTER

18 Cross-cultural communication

18.1 Introduction

It is not the objective of this discussion to provide information about different cultures, but only to put down some person-centred ideas (guided by the propositions) for facilitators who communicate with individuals, groups or communities with cultural experiences different from their own.

During our person-centred journey, we have developed an awareness of the uniqueness of the experiences of all people and their values. The value of uniqueness (individualisation) is relevant for every client with whom the facilitator communicates, but it is of particular importance with people from other cultures. Instead of viewing cross-cultural communication as an obstacle, we should rather try to learn about and develop appreciation for the person's culture, making the process an enriching experience for all people involved.

Working cross-culturally from a person-centred perspective implies that:

- Any person who is considered to be from another culture (in other words, a different culture from that of the facilitator) should be understood from his or her own frame of reference.
- There is no recipe or method available to use – this is a person-centred process.
- The facilitator respects, values and appreciates the client and his or her own culture, resourcefulness and skills. The facilitator allows the client to show him or her how to cross the border into the client's frame of reference and world in a respectful manner.
- The process of finding common ground and understanding is a learning process for both the facilitator and the client.
- To assume is to stereotype. If, however, the facilitator is able to admit that he or she does not know something, that facilitator opens the door to discovery, construction, learning and appreciation.

Working cross-culturally also implies that we as facilitators have to symbolise our own prejudices and biases toward people from other cultures. Mary Catherine Bateson (1994: 17), an anthropologist, described how she dealt with her experiences in a community in the Philippines that was very different from her own life in the United States.

> *A death occurred down the street where the houses were poorer and more rural in style. The family I had been living with would be going to the* pagla-lamay *or 'wake' and they urged me to come. I did my best to prepare for my part, asking a series of questions about what would be happening, and got instructions on how to give an* abuloy, *a 'contribution' of less than a dollar, to the young woman whose mother had died. We went together to the house, staying until late in the night.*

She said that when she came back she wrote two kinds of notes:

> *One narrative describes the body laid out in its coffin, surrounded by lamps. The relatives had gathered, and neighbours were coming and going, expressing condolences, and offering money, and then standing and gossiping. Boys and girls were playing word games and flirting at the door, and gambling tables and barbeques were set up outside, with general merriment continuing through the warm night, noisily audible in the room where the body was laid out. The other kind of notes concerned my own feelings: my reluctance even to go to this house, intruding on the grief of others; my embarrassment over the act of giving the* abuloy.

She wrote how different these practices were from what she was used to. In writing in this way, Bateson tried to symbolise her own experiences, and tried to get to an understanding of the practices and beliefs of the culture in which she was involved. From a person-centred perspective, the facilitation of change or development takes place through dialogue. This transformation or change occurs when there is symbolisation of the unsymbolised experiences, and change in the thoughts, perceptions, values and behaviour that have formed the prevailing vision of reality (Natiello 1990: 283). We as facilitators cannot change people's behaviour, but we believe that by facilitating the participatory development of new or different frames of reference (personal realities) about themselves and their situations, people will become empowered and have a vision of how to change or better their own situations. If we listen, ask, explore and learn, people will show us the appropriate way to collaborate with them in their endeavours to grow and develop.

18.2 A person-centred perspective on culture

We can describe culture as being person centred. By this, we mean that culture exists in the minds of people, in their feelings, meanings, values and behaviour. Culture is individual. It distinguishes us from others. Culture shifts the focus from the problem to the person and also determines our understanding of other people's behaviour (refer to Proposition 1, Proposition 2 and Proposition 6). Furthermore, culture is seen as always in flux; it is forever changing and adapting to new information (Proposition 1). Even more important is the fact that no two people share exactly the same cultural world. Although two people may come from the same ethnic group, they will still have different perspectives (Proposition 2) and experiences of the culture.

Authors such as Le Croy (1992) and Egan (1994) take this approach (particularly Proposition 2) so seriously that they see working cross-culturally as more than just working with people from other cultures. Le Croy (1992: 215), for example, mentions differences such as gender, sexual orientation, and socio-economic, cultural and racial differences. These differences may influence each person. According to Egan, every person can be seen as coming from a different cultural background.

> *Any two-way conversation – even one between two identical twins – is, in a very real sense, a cross-cultural event, because each person is a different individual with differences in terms of personal assumptions, beliefs, values, norms and patterns of behaviour.*
>
> [EGAN 1994: 52]

This implies that the facilitator should be sensitive towards each person, sharing perspectives with each person, group or community. Apart from individual culture, every group and community also has its own culture or frame of reference. This culture is part of the group or community's decisions and behaviour (Proposition 2 and Proposition 7).

18.3 Working cross-culturally

18.3.1 Cross-cultural communication and the facilitator

If the facilitator feels relatively good about him- or herself and his or her own value systems, the facilitator might be in a position to be more open and not be threatened by the different value systems of people from other cultures (or even the same culture). The facilitator can be more accepting and open to listening to the person, group or community in front of him or her, without having the need to change (or confront) the value system of that person, group or community.

The theory (thinking or perception), values and skills (action) used when working cross-culturally are exactly the same as when working with people from your own cultural group. Empathy is empathy – a 'way of being' – regardless of the people with whom we are in contact. We might simply have to adapt the phrasing or way of expressing our empathy.

Cross-cultural work sometimes offers the advantage that the facilitator is aware that he or she does not know what meanings clients attach to particular situations. The facilitator can then explore these meanings with his or her clients. When the facilitator and the clients come from the same culture, the facilitator is inclined to presume that he or she knows what meanings people attach to various situations, and therefore does not necessarily always explore them. The facilitator may make assumptions that have not been validated by his or her clients. For example, an Afrikaans-speaking farmer living in Namibia might indicate that the nearest town is close to his farm. The facilitator might think of 10–20 km as close, but the farmer may refer to 100 km as close. Distance in the context of Namibia is different from distance in Gauteng, the Karoo, the Netherlands or the United States.

As when working with people in the same culture, cross-cultural work requires that the facilitator determine what prejudices or stereotypes he or she has about other cultures, and why he or she feels different from them or feels threatened by them. Okun points out that the facilitator is often not even aware of his or her prejudices or discomfort. Subtle forms of racism occur:

> *... when helpers apply different strategies with clients from different ethnic groups, or when they modify the helping process in any way based on unsubstantiated attitudes and assumptions about race rather than on the nature of the helpee's problems (or person). Some helpers have been heard to say that responsive listening is not effective with black helpees, that directive, behavioral techniques are more effective; however, responsive listening has been found to be equally effective in developing helping relationships with all helpees ...*
>
> [Okun 1992: 245]

Empathy can, despite the beliefs of some facilitators, also be used in African cultural groups. It may be a question of phrasing things differently or using other ways of communicating, such as metaphors and stories, as the following examples illustrate.

Example 18.1

This example is from a context where an Afrikaans-speaking facilitator worked with a Setswana-speaking family. The following is an excerpt from an interview with the family. The facilitator paid attention to the mother's strong emotions about her husband who was, according to the mother, not much interested in her and the children.

Mother: He doesn't know what standard they are in.

Facilitator: That hurts you a lot.

Mother: *(Crying)* It is too much.

Facilitator: You feel that you take all the responsibility alone.

Mother: Yes!

Both the mother and the facilitator were able to speak English and could therefore communicate easily. What about clients who are less fluent in English and do not have the known affective words in their language? Wildervanck found the following:

> *According to the students, they found it difficult to translate the messages containing a verbal skill into their own black languages, saying that individual words of affect did not feature in these languages.*
>
> [WILDERVANCK 1989: 76]

Where the client and facilitator were young people who could both understand English, this was no problem, but as soon as the particular black language had to be used, especially in a more traditional situation, difficulties were experienced. To overcome the problem, the lecturer and the students went in search, among other things, of certain metaphors that could be employed as empathy. They found the examples given below.

Example 18.2

Mrs L, a woman from a rural village, came to the facilitator: 'My husband drinks home-brew all weekend. He has spent all the money ... Now we have no money for food and I have five children to take care of. He has also chased me out of the house.'

The students decided that the best empathic response would be to say: 'You have grabbed the clay cooking pot by its hot side.'

The inhabitants of rural villages usually cook their food in clay pots on open fires on the ground. The pots are usually placed at the perimeter of the fire. Consequently, one side of the pot always becomes much hotter than the other. If you take the pot by its hot side, you will burn your hands, indicating problems and frustration.

[WILDERVANCK 1989: 94–95]

Example 18.3

Iqhina liphum' embizeni.

Direct translation: The steenbok jumps out of the cooking pot.

This saying means that the person missed a wonderful opportunity, for example, a person failed to secure a job that he or she was convinced he or she would get.

[WILDERVANCK 1989: 94–95]

Example 18.4

U bva mikandoni.

Direct translation: To come from the breast milk. It means that a person takes after his or her mother. A father may complain about having the same problems with his daughter as with his wife. The facilitator may use this response to convey his or her understanding about the father's view of the problem.

[WILDERVANCK 1989: 94–95]

18.3.2 Crossing borders

When working cross-culturally, the facilitator, the person, the group or the community has to (dialogically) cross certain borders. By crossing borders, we do not mean invading the physical territory or the personal space of others, but rather going beyond our own mental and social borders, and reaching out to the worlds of others in a gentle and non-threatening way (Proposition 16). Borders are not seen as obstacles, but as learning experiences.

Lifschitz et al. (1992: 140) states that every therapeutic (or relationship) endeavour can be conceptualised as a journey across cultural borders, and hence is multicultural – although some journeys involve more borders than others. These borders might be more prominent when you are dealing with a person from another culture. However, they also exist when you enter a relationship with a person from your own culture. In this case, the client's own experiences and frame of reference (Proposition 2 and Proposition 7) form the borders that must be crossed.

The following issues are possible borders:

- Language, phrasing and non-verbal behaviour
- Frame of reference (including meaning, values, problems or solutions, humour and so on)
- Traditions and customs (for example, appropriate clothing, age and gender).

We will consider these issues in more detail below.

The language border

The language border might be a difficult one to cross, especially if the facilitator and the client do not share a common language. In this situation, the facilitator usually has to use a translator or interpreter. An interpreter or translator can be very useful in:

- Rephrasing what the facilitator says in a way that the person can understand
- Acting as a guide for the facilitator to follow in order to show respect for the client's culture.

However, we have to take some issues about the translator into consideration:

- Translators translate according to their own personal frames of reference.
- Translators may add their own experiences, interpretations, prejudices and comments.
- Confidentiality may be violated.

If there are such language difficulties that the facilitator is forced to use a translator, the following advantages exist:

- The facilitator has to use very clear and simple language.
- The facilitator must continually check with the client whether he or she understands the client correctly. This forces the facilitator to work from the frame of reference of the client.
- The facilitator has to be creative in the use of alternative communication media like play and mime.

If used with great care and sensitivity, this way of working can be empowering for clients when they have to explain and guide facilitators through their cultures or frames of reference.

The frame-of-reference border

> *If the world view of two people engaged in dialogue differs very greatly, communication is often difficult or can be hampered. The different presuppositions, beliefs, understandings and concepts in the minds of the participants distort the presentation and reception of the communication ... However, it is possible for people holding totally divergent world views to engage in meaningful communication. This can be achieved if both people consciously attempt to understand each other's frame of reference and subject all stereotyped ideas and perceptions to careful scrutiny during the dialogic encounter.*
>
> [Ayee 1993: 16]

Example 18.5

Here is an example of how a facilitator did not try to understand the perception of a particular person. A job-placement counsellor describes a night-shift technical job to a Russian immigrant, a 34-year-old woman named Anya. The client listens politely and, through an interpreter, explains why she can't consider night work.

Anya: I no work night. My mother needs me. I must take care my mother.

Counsellor: You're feeling responsible for your mother and as much as you need a job, you're not sure how you can do this. It must be difficult for you, being in a new country with strange ways and needing to find a job, but still meet your family obligations.

Anya: I need work, yes, I need money. I need to be a good daughter.

Counsellor: I admire your sense of loyalty, Anya. But I am concerned about how we're going to be able to find a job for you. It's been over a month since you first came in and this is the first time a job for which you are qualified has come up. You must realise this. I don't know if or when another opportunity will arise.

Anya: I need work ... I need take care of mother ... I need make life.

[From Okun. *Effective Helping*, 4E. © 1992 Wadsworth, a part of Cengage Learning, Inc. Reproduced by permission. www.cengage.com/permissions]

The counsellor is, to some extent, sensitive towards the dilemma in which Anya finds herself, but according to Okun, the counsellor is reasoning from his frame of reference. To his mind, employment should be the first priority for Anya. However, he would not be helping her by coercing her into accepting the job. This would simply aggravate her dilemma. She may accept the job, and then not arrive on the second day or ever again. She would then be seen as lazy or work-shy with no account being taken of the difficult situation in which she finds herself. It would be more useful if the counsellor were to explore her confusion instead of pressuring her to take the job. He could also show respect for her loyalty towards her mother and the expectation that she take care of her mother.

It is crucial for the facilitator to cross the border by learning about his or her client's frame of reference. The facilitator must try to understand and respect the client's behaviour from the client's point of view. The person, group and community are the experts on their own frames of reference. Let them guide us.

Example 18.6

A facilitator working at the cancer association had a client who had had a mastectomy. The client believed that this was the result of a spell cast by her husband to prevent her from being desirable to other men. The facilitator also discovered that the local community believed that women with cervical cancer were being punished for being unfaithful to their husbands.

The traditions-and-customs border

Respecting the client's customs and ways of communicating can concern the following aspects of the particular culture:

- Making or avoiding eye contact
- Who should sit, stand or walk first
- How a man should act towards a woman and how a woman should act towards a man
- How adults and children should act towards each other.

Example 18.7

A story is told of a man visiting a family from a different culture. In his culture, the man takes the tea tray from the woman when she enters the room and holds it for the guests to help themselves. When the mother of the family entered the room with the tray, the visitor jumped up politely to take it from her, upon which she berated him by saying: 'Sit, you glutton, you will get yours in a minute!', because according to her culture, the custom is for the woman to serve her guests.

Le Croy (1992: 215) regards the attitude of the facilitator as the most important factor in cross-cultural work. This links with the credo of James Yen. He said: 'Go to the people, learn from the people.' The facilitator should move into a community, group or family, and let them guide him or her through their customs and ways of communication. The facilitator must learn from them appreciatively and respectfully.

Activity 18.1

McGoldrick (1982: 27) proposes the following important activities that may be used during training in cross-cultural work:

1 Discuss your own experience or feelings of being stereotyped, for example, as a Jewish person, a Greek person, an Afrikaner, a woman, an African person, a Xhosa person, a Zulu person, a German or an American.

2 Explain which person in your family (or context) has had the greatest influence on your ethnic or cultural identity.

3 If your family were to consult a facilitator, which type of approach would they prefer and what would they find acceptable? For instance, what should the facilitator do and not do? Compare your own ideas about this question with the ideas of your own family.

Mother: Yes. *(Starts crying)*

Son: Mother, I do love you and I do care about what happens to you.

Facilitator: You want your mother to know that she and her future are very important to you.

Mother: Yes, but what about the present?

Son: I see only that you are living in dangerous conditions now.

Facilitator: It seems that you two have different priorities that concern you. You, Mr Z, care about your mother's safety, but you, Mrs Z, have something else that is important to you here and now, but that you have difficulty discussing.

Son: Mother, is it something I can help with?

Mother: There you go again, trying to help me as if I can't help myself.

Facilitator: Mrs Z, you feel that you can take care of this matter on your own, yet something keeps you back?

(Silence)

Mother: I can only tell you that it concerns your dead father. I still feel his presence in this house and I have to talk this matter over with him. I can't just go and leave him here. That is all I am prepared to say now.

It turned out later that the woman talked regularly with her dead husband and feared reprisals from his spirit if she just left. She then consulted a traditional healer, who helped her with a ritual that would enable her to make peace with her dead husband. This was the tradition in her culture. Her son, being of a different generation and not sharing her beliefs, was unaware of this tradition.

19.2.2 Proposition 3 in the conflict situation

This proposition helps us to keep in mind that we are concerned with the whole world of the people in conflict, not just the content of the issue at hand. It is also useful in reminding us that we are dealing with the whole person, which places the propositions that follow below in a meaningful context.

The facilitator's responses are then directed at all that the people bring and imply, and not just to the conflict situation itself. As we will see under Proposition 11 and Proposition 13, there might be extraneous aspects, not directly related to the conflict as defined consciously, which have some bearing on the situation. This would necessitate the use of basic as well as advanced communication skills with all the parties concerned.

19.2.3 Proposition 4 in the conflict situation

Is the issue or conflict related in any way to the maintenance, protection or defence of the organism or person(s)? What are they afraid of losing?

For each person, the conflict could be a way of fighting to maintain or actualise the self. If the facilitator understands this, and communicates his or her understanding to the clients involved, they might come to understand themselves and each other a bit better.

19.2.4 Proposition 5 in the conflict situation

What need is motivating the behaviour of the people in conflict? It could be related to the need referred to above, that is, to maintain or protect the self, or it could be some other need. It could be an unsymbolised need, as we will see under Proposition 11 and Proposition 13. Whatever the case may be, the facilitator needs to understand the symbolised need as well as unsymbolised needs fully. At some stage, the facilitator must communicate this understanding to the parties concerned.

19.2.5 Proposition 6 in the conflict situation

Emotion accompanies the behaviour. Thus, if the emotion is intense, the need is very important to the person(s). We need to hear what is important and how important it is to the client.

If there is intense anger, then the need motivating the behaviour is probably very important to the person (whether he or she knows it or not, in other words, whether it is symbolised or not). Here it is important to understand and fit with the intensity of the expressed emotion (and thus the seriousness of the felt need and behaviour to meet the need). In conflict situations, the facilitator may feel threatened by the emotion, especially if it consists of anger. The facilitator might then experience a need to calm the situation, motivating the clients to behave in a way that will 'pour oil on troubled waters'. However, if the clients do not see that the facilitator fully understands the depth of their feelings, they might shout even louder in order to be 'heard', that is, to be understood. The facilitator will need a lot of courage to stay with the emotion, to understand it fully and to show this understanding to the clients.

Example 19.2

The clients are shouting at each other. Here are several possible responses from the facilitator.

Facilitator: *(In a loud voice)* You two are really extremely angry with each other. You feel like shouting the house down.

or:

Your anger is so strong that you can hardly contain it.

or:

This is a very serious matter to you and it feels like no one hears just how important it really is!

or:

You really want the other one to listen to you, to understand what you are feeling, but no matter what you do, the message just does not seem to come across.

This kind of comment can be directed at both parties at once, if both are very angry. This kind of comment can also be used with group members and clients from a community who are fighting about some or other issue.

19.2.6 Proposition 7 and people in conflict

This proposition reminds us that it is very important to understand all the parties involved in the conflict from their own frames of reference, not that of any other person involved, including the facilitator. This implies that each person should be given the opportunity to express their experiences, no matter how threatening these experiences may be to the facilitator.

Conflict implies behaviour, that is, people disagreeing or fighting about something. This behaviour needs to be understood from the clients' frames of reference, and as mentioned under Proposition 5, in terms of the needs motivating the behaviour. This could be difficult for the facilitator, as he or she might believe one person is right and the other is wrong, but the facilitator must remember that his or her professional value system precludes any form of judgement. Instead, it urges the facilitator to enable the people in the conflict to find their own value system and way forward that fit with their selves.

Activity 19.2

Look at the examples given in this chapter. In each case, decide whether the facilitator was able to demonstrate understanding and acceptance to each person involved in the conflict.

19.2.7 Proposition 8 in the conflict situation

In order for the facilitator to understand what aspect of the self is being maintained (Proposition 4), he or she needs to gain some understanding of the self as experienced by the client concerned. Here the facilitator has to be careful not to see one person through the perceptions of another person. For instance, if the wife talks about her husband and who he is, the facilitator has to bear in mind that her experience of who her husband is is her reality. It tells us about how she views the world (and her husband), but it does not tell us how the husband sees himself. The same would apply if the husband told the facilitator about his wife.

Example 19.3

Wife: My husband is never at home these days. He has turned into a real workaholic, so that I don't see him any more.

Facilitator: *(To wife, not husband)* You really miss your husband. It seems to you that you are fighting a losing battle with his work for his attention. *(Basic empathy with wife's experience, emphasising her need for his attention)*

>>

Husband: But I work so hard because I have to provide well for you and my family.

Facilitator: *(To husband)* It is important for you to be a good provider, to look after your family's material needs. *(Basic empathy with husband's experiential world, and his need and self as a good provider)*

Wife: We also need you at home. It feels as though I am not married any more.

Facilitator: You don't feel like a wife any more. *(Advanced empathy with self of wife, her need to be a wife)*

Husband: I don't know which way to turn. I have to be a good provider, but that doesn't seem to be enough for you.

Facilitator: It seems to you that you are not giving enough to your family. No matter how hard you work and how much money you provide, something else is expected of you, which you just can't provide. *(Basic empathy with dilemma of husband who feels unable to give what is required of him)*

Wife: But money is not the issue here! We need your attention, your companionship.

Husband: But I have to work so hard to give you a good home and all the things that you want. I am tired after such a hard day's work.

Facilitator: There seems to be some misunderstanding between the two of you ... Mrs C, you seem to be asking for quality time with Mr C, and Mr C, you seem to feel that if you give this time to your family, you will fail at providing what you think they really need from you, that is, money. *(Advanced empathy, connecting their statements to create a theme of how time is spent)*

Wife: How did the money become such a big issue in our home?

Husband: But you and the kids keep on asking me for this, that and the other! I feel that I just can't keep up.

Facilitator: *(To husband)* And you would feel like a failure as a provider if you did not give them everything that they ask for? *(Advanced empathy with his fear of being a failed provider)*

Wife: I never realised how seriously you take this providing bit in our relationship. We don't always need to have whatever we say we want. Sometimes it is nice to dream. Also, it would not hurt the kids to wait, save or work for what they want.

Husband: But I would really like to give you whatever you want!

Wife: You spoil me. I realise that. But what I really want is to spend some time with you. For us to have some fun together.

Facilitator: Mrs C, you need time spent on doing things together as a family, while you, Mr C, feel your time is better spent on providing for the material

>>

things for your family. Mrs C, you want to provide a nice feeling of family togetherness, and you, Mr C, want to provide nice items for the family. For both of you, the family is important and you want to provide what you think it needs and what is best for it. You just have different ideas about what this 'best' consists of. *(Advanced empathy, connecting their needs and their ideas about the self of the family as a whole)*

The couple now have a better understanding of themselves, their needs and their fears. But as they were also listening to the facilitator's responses to each other, it enabled them to understand each other a bit better. In this example, the emphasis has now shifted from what they don't do or give each other and the family, to what they do and want for the family. Now they can more easily negotiate how each one can provide what is required without feeling like a failure.

The same applies to conflict situations in groups or in a community. If one group or community member talks about another person, be it another group member, another leader or a member of that community, he or she is revealing only his or her own perceptions and experiences, not what the other person is really like.

Example 19.4

Group member A is angry at group member B, because B told other people in the group about something A shared with B. Now A says that B is a big mouth. If the facilitator looks at what A is saying about herself, it seems that A values confidentiality, trusted B to keep a secret and now feels disappointed. B might respond that he did not think that telling other people in the group about what was shared violated the confidentiality of A's trust, as he also trusts the group. It seems that A and B have different perceptions of confidentiality, of the group, of trust, of friendship and of how to be a friend.

Example 19.5

One member of a community might describe another member as domineering and bossy, wanting to take over the arrangements for every meeting. The person under discussion might regard herself as assertive, as taking initiative and inspiring or leading her fellows in the project. Maybe both have the need to be active, to be recognised as important and valued members of the community. How they behave in order to fulfil this need might be different, however, as each person's sense of self is different, and behaviour mostly fits with the sense of self (see Proposition 12). Maybe one person expects the other person to behave in a certain way that is not in accordance with the other person's experience of the self.

ition 9 and Proposition 10 in the conflict situation

uld concern values taken over from others or an expectation that someone er a value from another. For instance, parents may expect their daughter believe in the same values that they believe in, while the daughter has developed other values in interaction with her peers. The parents could then say something like: 'We did not raise you in this way', or: 'Your friends have a bad influence on you.' The child may respond: 'You are trying to tell me what to do', or: 'You are just not giving my friends a chance', or 'My friends understand me better than you do'. The facilitator can hear that the way the parents feel they raised their child (values they hold) is important to them and they might fear that they have failed as parents (parental self) if the child does not hold the same values. They might also experience an emotion like fear of rejection by the child (whether it be rejection of their values or of themselves as parents, or both, if the identity of their selves as parents incorporates the values they hold). The child may be torn between the values experienced in interaction with the parents and the values experienced in interaction with the peer group. She may have symbolised that to be accepted by the peer group, she has to take over their values, whether she experiences them directly or not. Whether the values of the friends are directly experienced or not, the child seems to value (and need?) their friendship and acceptance. The intensity of the need will accompany the behaviour as expressed by the conflict (Proposition 6).

If we relate this idea to a group, we could use as an example a group member who has developed the value of swift and decisive actions to resolve problems. Another group member has developed the value of intense and thorough consideration of all the pros and cons of any proposal before taking action. These two people might get into conflict about what is to be done when. Although both people might have the best interests of the group in mind, their ideas about what is best might differ.

19.2.9 Proposition 11 in the conflict situation

The experiences of the people concerned may not be consciously symbolised. So although they may say that X is what the conflict is about, there might be other, unconscious experiences involved, which further complicate the conflict situation. Until these experiences are symbolised, the conflict might not be resolved.

This might manifest in a situation where the same issue is mentioned in arguments over and over again. Such repetition can be an indication that the discussion of the symbolised experiences is just not enough. There is thus a feeling of dissatisfaction with what is happening, but the people involved do not know why they are feeling dissatisfied.

This unawareness could also relate to Proposition 4 and Proposition 8. In other words, there is a struggle to maintain the self, but the specific experiences defining the self and/or the need to maintain it are not symbolised.

Example 19.6

The wife may say she is a homemaker so she has to stay at home and raise the children, like her own mother did. The husband concurs, as that is also what

>>

he experienced while growing up. Their symbolised view of a parent self is therefore that the mother stays at home while the father works. Yet when he gets home, he might complain about the amount of money she is spending, while she says he does not understand her needs and that she is tired of sitting at home all day, just to be blamed for their financial situation in the evening. The husband's unsymbolised need may be for an extra income to alleviate the financial burden, but that would threaten the symbolised self as discussed above. In addition, if the value of a wife staying at home was taken over from his parents, the husband might fear that he was betraying them, thus his self as a good child to his parents might also be threatened. His wife might feel disillusioned and/or bored with staying at home all the time, but to admit this would threaten her self. Depending on whether the value and self as homemaker were experienced directly or taken over from her parents, the same conflict regarding her parents might subconsciously be present as for her husband.

So facilitators should ask themselves what the conflict is about on a deeper, maybe even subconscious level, for all the people concerned.

The symbolised self can be understood and maintained by communicating it through basic empathy. The unsymbolised selves, however, can only be communicated by using the advanced skills.

19.2.10 Proposition 12 in the conflict situation

Behaviour usually fits with the self of the person, so the facilitator should ask:

- Who do the people involved experience themselves to be?
- In what way does the behaviour fit with their senses of their selves?

19.2.11 Proposition 13 in the conflict situation

Sometimes behaviour is motivated by unsymbolised experiences (see Proposition 11). The facilitator should ask whether any such experiences are involved. Is the conflict perhaps about denial of a behaviour that somebody is accused of, but denies strongly, because it does not fit with the symbolised self? See also Proposition 14 and Proposition 16 in this regard.

Example 19.7

The nurse and doctor at an Aids clinic were trying to get a male patient to admit that he had Aids. They had just told him that his blood tests had shown this to be so. He denied that it could be possible. Another member of staff was consulted and acted as facilitator. While listening to the patient, she heard him state repeatedly that he was a good husband and that he had not slept with anyone but his wife. She indicated to him that this issue of fidelity seemed important to him, more so than whether he had Aids or not. He was very upset and after a while he could verbalise that he was afraid

>>

that it might be said of him that he had slept with a widow before the required period of mourning had ended, which is absolutely forbidden in his culture. If people were to think this, then he would be cast out of the community. He was afraid that having Aids would be attributed to such a transgression. The patient was not immediately aware of this perception and how much he feared the community's reaction (as he perceived it); neither were the doctor and the nurse, as he was not immediately able to tell them about it. They were also not aware that such a perception about Aids existed. As the people involved in the conflict became more aware of each other's ideas, they were better able to understand and communicate with each other.

19.2.12 Proposition 14 in the conflict situation

Any experience that is inconsistent with the self can create tension. This could refer to the issue around which the conflict revolves, or, if the experience about which the conflict is centred is not symbolised, then that experience, as well as the conflict, could create tension.

Besides these aspects, it could be that the behaviour of the conflict itself (like fighting or disagreeing) does not fit with the self (see Proposition 13). This would mean that the conflict behaviour and the experience that the person is unable to control this (fighting) behaviour can add to the total stress of the situation.

Activity 19.3

What responses, in terms of basic and advanced empathy, could you make to the people concerned in the situations described below?

1 A woman says something like: 'I really don't know why I fight with my husband (child/mother-in-law). It is just not like me to do this, but I can't seem to help myself. It's driving me crazy.'
2 Group members say (to each other and/or the facilitator) that they just don't know why they are always arguing in this way because it does not happen in other situations. They feel like avoiding the sessions.
3 A community that is divided into different sectors is known for its high crime rate. A meeting was held at which members of all the sectors of the community discussed the high crime rate and what could be done about it. Each group maintained that crime was not so bad in its sector and so that group could not do anything about the situation.

19.2.13 Proposition 15 in the conflict situation

When people can symbolise the experience that threatens their selves, they can change (restructure) their selves to accommodate the experience.

Example 19.8

A woman whose symbolised self was that of a soft and yielding person might come to realise that there are some things she considers worth standing up for, and thus fighting for, if necessary. This does not mean that she is less feminine (as she fears), but that she is a feminine person who occasionally takes a firm stand. She found new behaviour to fit this new self. After conflict with the teacher of her child, during which she had shouted at the teacher, she said: 'I am sorry my vehemence surprised and hurt you. I know I do not usually come on so strongly, but I realise now that when my child is punished, I just see red. I now realise you did what you thought was best, but I really do wonder whether, between us, we can find a different way of punishing G that is less humiliating for him.'

19.2.14 Proposition 16 in the conflict situation

When the symbolised self is threatened, the person(s) will defend that self strongly. So is it possible that the selves of the people concerned are threatened in some way? How?

In a group, members could be fighting to protect their individual selves, but also the self or identity of the group as they perceive it. For instance, after one member suggests that they do something, others might respond that it is not what they are here for, or what they have been doing up till now.

19.2.15 Proposition 17 in the conflict situation

In a conflict situation, it is very important to create a context or environment in which the participants feel unthreatened by the facilitator.

The conflict is most probably an indication that a certain measure of threat already exists, either in the experiential world of the participants or as perceived by the other participants in the conflict situation. The facilitator needs to express understanding of this threat and enable participants to explore the origins of it, without either minimising or contributing to the threat. That is why the use of communication skills as discussed in Section A and Section B is so important. If one participant in the conflict feels threatened by the facilitator, he or she will not only feel threatened as a person, but might even blame the other participants for involving the facilitator, and withdraw from the session, more angry and hurt than before. Resolving the conflict might then become more difficult for everybody concerned.

19.2.16 Proposition 18 and Proposition 19 in the conflict situation

If the people involved in a conflict situation become more aware of who they are (their selves), their own experiences and their values, and give themselves permission to be and explore the whole range of their own experiences, they will probably feel less threatened by the other people in the conflict situation and the views of those people.

They will be able to accept themselves and not be threatened by unsymbolised experiences, whether these are their own experiences or those of the others involved, as perceived by themselves. By accepting who they are, they might allow others to be themselves without feeling the need to change the others. People might say something like: 'I understand now where you are coming from. I do not agree with you and I don't feel the same way. I think we can agree to disagree.'

Group and community members can use this kind of understanding as a basis for negotiation: 'We have come to realise that there are different needs in this group, and now all that remains is to find ways to meet all of these different needs without offending anyone.'

CHAPTER

20 The self of the facilitator

If we use the person-centred theory as the basis for our argument, then the propositions of the theory apply to the facilitator as well. After all, the facilitator is also a person, with unique experiences and perceptions that have to be dealt with in some way.

Can we evaluate ourselves in terms of this theory and see whether we are congruent with it? Be warned that such an exercise might be experienced as very threatening by some facilitators.

Here we can do an exercise by asking ourselves what we make of the concept of congruence.

- Do we use it to evaluate (and thus judge) our clients?
- Are we aware that it pertains to us?
- Are we true to ourselves and what we believe in?
- Do we maybe see our work as an opportunity to give clients 'a piece of our mind'?
- Are we aware of (most of) our own experiences, so that our behaviour towards our clients is not motivated by unsymbolised experiences? (See Proposition 1, Proposition 5, Proposition 11, Proposition 13 and Proposition 15.)
- How do we perceive people in general and our clients in particular? For instance, do we perceive people as self-determined with our whole being? (See Proposition 2, Proposition 3 and Proposition 4.)
- If we have some reservations in this regard, do we know what they are, why we have them and how they affect our interaction with our clients?
- What are our needs for helping others? Our needs motivate our behaviour during the helping process. If we are not aware of them, they might influence our behaviour without us having control of it. (See Proposition 5, Proposition 13 and Proposition 14.) For instance, do we need to be needed? If so, what implication does that have for the way in which we behave towards our clients so as to have this need met?
- Do we need to be in control of ourselves and/or other people, and how does this motivate our behaviour?
- How do we experience our selves?
- Can we make a distinction between our professional selves and our other selves (like mother/father, child or wife/husband)?

- Are there differences in the way we interact with our children, our spouses, our parents and our clients? If this is the case, can we still see ourselves as being congruent?
- How have our professional selves developed? Did we act as facilitators in interaction with our parents and/or friends while growing up?
- Did our experience or sense of who we are professionally develop in interaction with the people who were part of our training? This includes our first clients because this would have been an important experience, and if a negative value was taken over from it, similar situations might still (even unconsciously) threaten our professional selves today.
- What are our values regarding people in general, and clients and facilitators in particular?
- Are these values of our own experience, or have they been taken over from others, like lecturers, supervisors, colleagues, or important political and religious figures in our lives (past and present)?
- Does a client's statements or behaviour threaten our selves in some way, so that we feel a need to defend or explain ourselves? (See also Proposition 16.)
- Are we aware of any experiences that threaten us, and how we deal with them? Do we, for instance, blame them on the client?
- What can we do with experiences with which we are uncomfortable, without really knowing why? Are we even allowed to have such experiences?
- Do we expect ourselves to always feel good about ourselves and our clients? If yes, what happens if we do not feel this way?
- Can we accept and deal with most of our experiences, even troublesome ones? If not, what do we do with these experiences?
- Can we accept that other people are different from us, without wanting to change them or ourselves? If so, what implication does this have for our role as facilitators?

We would appreciate any feedback about the content of this book. Please forward your comments to the authors care of the publishers at: Oxford University Press (Southern Africa), PO Box 12119, N1 City, 7463, or by e-mail to oxford.za@oup.com.

Bibliography

Agere, S.T. 1981. 'The promotion of self-reliance and self-help organisation in community development in Zimbabwe: A conceptual framework'. *Community Development Journal.* 17(3): 208–215.

Anchin, J.C. & Kiesler, D.J. 1982. *Handbook of interpersonal psychotherapy.* New York: Pergamon.

Attwood, G.A. 2007. 'An action research study of the REFLECT approach in rural Lesotho' (Unpublished Doctoral dissertation). Johannesburg: University of the Witwatersrand.

Ayee, E.S.A. 1993. 'A participatory communication approach to rural community development'. (Unpublished thesis). Potchefstroom: PU for CHE.

Balgopal, P.R. & Vassil, T.V. 1983. *Groups in social work: An ecological perspective.* New York: Macmillan.

Barret-Lennard, G.T. 1988. 'Listening'. *Person Centered Review.* 4 (November): 410–425.

Bateson, M.C. 1994. *Peripheral visions. Learning along the way.* New York: Harper Collins.

Batley, K. 2007. *A secret burden: Memories of the Border War by South African soldiers who fought in it.* Johannesburg: Jonathan Ball.

Bawden, R. 1991. 'Towards action research systems'. In O. Zuber-Skerrit (Ed.) *Action research for change and development.* Sydney: Avebury.

Blakely, E.J. 1979. *Community development research: Concepts, issues and strategies.* New York: Human Science Press.

Boy, A.V. & Pine, G.J. 1983; 1990. *A person-centered foundation for counselling and psychotherapy.* Springfield, IL: Thomas.

Bradshaw, B. 1993. 'Management by objectives versus community'. *Together.* (July–September).

Brill, V.I. 1990. *Working with people: The helping process.* (4th edition). New York: Longman.

Bruwer, E. 1995. *Beggars can be choosers.* Pretoria: University of Pretoria.

Burkey, S. 1993. *People First: A guide to self reliant, participatory rural development.* London: Zed Books.

Burkitt, I. 2001. 'Traversing the swampy terrain of post modern communities: Towards theoretical revisionings of Community development'. *European Journal of Social Work* 4(3) 233–246.

Carter, B. & McGoldrick, M. 1989. *The changing family life cycle.* (2nd edition). Boston: Allyn & Bacon.

Chambers, R. 1983. *Rural development: Putting the last first.* London: Longman.

Chambers, R. 1994. *Challenging the professions: Frontiers for rural development.* London: ITP.

Chambers, R. 1997. *Whose reality counts? Putting the last first.* London: ITP.

Compton, B.R. & Galaway, B. 1984. *Social work processes.* (3rd edition). Homewood, IL: Dorsey.

Corey, G. 1985; 1990. *Theory and practice of group counselling.* Monterey, CA: Brooks/Cole.

Cormack, P. 1993. 'Letting the people tell'. *Together.* (April–June): 16–18.

Cormier, W.H. & Cormier, L.S. 1985. *Interviewing strategies for helpers.* Monterey, CA: Brooks/Cole.

Cornwell, L. 1986. 'Gemeenskapsontwikkeling: wetenskaplike konsep of metafoor?' (Unpublished Masters dissertation). Pretoria: Universiteit van Suid-Afrika.

Crocker, D.A. 1991. 'Toward development ethics'. *World Development.* 19(5): 457–483.

Cruikshank, J. 1994. 'The consequences of our actions: A value issue in community development'. *Community Development Journal.* 29(1): 75–89.

Davis, R. 1994. 'Getting inside: PRA as a first step'. *Together.* (July–September): 19–20.

Davison, C., Frankle, S. & Smith, G.W. 1992. 'The limits of life style: reassessing "fatalism" to the popular culture of illness prevention'. *Social Science Medicine.* 34(6): 675–685.

DeVito, J.A. 1991. *Human communication: The basic course.* (5th edition). New York: Harper Collins.
Douglas, T. 1976. *Groupwork practice.* London: Tavistock.
Dunham, A. 1970. *The new community organisation.* Ithaca, IL: Peacock.
Du Plessis, M.J.M. 2000. 'Die ontwerp van 'n gemeenskapsontwikkelingsmodel: 'n Maatskaplike werk persektief'. (Unpublished Doctoral dissertation). UOVS.
Du Plessis, R. 2002. 'The narrative approach and community development: A practical illustration'. *Africanus. Journal of Development Studies.* Vol 32(2): 76–92.
Edward, A.D. & Jones, D.G. 1976. *Community and community development.* The Hague: Mouton.
Egan, G. 1990. *The skilled helper: A systematic approach to effective helping.* (4th edition). Monterey, CA: Brooks/Cole.
Egan, G. 1994. *The skilled helper: A problem management approach to helping.* (5th edition). Monterey, CA: Brooks/Cole.
Egan, G. 2000. *The skilled helper: A problem management approach to helping.* (6th edition). Monterey, CA: Brooks/Cole.
Farber, B.A., Brink, D.C. & Raskin, P.M. 1996. *The psychotherapy of Carl Rogers – Cases and commentary.* New York: The Guilford Press.
Feuerstein, M.T. 1986. *Partners in evaluation: Evaluating development and community programmes with participants.* London: Macmillan.
Flood, M. & Lawrence, A. 1987. *The community action handbook.* (2nd edition). Sydney: Ncoss.
Freire, P. 1972. *Pedagogy of the oppressed.* New York: Seabury.
Freire, P. 1994. *Paolo Freire: On higher education: A dialogue at the National University of Mexico.* Albany: State University of New York.
Freire, P. 1998. *Pedagogy of freedom: Ethics, democracy and civic courage.* London: Rowman & Littlefield.
Friedman, J. 1984. 'Planning as social learning'. In D. Korten and R. Klaus. *People-centered development.* 273–279. West Hartford, CT: Kumarian Press.
Garvin, C.D. 1987. *Contemporary group work.* Englewood Cliffs, NJ: Prentice-Hall.
Gauteng Department of Social Development. 2008. 'Child-headed households in Gauteng'. (Unpublished research report). Pretoria.
Germain, C.B. 1980. 'Social work identity, competence and autonomy: The social work perspective'. *Social Work in Health Care.* 6(1).
Gilliland, B.E., James, R.K. & Bowman, J.T. 1989. *Theories and strategies in counseling and psychotherapy.* New Jersey: Prentice Hall.
Glassman, U. & Kates, L. 1990. *Group work: A humanistic approach.* London: Sage.
Gooddal, G. 1984. 'Political development and social welfare: A conservative perspective'. In D. Korten and R. Klaus. *People-centered development.* West Hartford, CT: Kumarian Press.
Hancock, M.R. 1997. *Principles of social work practice: A generic approach.* New York: Haworth.
Hanson, N.R. 1961. *Patterns of discovery.* London: Cambridge University Press.
Harman, W.W. 1988. 'Development for what? Emerging trends of promise and concern'. In J. Burbridge (Ed.) *Approaches that work in rural development.* Munich: Sauer.
Henderson, P. & Thomas, D.N. 1989. *Skills in neighbourhood work.* London: Allen & Unwin.
Hepworth, D.H. & Larsen, J.A. 1990. *Direct social work practice: Theory and skills.* Belmont, CA: Wadsworth.
Hersey, J. 1988. 'Jimmy Yen: Crusader for mankind'. *Reader's Digest.* April: 151–192.
Hope, A. & Timmel, S. 1984. *Community worker's handbook.* Books 1, 2 & 3. Parktown: The Grail.
Hope, A. & Timmel, S. 1995. *Training for transformation.* Book 1, 2 & 3. Gweru: Mambo.
Hugo, E.A.K., Schoeman, J.H. & Engelbrecht, J.F. 1982. *Gemeenskapswerk.* Pretoria: Heer.
Jackson, A.O. 1979. 'Die rol van die etnoloog in gemeenskapsontwikkeling'. (Lesing gelewer vir die vakkundiges van die Departement Plurale Betrekkinge).
Johnson, D.W. & Johnson, F.P. 1975. *Joining together: Group theory and group skills.* London: Prentice-Hall.
Johnson, D.W. 1981. *Reaching out: Interpersonal effectiveness and self-actualization.* Englewood Cliffs, NJ: Prentice-Hall.

Kadushin, A. 1990. *The social work interview.* (3rd edition). New York: Columbia University Press.
King, C. 1965. *Working with people in community action.* New York: Association Press.
Kirschenbaum, H.C. & Henderson, V.L. (Eds.) 1989. *The Carl Rogers' Reader.* London: Constable.
Kirschenbaum, H.C. & Henderson, V.L. (Eds.) 1990. *Carl Rogers: dialogues.* London: Constable.
Kishindo, P. 1993. 'The case of non-formal vocation education for out-of-school youths in rural Malawi'. *Development Southern Africa.* 10(3): 393–400.
Konopka, G. 1972. *Social groupwork: A helping process.* Englewood Cliffs, NJ: Prentice Hall.
Korten, D. 1984. *Community organising and rural development: A learning process approach.* West Hartford, CT: Kumarian Press.
Kotze, D.A. & Swanepoel, H. 1983. *Guidelines for practical community development.* Silverton: Promedia.
Kotze, P.M.J. 1989. 'Wanvoeding: 'n Kontekstuele benadering'. (Unpublished Masters dissertation). Pretoria: Universiteit van Suid-Afrika.
Lee, R.L. 2009. 'If you build it they may not come'. *Research on Social Work Practice.* 19(2): 251–26
Le Croy, C.W. 1992. *Case studies in social work practice.* Belmont, CA: Wadsworth.
Lietser, G., Rambouts, J. & Van Balen, R. 1990. *Client centered and experiential psychotherapy in the nineties.* Leuven: Leuven University Press.
Lifschitz, S., Kjoadi, D. & Van Niekerk, S.M.F. 1992. 'Three views of a psychotherapy service in Mamelodi'. In J. Mason, J. Rubenstein & S. Shuda (Eds.) *From diversity to healing.* Johannesburg: South African Institute for Marital and Family Therapy.
Louw, H. 2002. 'Process is power in small grassroots participatory development efforts'. *Africanus. Journal of Development Studies.* 32(2): 44–58.
Louw. H. 2007. 'Men at the margins: Day Labourers at Informal hiring sites in Tshwane'. (Unpublished Doctoral thesis). Pretoria: University of South Africa.
Martin, D.G. 1983. *Counselling and therapy skills.* Monterey, CA: Brooks/Cole.
Mavalela, H. & Schenck, R. 2002. 'The story of "Phela & Phedise" income generating project'. *The social work practitioner/researcher.* 14(1): 48–66.
Max-Neef, M. 1991. *Human scale development: Conception, application and further reflection.* New York: Apex.
McGoldrick, M., Pearce, J.K & Giordano, J. (Eds.) 1982. *Ethnicity in family therapy.* New York: Guilford.
Mda, Z. 1993. *When people play people: Development communication through theatre.* London: Zed Books.
Meador, B.D. & Rogers, C.R. 1973. 'Client-centred therapy'. In R.J. Corsini (Ed.) *Current psychotherapies.* Illinois: F.E. Peacock.
Menike, K. 1993. 'People's empowerment from the people's perspective'. *Development in Practice.* 3(3):176–183.
Meyers, B.L. 1994. 'From Lystra to Louga'. *Together.* (July–September): 3–5.
Meyers, B. L. 1999. *Walking with the poor: Principles and practice of transformation and development.* Maryknoll: World Vision.
Middleman, R.R. & Wood, G.G. 1990. *Skills for direct practice in social work.* New York: Columbia University Press.
Mitchel, W. 1987. 'Social work with communities'. In B.W. McKendrick. *Introduction to social work in South Africa.* Pinetown: Owen Burgess.
Natiello, P. 1990. 'The person centered approach, collaborative power and cultural transformation'. *Person Centered Review.* 15(3): 268–286.
Nell, D. 2007. 'An Exploratory study of the perceptions and experiences of people affecting and affected by day labourers at hiring sites in Tshwane'. (Unpublished Masters dissertation). Pretoria: University of South Africa.
Ngubane, H. 1977. *Body and mind in Zulu medicine.* London: Academic.
Ntsoane, D.G. 2001. 'Tsoga O Iterele: A reflection on a participatory action research process'. (Unpublished Masters dissertation) Pretoria: University of South Africa.

Odendal, F.F., Schoonees, P.C., Swanepoel, C.J., Du Toit, S.J. & Booysen, C.M. 1987. *HAT Verklarende woordeboek van die Afrikaanse taal.* Johannesburg: Perskor.

Okpala, D.C.I. 1992. 'Planning and development in Africa'. *Third World Planning Review.* 14(1): iii–vii.

Okun, B. 1992. *Effective helping: Interviewing and counseling techniques.* (4th edition). Monterey, CA: Brooks/Cole.

Ox, E. & O' Neill, M. 2002. 'Establishing of a creche in the Popo Molefe informal settlement using a people-centred participatory approach'. *Africanus. Journal of Development Studies.* 32(2) 59–75.

Parkash, M.S. & Esteva, G. 1998. *Escaping education: Living as learning within grassroots cultures.* New York: Lang.

Parnes, S. 1981. *The magic of your mind.* New York: Creative Education Foundation.

Pierce, D. 1989. *Social work and society: An introduction.* New York: Longman.

Pitt, B. & Michel, M. 1992. *Making workshops work.* Cape Town: Erip.

Pradervand, P. 1990. *Listening to Africa: Developing Africa from the grassroots.* New York: Praeger.

Pretty, J., Gujit, I., Thompson, J. & Scoones, I. 1996. *A trainer's guide to participatory learning and action.* London: IIED.

Rahim, S.A. 1994. 'Participatory development communication'. In S. White (Ed.) *Participatory communication.* New Delhi: Sage

Rahman, M.A. 1993. *People's self-development: Perspectives on participatory action research.* (2nd edition). London: Zed Books.

Reid, K.E. 1991. *Social work practice with groups: A clinical perspective.* Monterey, CA: Brooks/Cole.

Rennie, D.L. 1998. *Person-centred counseling – an experiential approach.* London: Sage.

Rogers, C.R. 1951. *Client-centered therapy.* Boston: Houghton Mifflin.

Rogers, C.R. 1974. *Encounter groups.* Middlesex: Penguin.

Rogers, C.R. 1977. *Carl Rogers on personal power: Inner strength and its revolutionary impact.* London: Constable.

Rogers, C.R. 1980. *A way of being.* Boston: Houghton Mifflin.

Rogers, C.R. 1987. *Client centered therapy: Its current practice, implications and theory.* London: Constable.

Rogers, C.R. 1989. 'Do we need a "reality"?'. In Kirschenbaum, H.C. & Henderson, V.L. (Eds.) *The Carl Rogers Reader.* London: Constable.

Rogers, C.R. 1990. 'Client-centred therapy'. In Kirschenbaum, H.C. & Henderson, V.L. (Eds.) *Carl Rogers dialogues.* London: Constable.

Rogers, C.R. & Freiberg, H.J. 1983. *Freedom to learn.* (3rd edition). New York: Merrill.

Rubin, H.J. & Rubin, I. 1986. *Community organizing and development.* Columbus, OH: Merrill.

Schwartz, W. & Zalba, S.R. 1971. *The practice of group work.* New York: Columbia University Press.

Schenck, C. J., Louw, H. & Nel, H. 2009. 'People centred community practice: A handbook for beginners'. (Unpublished) Pretoria: University of South Africa.

Shiffman, R. 1995. 'Urban poverty – the global phenomenon of poverty and social marginalisation in our cities'. (Keynote address at SCUPAD conference). New York.

Shrivastava, O. 1989. 'Participatory training – some philosophical and methodological dimensions'. *Adult Education and Development.* 32: 3–21.

Shulman, E.D. 1982. *Intervention in human services.* (3rd edition). St Louis: Mosby.

Shulman, L. 1979. *The skills of helping: Individuals and groups.* Ithaca, IL: Peacock.

Soal, S. 2004. *Holding infinity: Guiding Social Processes.* CDRA: Cape Town.

Soal, S. & Reeler, D. 2009. 'Freedom, inclusion and sufficiency – another look at what really matters'. (Online at www.cdra.org.za). CDRA: Cape Town.

Swanepoel, H. 1992. *Community development: Putting plans into action.* Johannesburg: Juta.

Swanepoel, H. & De Beer, F. 1994. *Guide for trainee community development workers.* Johannesburg: Southern.

Sykes, J.B. 1982. *The Oxford Dictionary of Current English.* Oxford: Clarendon Press.

CDRA. 2009. *Barefoot Guide.* (Draft book on www.cdra.org.za). Cape Town.

Thomas, P.N. 1994. 'Participatory development communication: Philosophical premises'. In S. White (Ed.) *Participatory comunication.* New Delhi: Sage.
Tolan, J. 2003. *Skills in Person-Centred Counselling and Psychotherapy.* New Delhi: Sage.
Tubbs, S.L. & Moss, S. 1991. *Human communication.* (5th edition). New York: McGraw Hill.
Van der Kolk, C.J. 1985. *Introduction to group counselling and psychotherapy.* London: Thomas.
Van Niekerk, A.J. 1992. *Saam in Afrika.* Cape Town: Tafelberg.
Wenresti, G.G., Vincent, C.E. & Nestor, C.B. 1995. 'Rapid rural appraisal and participatory research in the Philippines'. *Community Development Journal.* 30(3): 265–275.
Weyers, M.L. 1987. 'Die plek en rol van skakelwerk in gemeenskapswerk: 'n Maatskaplike werkondersoek'. (Unpublished Doctoral dissertation). Pretoria: Universiteit van Pretoria.
Wildervanck, J. 1989. 'Toward an ecology of communication and its implications for social work interviewing'. (Unpublished Masters dissertation). Pretoria: University of South Africa.
Wood, J.K. 1995. 'The person centered approach: Toward an understanding of its implications'. *The Person-Centered Approach Journal.* 2(2).
Wood, J.K. & Jatoba, E. 1994. 'The person-centered approach's greatest weakness: Not using its strength'. *The Person-Centered Journal.* 1(3): 96–104.
Yaccino, T. & Yaccino, D. 1994. 'Insiders and outsiders: Are we asking the right questions?' *Together.* (July–September): 14–16.
Yaron, G., Janssen, G. & Maamberua, U. 1992. 'Rural development in the Okavango Region of Namibia: An assessment of needs, opportunities and constraints'. (Research report). Windhoek.
You. 23 March 1994. p. 187. Cape Town: Naspers.
Zeig, J.K. 1987. *The evolution of psychotherapy.* New York: Brunner/Mazel.

Index